Railway Track Diagrams
Book 4: Midlands & North West
Edited by Martyn Brailsford

Preface

Quail Track Diagrams have been published since 1988 and provide a reference to Enthusiasts and Industry alike. Originally drawn by cartographer John Yonge of the Quail Map Co and edited by the late Gerald Jacobs, the updating and publication of these titles were taken over by TRACKmaps in 2004. Now a de-facto standard for a wide range of users from train staff and infrastructure managers to railway enthusiasts and modellers, they contain information which may exist elsewhere and in other forms but are unique in making it all available in one easily portable volume.

TRACKmaps December 2018

Introduction to this Edition

This book has been partly reorganised to contain track diagrams for all lines forming the London North Western and East Midlands Routes of Network Rail plus small adjoining sections of adjacent routes. In addition a number of private railways and tramway systems are included. The maps are, in general, up to date as at December 2018.

The reorganisation has seen Mid and North Wales move to Book 3 and in return, the Chiltern Lines move into this book along with the line from Bromsgrove to Barnt Green. As part of this process the opportunity has been taken to reorder pages into a more logical and usable order along main routes. A number of maps have been redrawn, with Central Manchester and Stockport now appearing on one map, while Nottingham's tram system has a page of its own.

In the five years since the last edition was published the pace of change has not diminished. The Ordsall Chord in Manchester has opened along with phase 1 of the East West Project (Bicester – Oxford), while capacity improvements have seen Kettering to Corby redoubled, Roby to Huyton quadrupled and Norton Bridge Junction completely rebuilt. Stations have not been forgotten and significant alterations have taken place at both Liverpool Lime Street and Derby, while a number of new stations have opened including Kenilworth and Ilkeston, or have been moved as at Bromsgrove. New depots have been built to service passenger stock, including those at Banbury and Widnes, while freight sees the Daventry complex expanded and a new terminal being built at Kegworth. In addition, expansion of the electrified network continues with a number of schemes either completed or in progress. Signalling continues to be consolidated into the centres at Rugby, Birmingham, Manchester and Derby. Most of the tram systems in this book have also seen expansion during the period.

Acknowledgements

The Editor is indebted to Network Rail and its staff for access to industry documents and there are many other contributors to this publication; some significant in providing layouts, site checking or proofing details and some in smaller ways giving personal observations, answering individual questions or giving access to engineering drawings and construction diagrams. The editor is particularly grateful for the assistance of Kevin Adlam, Peter Green, Bernard Lovelock, Richard Maund, Robin Morel, Myles Munsey, Adrian Nicholls, Geoff Noakes, Andrew Taylor and David Tillotson together with representatives of various heritage lines. Acknowledgement is also due to Phil Deaves whose website on railway codes has been invaluable for sorting out ELR queries, to Peter Scott, the editor of Minor Railways and to the Branch Line Society.

The Editor would also like to thank cartographer Leanne Kelman on whom the extensive changes to the layout of book have fallen.

Martyn Brailsford

1st Edition 1990 (reprinted 1996)   3rd Edition 2013 (reprinted 2017)
2nd Edition 2005   4th Edition 2018

© TRACKmaps 2018

Published by TRACKmaps, PO Box 5259, Beckington, Frome, BA11 9DD. Website: www.trackmaps.co.uk

Edited by Martyn Brailsford

Cartography & typesetting by Leanne Kelman   Printed by Brightsea Print Group, Clyst Honiton EX5 2UL
Cover design by Jan McFarlane at ArtWebCo, Swindon SN2 8YY
Cover photography, see opposite

Publisher's Note
Every effort has been made by the Editor to ensure the accuracy of the information in the book is as correct as possible at the time of going to press. Notwithstanding, the Publishers welcome corrections, updates or suggestions for application to future editions. Contributions are preferred through the Contact Us page on the website or by post to the address above.

KEY

————	Running Line
————	Siding
————	Electrified overhead (25kV AC unless stated)
————	Electrified 3rd rail (750V DC)
————	Electrified 4th rail (LUL) (630V DC)
————	Electrified, overhead & Conductor rail
··············	Proposed or under construction.
——●——	Line obstructed
——○- - -	Line 'in situ' but out of use, partly dismantled, buried, or overgrown
——·——	Change of Signalling mandate
LNW ‖ WR	Network Rail Territory boundary
(OS) │ (MJ) WMSC	Signal control limits (Within an area, plates on automatic signals may reflect actual line description)
Diamond	Diamond Crossing / Switch Diamond
—│- - -│—	Tunnel
Viaduct	Viaduct or Bridge under Rail
—Ⅰ—	Selected Motorway / Trunk Road bridges over rail
——┼——	Network Rail operated level crossing
——│——	User-worked crossing with Telephone
←——→	Track signalled in both directions (a double arrow indicates normal direction of travel)
—⋈—	Private siding boundary, or gate
⌐———	Sand Drag / Trap Point
—○—	Turntable / Friction Arrester, Buffer or other stop
—‡—	Gantry Rails (Freightliner Terminal)
—×—×—×—	Fence
⋀⋀⋀⋀⋀⋀	Wall / Bank / Cliff
▲	Hot Axle Box Detector (HABD), Wheel Impact Load Detector (WILD) or Wheelchex Device

86.34 *(Not italic if Station mileage)*	Distance in Miles and chains from specified zero 1 Mile = 1760 yards / 1.6km 80 chains = 1 Mile 1 chain = 22 yards / 20.11m
57.600	Distance in Kilometres
│ 93	Whole mileposts, shown on the appropriate side of the line
│ 32	Whole kilometre posts
81.30⌐	End of mileage run
113.76 / 105.70 COM	Lineside mileage change
LEC 2	ELR-Engineer's Line Reference (Prefix and suffix numbers indicate sub-divisions and their boundaries)
[NW 5009]	Line of Route Code
3	Platform with number (May be supplemented by sub-divisions. e.g. (a), (b), (c), 'N' or North etc)
⑦	Indicates number of carriages per platform (approx 20m lengths)
⬚	Proposed platform
▭	Former Royal Mail platform
▭	Platform out of use
⌂	Other feature (labelled)
▨	Loading bank / dock
Blea Moor (BM) ⊠	ASC, IECC, SB, SC, SCC or ROC with code (underlined text relates)
◨	Control Panel
◆	Gate Box
□ ⊙	Ground Frame GF / Ground Switch Panel GSP or Shunting Frame SF. ⓢ Indicates 'Shut in' facility
✳	Radio electronic token block / Token exchange point
¶	Proposed closure
○	Water tower
⋀	Summit, height in feet
(Sydney Bridge Jn) ●	Indicates a former Jn, Station or Signal Box

Guide references are given to pre-nationalisation, pre-grouping and sometimes pioneer railways e.g. LMS: L&Y

Traditional line descriptions may be quoted, e.g. *JEWELLERY LINE*

GENERAL ABBREVIATIONS

AA	Acid Application	ft	Feet	Qy	Query concerning distances etc, unresolved
ABP	Associated British Ports	GC	Gantry Crane	REC	Reception
AC	Alternating Current	GDS	Goods	RETB	Radio Electronic Token Block
ARR	Arrival	GL	Goods Loop	REV	Reversing or Reversible line
ASC	Area Signalling Centre	GS	Goods Shed	ROC	Rail Operating Centre
bdy	Boundary	H	Headshunt	RR	Run-Round
BCH	Branch	HABD	Hot Axle Box Detector	S	South
BR	British Rail	HH	Hopper House	S & T	Signal & Telegraph
CET	Controlled Emission Toilet Discharge	HL	High Level	SB	Signal Box or Southbound
CL	Crossing Loop on Single Line	HST	High Speed Train	SC	Signalling Centre
COM	Change of Mileage	IECC	Intergrated Electronic Control Centre	SCC	Signalling Control Centre
CR	Cripple Siding	IET	Intercity Express Train	Sdg(s)	Siding(s)
CW	Carriage Washer	Jn	Junction	SD	Sand Drag
C&W	Carriage & Wagon	Jt	Joint	SIMBIDS	Simplified Bi-Directional Signalling
D	Connections Disconnected	km	kilometres	SN	Shunt Neck
DA	Down Avoiding	LC	Level Crossing (locally operated)	SP	Switch Panel
DC	Direct Current	LHS	Locomotive Holding Siding	SS	Shunt Spur
DE	Down Electric	LL	Low Level	TA	Tamper siding
DED	Diesel Electric Depot	loe	limit of electrification	TB	Turnback Siding
DEP	Departure	LP	Loop	TEP	Token Exchange Point
DF	Down Fast	LPG	Liquified petroleum gas	TL	Traffic Lights
DG	Down Goods	LS	Locomotive Shed	TMD	Traction Maintenance Depot
DGL	Down Goods Loop	LW	Locomotive Washer	T&RSMD	Traction & Rolling Stock Maintenance Depot
DL	Down Loop	M	Middle	U&D	Up & Down
DM	Down Main	M ch	Miles and Chains	UA	Up Avoiding
DMD	Diesel Maintenance Depot	M&EE	Mechanical & Electrical Engineer	UE	Up Electric
DMUD	Diesel Multiple Unit Depot	MGR	'Merry-go-round'	UF	Up Fast
DN	Down	MN	Main	UFC	Underframe Cleaning
DPL	Down Passenger Loop	MOD	Ministry of Defence	UFN	Until Further Notice
DR	Down Relief	MU	Maintenance Unit	UG	Up Goods
DRS	Down Refuge Siding	N	North	UGL	Up Goods Loop
DS	Down Slow or Down Siding	NB	Northbound	UH	Unloading Hopper
DSB	Down Surburban	Ng	Narrow Gauge	UL	Up Loop
DT	Down Through	NIRU	Not in regular use	UM	Up Main
E	East	NR	Network Rail	UPL	Up Passenger Loop
EB	Eastbound	NT	No Telephone (on LC)	UR	Up Relief
EGF	Emergency Ground Frame	OHC	Overhead Crane	URS	Up Refuge Siding
EMD	Electric Maintenance Depot	OHLE	Overhead Line Equipment	US	Up Slow or Up Siding
EMUD	Electric Multiple Unit Depot	oou	Out of Use	USB	Up Suburban
Engrs	Engineers' Sidings	ONS	Overhead Neutral Section	UT	Up Through
eol	End of Line	OTM	On-track Maintenance	V or Vdct	Viaduct
ERTMS	European Rail Traffic Management System	P	Points padlocked	W	West or Wash Point
ESP	Emergency Signalling Panel	PAD	Prefabricated Assembly Depot	WB	Westbound or Weighbridge
ETCS	European Train Control System	PL	Passenger Loop	WD	War Department or Wheelchex Device
FA	Flushing Apron	PSB	Power Signal Box	WILD	Wheel Impact Load Detector
FP	Fuelling Point or Footpath	PW	Permanent Way	WL	Wheel Lathe
				yds	yards

SUPPLEMENTARY ABBREVIATIONS FOR THIS BOOK

AR	Network Rail Anglia Route	L&Y	former Lancashire and Yorkshire Railway
BCN	Birmingham Canal Navigation	LUL	London Underground Limited
Cal	former Caledonian Railway	MD&HC	Mersey Docks & Harbour Co.
CTRL	Channel Tunnel Rail Link	M&C	former Maryport and Carlisle Railway
CLC	former Cheshire Lines Committee	MSC	Manchester Ship Canal
EM	Network Rail East Midlands Route	MSJ&A	former Manchester South Jn & Altrincham Railway
GC	former Great Central Railway	Met	former Metropolitan Railway
GE	former Great Eastern Railway	Mid	former Midland Railway
GN	former Great Northern Railway	NB	former North British Railway
GSW	former Glasgow & South Western Railway	NE	former North Eastern Railway
GW	former Great Western Railway	NS	former North Staffordshire Railway
KT	Network Rail Kent Route	N&SWJn	former North and South Western Jn Railway
LBSC	former London, Brighton and South Coast Railway	S	former Southern Railway
LCD	former London, Chatham and Dover Railway	SC	Network Rail Scotland Route
LMS	former London Midland and Scottish Railway	SE	former South Eastern Railway
LNE	former London and North Eastern Railway	SX	Network Rail Sussex Route
LNE	Network Rail London North East Route	WA	Network Rail Wales Route
LNW	former London and North Western Railway	WL	former West London Joint Railway
LNW	Network Rail London North West Route	WLE	former West London Extension Joint Railway
LPTB	former London Passenger Transport Board	WR	Network Rail Western Route
LSW	former London and South Western Railway	WX	Network Rail Wessex Route

LEVEL CROSSING ABBREVIATIONS

Abbreviation	Description	Abbreviation	Description
(ABCL) *	Automatic Barrier Crossing, Locally monitored	(MWL) *	Crossing with Miniature Warning Lights
(AHBC) *	Automatic Half-Barrier Crossing	(OC) or (OPEN)	Open Crossing (non-automatic), without barriers or gates
(AOCL) *	Automatic Open Crossing, Locally monitored	(OMSL)	Crossing with Overlay Miniature Stop Lights
(AOCL+B)	AOCL with Barriers	(RC)	Remotely Controlled crossing with barriers
(AOCR)	Automatic Open Crossing, Remotely monitored	(R/G) *	UWC with Red and Green warning lights operated by approaching
(BW)	Bridle Way (generally shown if telephone provided)		trains
(CCTV)	Full barrier crossing with Closed Circuit Television monitored by Signaller	(TMO)	Traincrew Operated crossing
(FP)	Footpath crossing (generally shown if telephone provided)	(TMOB)	Traincrew Operated Barrier
(MCB)	Manually controlled Crossing with Barriers	(TMOG)	Traincrew Operated Gates
(MCB-OD)	MCB with Obstruction Detection	(UWC)	User-Worked accommodation or occupation crossing, with telephone
(MCG)	Manually controlled Crossing with Gates	(UW~)	User-Worked crossing where ~ is substituted with 'B' Barriers, 'G' Gates,
(MGH)	Manned Gates, Hand worked		'K' Kissing gates or 'W' Wickets
(MGW)	Manned Gates with Wickets	(WL)	Barrow or Foot Crossing with White Light indicators
(MSL) *	Crossing with Miniature Stop Lights		

* (-X) shown after these abbreviations (e.g. AHBC-X) indicates that the crossing works automatically for movements in the wrong direction.

In some cases, the code of the controlling signal box may be shown, e.g. Cresswell (AHBC)(CL).

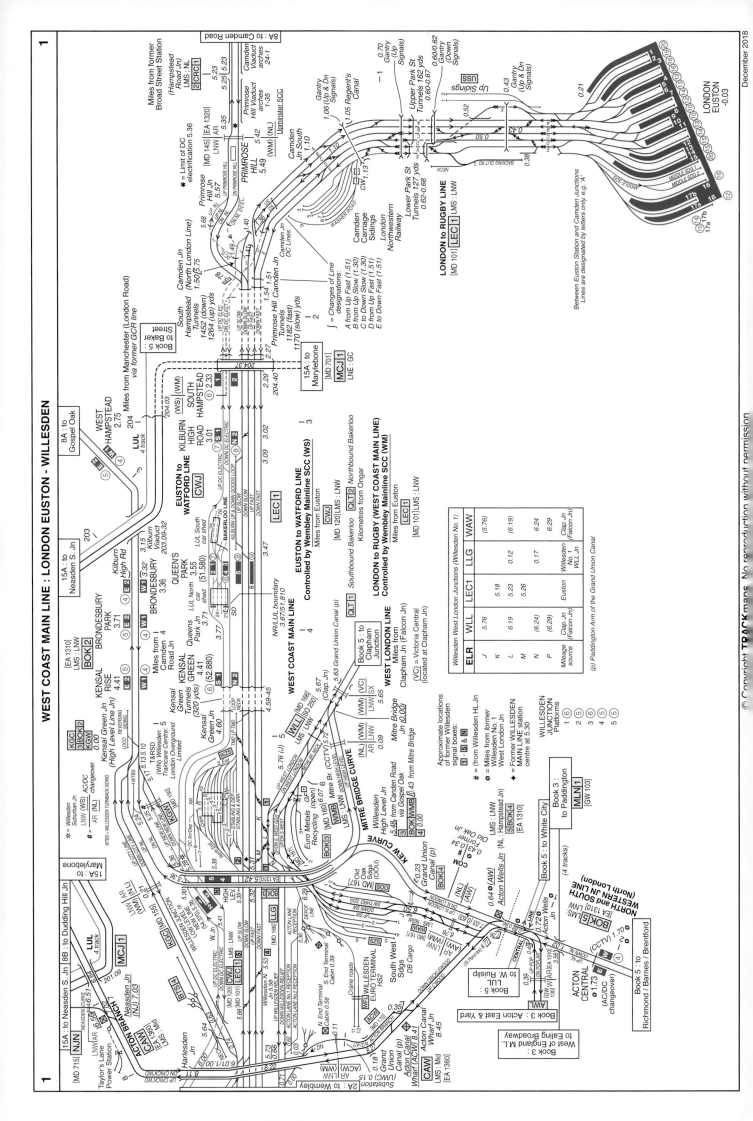

WEST COAST MAIN LINE : LONDON EUSTON - WILLESDEN

December 2018

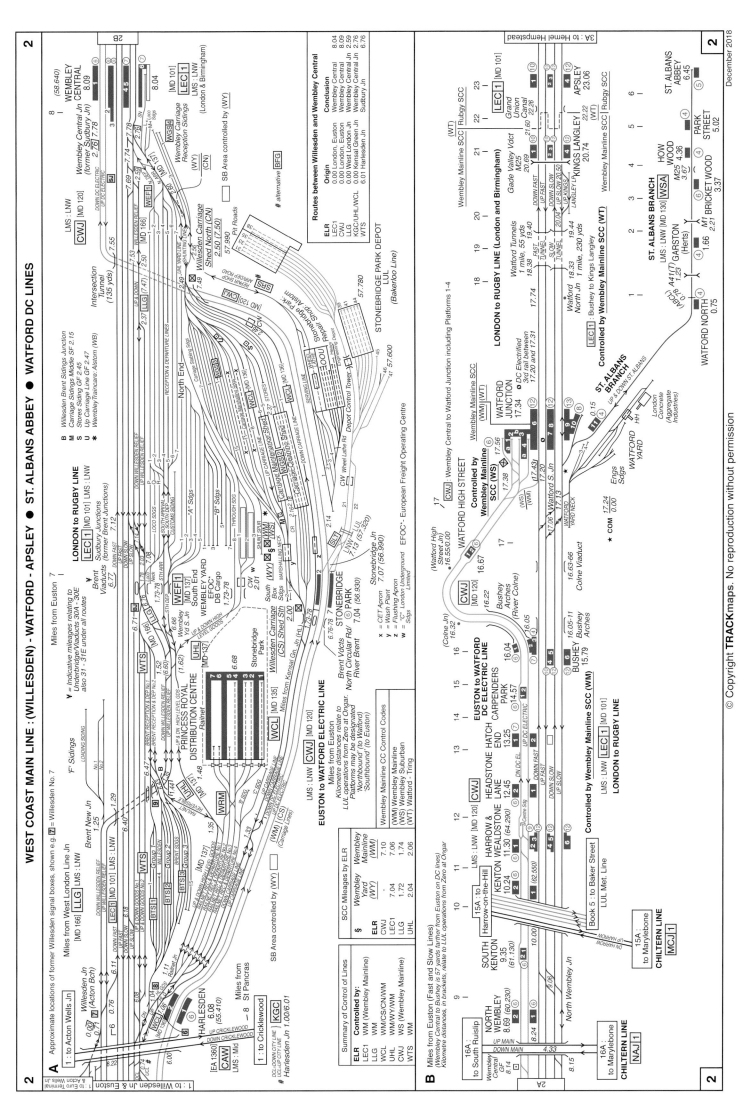

WEST COAST MAIN LINE : (WILLESDEN) - WATFORD - APSLEY ● ST. ALBANS ABBEY ● WATFORD DC LINES

© Copyright TRACKmaps. No reproduction without permission

December 2018

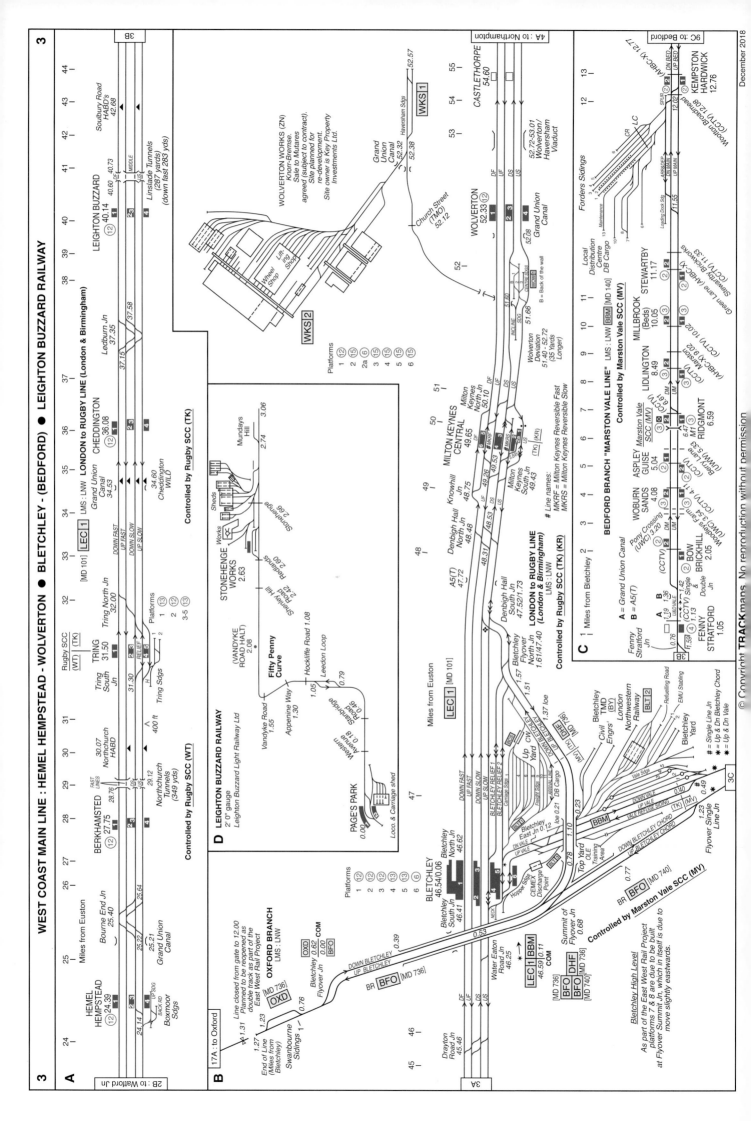

WEST COAST MAIN LINE : HEMEL HEMPSTEAD - WOLVERTON ● BLETCHLEY - (BEDFORD) ● LEIGHTON BUZZARD RAILWAY

December 2018

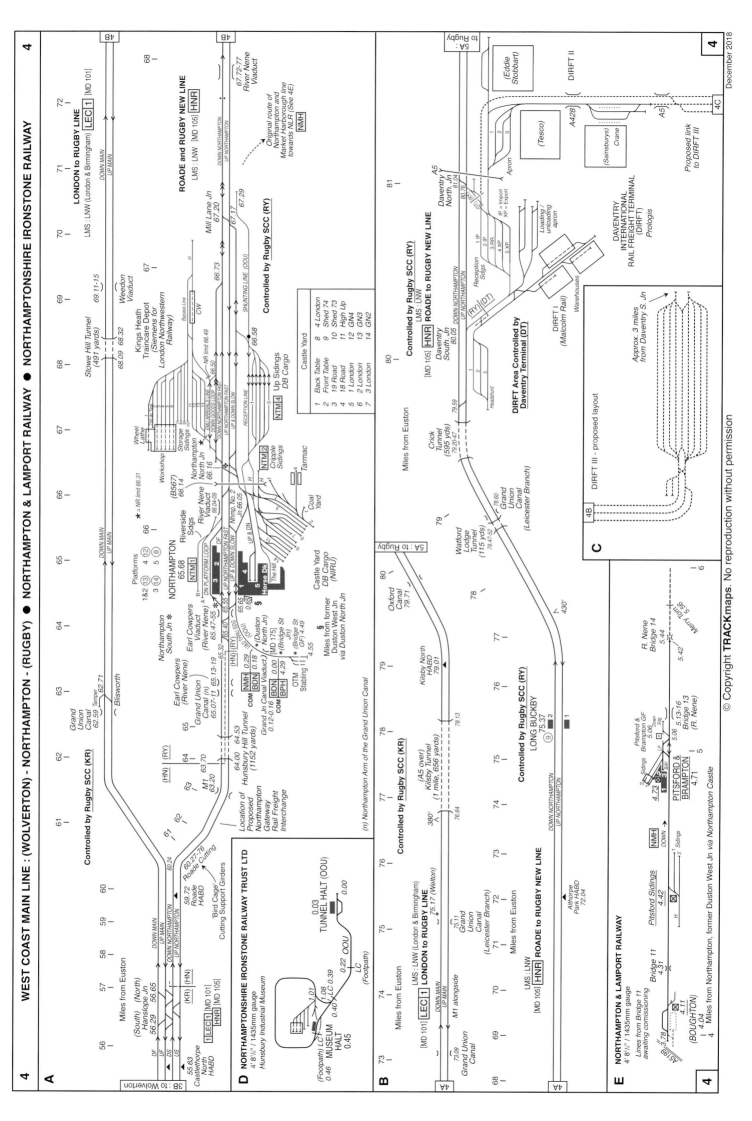

WEST COAST MAIN LINE : RUGBY - NUNEATON - TAMWORTH ● BATTLEFIELD STEAM RAILWAY

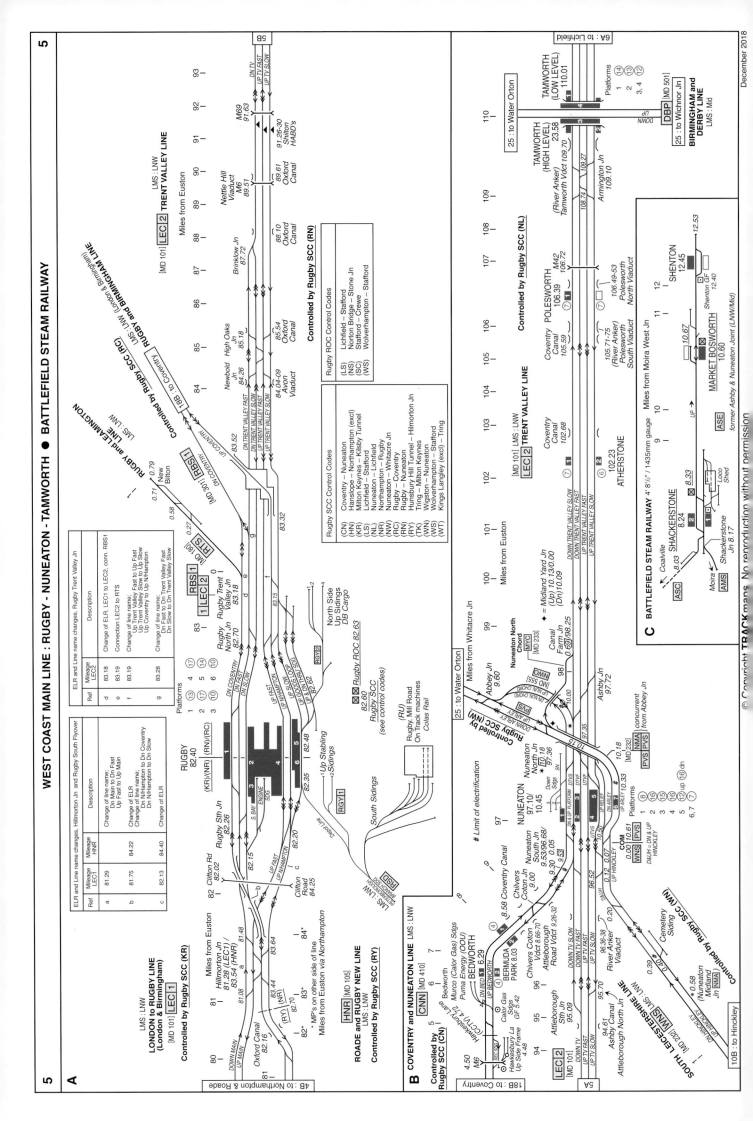

A

LMS : LNW
LONDON to RUGBY LINE
(London & Birmingham)
[MD 101] LEC 1

Controlled by Rugby SCC (KR)

Miles from Euston

ELR and Line name changes, Hillmorton Jn and Rugby South Flyover

Ref	Mileage HNR	Description
a	81.29	Change of line name: Dn Main to Dn Fast Up Fast to Up Main
b	81.75	Change of ELR Change of line name: Dn N'hampton to Dn Coventry Up N'hampton to Up Fast
c	82.13	Change of ELR

ELR and Line name changes, Rugby Trent Valley Jn

Ref	Mileage LEC2	Description
d	83.18	Change of ELR, LEC1 to LEC2, conn. RBS1
e	83.19	Connection LEC2 to RTS
f	83.19	Change of line name: Up Trent Valley Fast to Up Fast Up Trent Valley Slow to Up Slow Up Coventry to Up N'hampton
g	83.28	Change of line name: Dn Fast to Dn Trent Valley Fast Dn Slow to Dn Trent Valley Slow

HNR [MD 105]
ROADE and RUGBY NEW LINE
LMS : LNW

Controlled by Rugby SCC (RY)

B

COVENTRY and NUNEATON LINE LMS : LNW
CNN [MD 410]

Controlled by
Rugby SCC (CN)

18B : to Coventry

Controlled by Rugby SCC (RC)
RUGBY and LEAMINGTON LINE
LMS : LNW

RUGBY and BIRMINGHAM LINE
LMS : LNW

Controlled by Rugby SCC (RN)

Rugby SCC Control Codes

(CN)	Coventry – Nuneaton
(HN)	Hanslope – Northampton (excl)
(KR)	Milton Keynes – Hilmorton Jn
(LS)	Lichfield – Stafford
(NL)	Nuneaton – Lichfield
(NR)	Northampton – Rugby
(NW)	Nuneaton – Whitacre Jn
(RC)	Rugby – Coventry
(RN)	Rugby – Nuneaton
(TK)	Hunsbury Hill Tunnel – Hilmorton Jn
(RY)	Tring – Milton Keynes
(WN)	Wigston – Nuneaton
(WS)	Wolverhampton – Stafford
(WT)	Kings Langley (excl) – Tring

Rugby ROC Control Codes

(LS)	Lichfield – Stafford
(NS)	Norton Bridge – Stone Jn
(SC)	Stafford – Crewe
(WS)	Wolverhampton – Stafford

Controlled by Rugby SCC (NL)

C **BATTLEFIELD STEAM RAILWAY** 4' 8½" / 1435mm gauge

Controlled by Rugby SCC (NL)

25 : to Water Orton

TAMWORTH (LOW LEVEL) 110.01
Platforms
1 ⑭
2 ⑲ ⑫
3, 4

TAMWORTH (HIGH LEVEL) 23.58

DBP [MD 501]
BIRMINGHAM and DERBY LINE
LMS : Mid

25 : to Wichnor Jn

6A : to Lichfield

December 2018

© Copyright TRACKmaps. No reproduction without permission

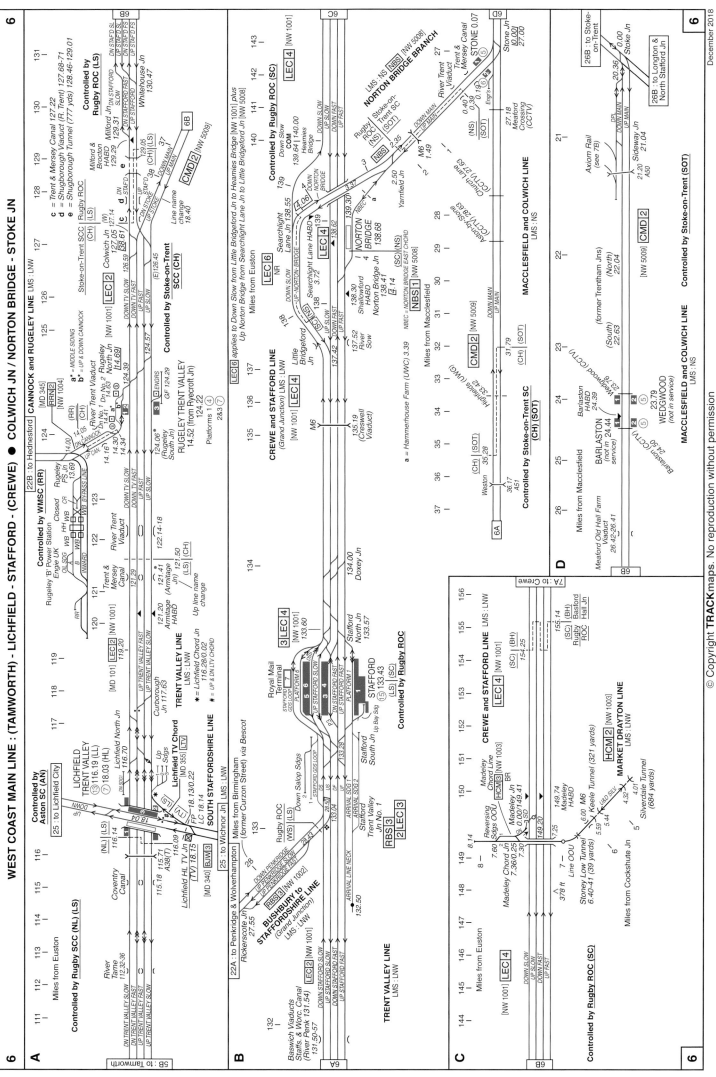

WEST COAST MAIN LINE : (TAMWORTH) - LICHFIELD - STAFFORD - (CREWE) ● COLWICH JN / NORTON BRIDGE - STOKE JN

December 2018

CREWE

A   **B**

CREWE WORKS (ZC)
Bombardier Transportation

Traverser
Engine Services
Test Stand
Repairs
Electrical Reprs
Wheel Shop
Bogie Shop

28C : to Chester

DOWN MAIN
UP MAIN
159.55
159.01
158.77

Crewe Steelworks (SW) 159.41

Colas Training School

West Side
East Side
Apron
Wheel Lathe
1 - THRO
2 - THRO
DEPARTURE LINE
ARR LINE EAST

CREWE and CHESTER LINE
LMS : LNW

CREWE and SHREWSBURY LINE LMS : LNW

Book 3 : to Nantwich & Shrewsbury — 3
— 2
— 1

(SC) Wales ROC

[GW 735] WA
[NW 1007]
(SC) (GL)
Willaston (CCTV) (Gresty Lane) 2.41
3.10
loe 1.41
[NW 1007]

Gresty Lane Down Sidings
Sdgs 1-5 AmeyColas
Crewe PAD
Gresty Lane Down Sidings GSP

Controlled by Gresty Lane SCC (GL)

Gresty Green Sidings
Axiom Rail
Gresty Green West Jn 1.18
Gresty Green East Jn 0.60
GBN = GRESTY BRIDGE NECK

Gresty Bridge Depot
Direct Rail Services (CR)
Gresty Road
Freightliner Basford Hall TMD

BASFORD HALL YARD

Basford Hall Down Sdgs

* also equipped with DC conductor Rail
Z = WISTASTON ROAD 159.24 (EMD Platform)

5-8 = SHED ROADS 1-4
11 = ELEC LOCO RR

Crewe Electric EMD (CE)
DB Cargo

Line ELR's
[BHI] 157.74-158.76
[CIL] 157.64-158.24
[LLI] 157.72-158.73

Gresty Lane SCC (GL) and Crewe Signalling Control Centre

[CNH1] [NW 3001]

[CE] 158.21
[CSG] [SYC] [GSG]
157.47 0.33 0.00

Salop Goods Jn (SG) 157.71 (GL) 0.37

Crewe Diesel Depot (CD)
Locomotive 158 Services Ltd

Carriage Shed
North End 12
South Yard
Crewe Down Holding Sdgs

Salop Goods Loop Jn
Coal Sidings (DRS)

CREWE 158.03

Platforms
Up Dn
1 [15][16]   7
2 [7]   8
3 [4]   9
4 [5][13]   10
5   11
Manchester 6 [12][15]   12 [21]
Liverpool/Chester 6 [19][22]

Crewe North Jn 158.18
[CNH1] [LEC][5][CMP1]

EMD STABLING SDG

CREWE JUNCTIONS
A Stoke Line Jn
B Shrewsbury Line Jn
C Chester Line Jn
D Manchester Line Jn
* = Crewe Carriage Sheds (1 & 2) (CP)

CREWE and STOCKPORT LINE LMS : LNW

Crewe South Jn 157.60
Stoke Line Jn 157.53

North Stafford Jn (Crewe) 7.52
Arriva Traincare Maintenance Depot (CP)
A5020 7.43
Wheel Lathe Shop

CREWE BRANCH (NS) LMS : NS
[KCS][1&2]
[NW 1005]

Basford GF Wood 157.03

New Middle Sdgs
Basford Hall Up Sdgs

UP ARRIVAL No 2
UP ARRIVAL No 1
UP LOOP

Crewe Sorting Sidings North SB (NH) 157.23
M = (Crewe Sorting Siding Middle) 156.66
‡ = Crewe Sorting Sidings Down Sdgs

[BHI] [NW 1009]

[LEC][4] [NW 1001]

CREWE and STAFFORD LINE (Grand Junction) LMS : LNW

Basford Hall Jn (BHI) 156.23
156.51 (A500)
156.25 156.20 156.23
156.16 156.08 156.05

Lower Radway Green (UWG) 4.26
Barthomley Jn 4.67
M6 4.37
Barthomley 4.77

RADWAY GREEN 4.03
DN MAIN UP MAIN

Miles from Euston 156
157
158
159

Miles from Kidsgrove Jn

6C : to Stafford
42A : to Kidsgrove

29A : to Winsford
42B : to Sandbach

CREWE and BIRDSWOOD LINE (Grand Junction)
LMS : LNW
[LEC][5][CGJ][1]
[NW 1001]
158.73 158.77

Crewe Coal Yard (CY) 158.68
[BHI] [CMP1]
(Sydney Bridge Jn)
158.57
DN WILMSLOW
UP WILMSLOW

Railway Age Heritage Centre
Boiler Shop
Exhibition Hall
Tunnel (394 yards)
DOWN MANCHESTER LOOP
UP MANCHESTER LOOP

CREWE and STOCKPORT LINE LMS : LNW
[CMP1] [NW 5001]

6D : to Stoke
[CMD][2] [NW 5009]

Sideway Jn 21.04
Wshop two
Traversers
Paint Shop
Wheel Bay
Bogie Shop
Main Workshop one

Stoke on Trent Works Axiom Rail (ZJ)

Gas freeing, purging & steaming sidings
P = Paint Booth
s = Shotblast Booth
z = Hoist

Trent & Mersey Canal

6D : to Wedgewood

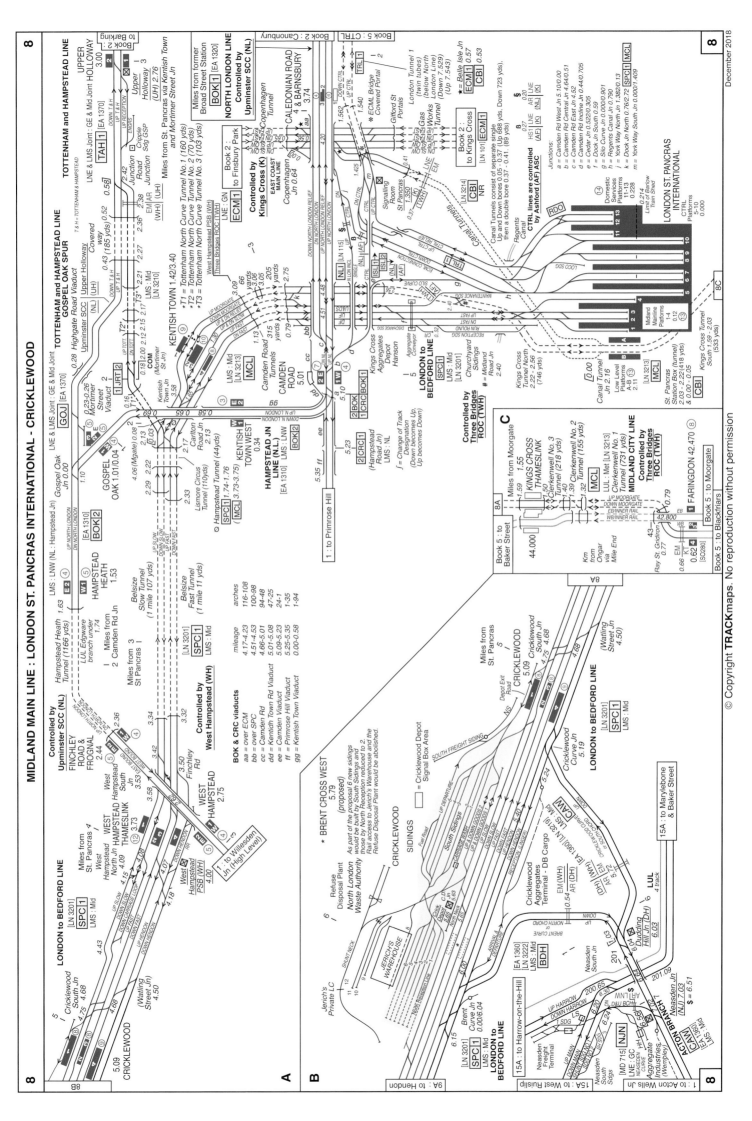

MIDLAND MAIN LINE : LONDON ST. PANCRAS INTERNATIONAL - CRICKLEWOOD

December 2018

MIDLAND MAIN LINE : HENDON - BEDFORD - WELLINGBOROUGH ● RUSHDEN ● LUTON DART

A

8B : to Cricklewood & St. Pancras

Controlled by West Hampstead PSB (WH)

[LN 3201] SPC 1 LMS : Mid

LONDON to BEDFORD LINE

Book 5

LUL to Edgware

HENDON CHORD
UP HENDON 7.06 DOWN HENDON
DOWN FAST 7.35
UP FAST 7.35
DOWN SLOW
UP SLOW

6.58 DOWN HENDON
6.21-6.31
Welsh Harp/Brent 6.79
River Brent
Viaduct

(8) HENDON 6.79

Silkstream Jn 29.19 (7.72)
7.36
7.75
7.43
7.78

MILL HILL BROADWAY 9.28
4   2 3   1 (12)

8.73

Stonefield/Deans Brook Viaduct 10.32-36
M1 11.26
New Tun. Old Tun.
11.38 12.06
Elstree Tunnels (1058 yards)

ELSTREE & BOREHAMWOOD 12.35
4   2 3   1
(9) Fast lines   (12) Slow lines

13   14   15

14.33
Radlett Jn 14.33
14.55
RADLETT 15.17
16.50 17.09
16.30
18.00

2 3   1 (12)
(8) Fast lines   (12) Slow lines

R. Colne M25
A414 18.37

CR Radlett : Napsbury HABD
Tarmac
Reception Road
Stone Sdg 16.27

ST. ALBANS CITY 19.71
4   2 3   1 (12)
TB 20.09

Centre Sdg

20   21   22   23   24

Harpenden Jn 24.25 24.34
24.13
24.51 HARPENDEN
9B   4   2 3   1 (12)

Miles from St. Pancras

25   26   27   28

(Old Harpenden Jn) 25.20

Chiltern Green HABD 27.69 28.76 A1081
26.66 26.72
River Lea Hyde/Chiltern Green Viaduct

B

9A

Controlled by West Hampstead PSB (WH)

[LN 3201] SPC 1 LMS : Mid

LONDON to BEDFORD LINE

LUTON AIRPORT PARKWAY 29.19 (12)
4   2 3   1

Luton DART see 9E

29   30

Luton South S   N Platform Sub-divisions
CARRIAGE SDG
30.00 30.12 (12) (12)
30.12   4   3   2   1 LUTON 30.19 (12)
30.52
LOOP
Luton North Jn

Luton Up Sdgs GF 29.69 29.70
Crescent Road Yard Tarmac

DOWN FAST
UP FAST
DOWN SLOW
UP SLOW

Limbury Road North GF (Down Line) 31.69
Limbury Road (Ledgrove Road) (Up Line) 31.45
SDG 1

* Access to/from Down Slow only
Aggregates Discharge Breedon

31   32   33

LEAGRAVE 32.30 (12) (3, 9)
4   2 3   1
33.05   33.28

Leagrave Jn 33.18
403 ft 33.60

34   35   36   37

Sundon Jn 35.49
UP SUNDON LOOP

Harlington Jn 37.00

HARLINGTON 37.22
4   2 3   1 (12)

38   39   40

FLITWICK 40.18
9C   4   2 3   1 (12)

C

9B

[LN 3201] SPC 1 LMS : Mid

LONDON to BEDFORD LINE

Flitwick Jn 40.35 40.47 40.60

DOWN FAST
UP FAST
DOWN SLOW
UP SLOW

41   42   43   44   45   46   47

Ampthill Tunnels (715 yards) 42.19 42.52

Miles from St. Pancras

47.18
Hopper Elstow: Tarmac
47.74 A421

48
14.64
48.23   48.45   48.60   48.27   48.77

Bedford South Jn 48.60

REC. ROAD 49
DOWN BEDFORD
UP BEDFORD

BEDFORD BRANCH
Controlled by Marston Vale SCC (MV)

Double to Single Jn 15.67
15   Miles from Bletchley

River Great Ouse Viaduct 49.33-49.38

49.41   49.46   50.06

Great Ouse
Holding Sdgs   4x4   Shed
CET Discharge Points
CW   CAULDWELL EMUD
Thameslink (BF)
* = Carriage Washer Bypass
≠ = Carriage Washer Rd

49.60 16.51
16.52 (former Hitchin Branch Jn)
49.64 16.55

16.05 BEDFORD ST. JOHNS (12) (2)
16.07   16.08   16.32   16.60

(WH) [MV] [MD 140]
LMS : LNW

D

9C

[LN 3201] SPC 2 LMS : Mid

LEICESTER and HITCHIN LINE

Bedford North Jn 50.35
BEDFORD 49.65 50.00
(16.60 from Bletchley)
4   2 3   1a   1 (12) (13)

[LN 3201] BBM

Bedford Station Jn 50.46
SPC 1 BBM
a. 49.60 16.51
b.   16.52 (former Hitchin Branch Jn)
c. 49.64 16.55
d. UP & DN BLETCHLEY BBM
e. UP & DN BLETCHLEY GOODS BBM

50.72-50.79 Bromham Viaducts
51.50 (Oakley Jn)
River Ouse 51.50

50   51   52   53   54   55   56

51.78-52.04 Clapham (River Ouse) Viaducts
53.60   53.29-35 Oakley Viaducts
54.17-25 Milton Ernest Viaducts
Oakley HABD
56.16-56.25 Sharnbrook Viaducts

Radwell Viaducts 54.76½- 55.03

DOWN FAST
DOWN SLOW
UP SLOW

Line between Bedford and Corby planned to be electrified in 2020

E Luton DART (Direct Air-Rail Transit)

MID-STAY CAR PARK (proposed)

LUTON AIRPORT CENTRAL TERMINAL
Under Construction, due to be open 2021

Maintenance Area 2.079
2.000
1.560

LUTON AIRPORT PARKWAY 0.000

F RUSHDEN HISTORIC TRANSPORT SOCIETY

4' 8½" / 1435mm gauge

2.66
2.53
2.30 RUSHDEN
2.27

HFB LMS : Mid
10A : to Kettering

Miles from Irchester Jn

D (lower)

9B

Controlled by East Midlands CC (LR) (located at Derby)

LEICESTER and HITCHIN LINE

West Hampstead PSB (WH)
EMCC (LR)

SPC 2 [LN 3201] LMS : Mid
WYM [LN 3201] LMS : Mid

Sharnbrook Summit 315 ft 59.51
Sharnbrook Tunnel 59.00 59.09
* also known as Sharnbrook Tunnel

Wymington 60.05 60
WYMINGTON Deviation (1 mile, 90 yds)
Wymington Tunnel 58.60

(LR) (BK)
SLOW LINE
COM (Slow Lines) 62.05 62.00

River Ise 65.09
WELLINGBOROUGH
Wellingborough North Jn 65.27
Wellingborough South Jn 64.26 64.78
(Irchester Jn) 63.60-63.67
Irchester 63.54
River Nene A45 63.38
River Nene Wellingborough Viaducts

60   61   62   63   64   65   66

Miles from St. Pancras

63   64
64.51-64.57 Wellingborough (late 2019)

WELLINGBOROUGH UP SIDING
WELLINGBOROUGH UP DEP
DOWN GOODS LOOP
65.38 UP & DOWN SLOW

P1/2 (10) being rebuilt to (12)
P3 (5)
Wellingborough Down Sidings

Wellingborough Goods 2 65.72

Neilsons Sidings (Wellingborough) GBRf 66.35
66.21
Crane 66.25

RR

Line between Bedford and Corby planned to be electrified in 2020
Line between Sharnbrook Jn and Kettering South to be re-quadrupled late 2019.

C (lower / 9B)

West Hampstead PSB (WH)

DOWN FAST
UP FAST
UP & DN SLOW (future)
DN SLOW
USLOW

Sharnbrook Jn 56.44 56.52 56.59 56.66

57   58   59

Line between Sharnbrook Jn and Kettering South to be re-quadrupled late 2019.

December 2018

A — LEICESTER and HITCHIN LINE

Controlled by East Midlands CC (located at Derby)

9D : to Wellingborough
10B

SPC 3 [LN 3201]   LMS : Mid

Harrowden Jn HABD 67.36
Harrowden Jn 66.68

Line between Sharnbrook Jn and Kettering South Jn to be re-quadrupled late 2019.

Kettering South Jn 70.54
70.51 70.55 70.60 70.63
Engrs
Kettering Stabling Sidings (planned)

Kettering Jn 72.01
4 72.18 2 72.23 1
DOWN FAST / UP FAST / DOWN SLOW / UP SLOW

Kettering 72.01
Kettering North Jn 74.02 74.04/74.09
Kettering Station Jn 73.47 73.59/73.64 73.68/73.68 73.68
(Glendon North Jn) 74.77
A43
(LR)(KM) East Midland CC

LEICESTER and HITCHIN LINE

Line between Bedford and Corby planned to be electrified in 2020

Geddington/ Harpers Brook Viaduct 77.38-50
Geddington HABD 77.08
Glendon Viaduct (R. Ise) 75.22-75.26
Desborough Summit 436 ft 78.39

DOWN MAIN / UP MAIN
MARKET HARBOROUGH 82.74
82.54 (Market Harborough) 1 10
82.69 R. Welland
Little Bowden 82.28/33
(R)(FP)
H P 2 6
(Glendon North Jn)

KETTERING and MANTON LINE   GSM1 [LN 3601]   LMS : Mid
Controlled by East Midlands CC (KM)

East Langton HABD 86.20
Seaton Tunnel (206 yds) 86.24/86.33 85.18-76 87.30
Harringworth Vdct max height 70 ft Welland Valley Vdct 88 acres
Seaton Vdct (1mile, 82yds) Glaston Tunnel 88.33

Corby Tunnel (1mile, 160yds) 80.18
Gretton Viaduct 83.05 - 83.08

B

Controlled by East Midlands CC (LR)

5B : to Nuneaton
to : Nuneaton
10A

Paget Hall Farm 2.24
Jericho (UWC) 3.31
DN H.
UP H.

HINCKLEY 4.00
Hinckley Canal 2.62
EM | LNW
EMCC (CT) | (WN) Rugby SCC

M69 7.46
Holts (UWC) 9.8

River Soar
Croft Quarry | Aggregates Industries
9.44
Loading Hopper 10.04
10.20

NARBOROUGH 11.67
12.15 2 1
M1
12.42 former GC River Soar Overbridge) 12.17 Narborough HABD
(CT) 12.35 Hinds
12.75 former GC River Overbridge) (107.24)

LN 3232 WNS LMS : LNW
SOUTH LEICESTERSHIRE LINE
Miles from Nuneaton (South Jn) 11

14B : to Coalville & Burton
LMS : Mid KSL [LN 3525]
LEICESTER and BURTON LINE

LN 3232 WNS
SOUTH WIGSTON 14.67
Glen Parva Jn GSP 14.53
Glen Parva Jn 14.57
WIGSTON NORTH CURVE LMS : LNW
95.76 (15.33) Wigston North Jn
96.02 (15.36)
SPC 4 [LN 3201]

[LN 2231] WGP LMS : Mid
WIGSTON SOUTH CURVE
Wigston South Jn 95.37
Kilby Bridge 93.40
95.38
3 SPC 4 [LN 3201] LMS : Mid

Kibworth 370 ft 89.54

Knighton Tunnel (104 yds) 98.02
Knighton Vdct 97.45
Knighton South Jn 96.74
former London Rd Jn 98.36/98.36 98.07
Leicester South Jn 98.74/99.07

◊ LEICESTER 99.07 99.00
Leicester North Jn 99.18
4 SPC 5 [LN 3615]
✱ All Platforms subdivided (a) south (b) north
Platforms 2-4 1 13 5 14
Leicester Sidings
A Under the Box
B Accident Van Road
C Old Shed Side
D Coal Road 1
E Coal Road 2
F Coal Road 3
G Slip Road
H Pass Pit Road
J Goods Pit Road
K Fuel Road 1
L Fuel Road 2
M Shop Coal Road
N Long Coal Road
Bell Lane 99.59
No.5 TOP SDG 100.00
SHUNT NECK 100.20
Humberstone Road (100.20)
Humberstone 100.31

Loco Sidings (LR) UK Rail Leasing

MELTON MOWBRAY 104.76/105.22
Melton Jn & GF 105.70
Melton Stn 105.22
River Eye 105.33
103.75 103.62 104.19 104.22 105.09 105.11-/105.17

Carriage Sidings
DALBY'K K
WILD Thurmaston 101.78

C — CORBY CORUS BRANCH / CORBY AUTOMOTIVE BRANCH

BSC 10A
Water Works
Scrap Tata Steel Corby
Coil Unloading Pad -2.62
Overhead Crane
Exchange Sdgs 2.29
2.75
A427 / A6086 / A14
Corby Euro-Hub Freight Park Automotive Terminal (OOU)
Ramps
[LN 3605] [LN 3610]
CORBY AUTOMOTIVE BRANCH
DN & UP BSC BCH
1.10

Corby (Corby Loop)

10C BSC
Corby Station South Jn 79.30 79.40
Corby Station North Jn 79.56 79.62/79.68
Spring Corby Run Point Round Sdgs 79.56
79.19 79.24 79.34 79.50
10.00 79.62/79.68 80.18
357 ft 78.65/78.39
NR Bdy 0.16
DN CORBY / UP CORBY

SPC 3 [LN 3201] LMS : Mid
LEICESTER and HITCHIN LINE

Kettering and Manton Line (B cont.)

[LN 3601] GSM2 LMS : Mid
Manton Jn 0.00/90.23
PMJ Manton Jn GF 0.14
Manton Jn (MJ) 90.16
Manton Tunnel (749 yards) 90.06
90.06 90.16/90.18 90.06

Wing Tunnel (353 yds) 89.73
Wing Viaduct 89.39 89.54 89.22
River Chater 90.50 90.58/90.62 89.62
Manton North Jn 91.05

SYSTON and PETERBOROUGH LINE

Rutland Water
Oakham Tunnel (49 yards) 92.96/96.19

Gunthorpe (BW - OMSL) 91.24
Goodridges (UWC) 91.61
Pattersons (UWC) 92.00
Egleton (UWB) 92.27
OAKHAM 93.61
Brooke Road (CCTV) 93.22
Oakham Crossing (OMJ) 93.56
5 2 6

Langham Jn (LN) 95.06
Ashwell Gate House (MCBR) 96.47
Ashwell (AL) 96.67
Ashwell Branch Jn 97.22
97.22✱ (Ashwell) #
Whissendine (WE) 99.15
Whissendine (MCG) 99.01
River Eye 99.01/99.15

= Junction with [ASB] to Cottesmore (see 10D), Rutland Railway Museum

Book 2 : to Peterborough
EM LINE | LN
(P) Peterborough

Uffington (UN) 12.75
Hoods Mill (UWC) 11.77
✱ Uffington & Barnack
Stamford Tunnel (341 yds)
STAMFORD 10.11
River Chater Meadows Exchange Sdgs 10.20-/.39
River Chater GF 7.60
Ketton Cement Works Hanson Cement (Heidelberg)
Loading Silos
Ketton (K) 6.60
Luffenham (CCTV) 5 - 5.13
Naylors (UWC) 5.46
River Chater 6.53
Wing (UWC) 1.03
Pilton Sdg 1.26
9.13 10.20/.39
A1

SYSTON and PETERBOROUGH LINE
Miles from St Pancras via Corby
Miles from Manton Jn

11C : to RIDC Melton
10

D — RUTLAND RAILWAY MUSEUM

4' 8½" / 1435mm gauge
ASB
Former Iron Ore Loading Dock 0ch
COTTESMORE 9ch
'Rocks By Rail'
ASB former Oakham Canal 1802-1846

SEN 11A : to Loughborough
Ashwell Branch Jn (to 10B)
Syston North Jn 104.25
SPC 5 GSM3 [LN 3615]
Syston South Jn 103.62 103.72
SYSTON 103.63
2 GSM3 [LN 3615] (Leics) 113.36
SPC 5 [LN 3201]
Controlled by East Midlands CC (LR)

UP N. CURVE 49ch 0.00
DOWN UP N. CURVE
UP FAST / DOWN FAST / UP & DOWN SLOW
Ratcliffe (UWC) 40ch 32ch

Syston East Jn 104.22
DOWN FAST UP & DOWN SLOW
Broome Lane (AHBC) 106.00

Miles from St Pancras via Leicester

Melton Mowbray — Grange (UWC) 105.70
Sysonby 105.17
(Corby) 105.70 105.31
mileage meet

Sysonby GF & GF
Frisby (MCB)
Saxby
Brentingby (UWC) 102.38
Ashfordby (UWW) 103.01
River Eye

2 GSM4 [LN 3620] 11C : to RIDC Melton

Mill Deeping (UWC) 113.01/110.41
Asfordby (AHBC) 106.00
Brooksby (AHBC)
(FY) SB (LR) EMCC

December 2018

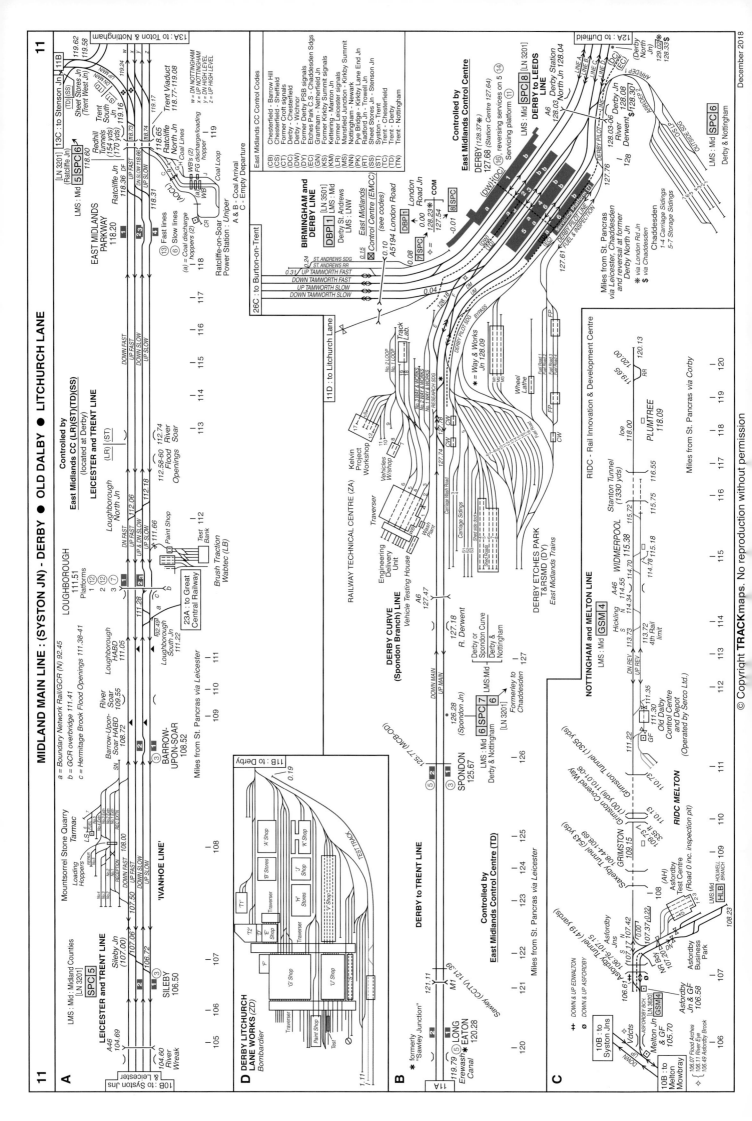

MIDLAND MAIN LINE : (SYSTON JN) - DERBY ● OLD DALBY ● LITCHURCH LANE

December 2018

© Copyright TRACKmaps. No reproduction without permission

A

Controlled by East Midlands Control Centre (DC)

14D: to Rowsley South (Peak Rail)

MATLOCK 145.00
Platform 1 & 2
High Tor Tunnels
145.03 Matlock GF
145.05
144.60 Boathouse
Bridge Road
cablecar line

CROMFORD 143.10
Wirksworth Tunnel (764 yards)
143.48
1 AJM LMS : Mid [LN 3246]

RAVENSTOR 141.79
WIRKSWORTH 141.34
Incline 141.79

WHATSTANDWELL
Lea Wood Bridge 141.58
Lea Wood Tunnel (315 yds)
High Peak Jn 141.23
Whatstandwell Tunnel (149 yds) 140.06

Miles from St Pancras via Leicester & Chaddesden

d = River Derwent Viaduct 140.51
e = Cromford Viaduct 143.03-06
f = High Tor No. 1 Tunnel (321 yards) 144.06-20
g = High Tor No. 1A Tunnel (58 yards) 144.21-24
h = High Tor No. 2 Tunnel (378 yards) 144.24-41
j = Holt Lane Tunnel (126 yards) 144.65-70

AMBERGATE and ROWSLEY LINE

DERBY and LEEDS LINE

AMBERGATE 138.18
Toadmoor Tnl (129 yards) 138.07-12
Wingfield Tunnel (261 yards)

River Amber 140.40

BELPER 135.55
Belper Yard
Belper GF 134.61
SPC 8 LMS : Mid [LN 3201]

Milford Tunnel (855 yards)
Swainsley Viaduct (River Derwent) 134.57-61

SHOTTLE 136.43
IDRIDGEHAY 138.04
LC 138.07
Engrs

DUFFIELD 133.08
Duffield Branch Jn 133.07
Duffield South GF
North GF
HABD

Controlled by East Midlands Control Centre (DY)

DJW

Burley Viaduct (River Derwent) 131.54-58
EMCC (DC) (DY)
SPC 8 LMS : Mid : North Mid [LN 3201]

Breadsall Jn 130.50
(Little Eaton Jn) 131.06
A38 130.49

DEX
former Derby Friargate Line overbridge 129.22

St Mary's North Jn 129.60
St Mary's South Jn 129.06

Miles from St Pancras via Leicester & Chaddesden

DERBY and LEEDS LINE

Nottingham Road Viaduct 128.40-43

11B : to Derby

DERBY and LEEDS LINE (North Midland)

Controlled by East Midlands CC (DC)(TC)
Main Lines (DC) - Erewash Lines (TC)

Book 2 : to Chesterfield

Down Sdgs 145.60

Chesterfield 145.21
Chesterfield South Jn 146.00
former LMR/ER Regional Bdy) (Horns Bridge) 144.68

Clay Cross North Jn 142.77
Clay Cross (R. Rother 143.12) South Jn 142.64

SPC 9 LMS : Mid : North Midland [LN 3201]
8 SPC TCC [LN 3207]

(Clay Cross South Jn)
147.69 142.10
DCCL = DOWN CLAY CROSS LOOP

DN MAIN
UP MAIN

Clay Cross Tunnel (1 mile, 24 yards) 147.22

EMCC (DY) (DC)

Miles from St Pancras via Leicester & Chaddesden

River Amber 140.40

141.43 (Coney Green Jn) 146.21

DOWN MAIN 144.18
UP EREWASH 147.69

ERWASH VALLEY LINE

HAMMERSMITH 136.04
S & T Depot
RR 135.78
136.10
SOUTH LINE
NORTH LINE
causeway (Butterley Reservoir) 135.63-74

a = former Kilby Bridge SB
b = former Ais Gill SB
c = former Kettering SB

BUTTERLEY 135.57
LC 135.51
b
Carriage Shed

MIDLAND RAILWAY-BUTTERLEY
Midland Railway Trust Ltd
4' 8½" / 1435mm gauge
APB LMS : Mid

(SK)
Matthew Kirtley Museum, with loco running & repair shops
Richard Levick Workshop
Butterley Works Branch
West Shed
Historic carriage & wagon repairs
Brands Crossing 0.10
Butterley Park 0.03 0.00
Brands Siding 0.17
LC 0.20
Engrs
Diesel Shed 0.21
SWANWICK JN 134.79
APB LMS : Mid
Swanwick Branch 134.66
SWH

GOLDEN VALLEY LIGHT RAILWAY 2' 0" gauge
Newlands Inn
0.64
0.15
LC's
134.75

(Pye Bridge Jn) 133.67
Riddings 0.22
CPC
0.00 0.07
Ironville GF 133.18
Ironville Jn (old) 133.20
APB CPC APB

Ironville Jn (new) 133.18
R. Erewash 132.67
Codnor Park Jn 132.76
APB TCC TCC

LMS : Mid
Stoneyford Sidings (OOU)
(Disused) Cromford Canal 132.67
1 = CR
2 = RR
3 = Loading Line

LMS : Mid
EREWASH VALLEY LINE
DOWN EREWASH FAST
UP EREWASH FAST
UP & DN EREWASH SLOW
TCC [LN 3207]

LANGLEY MILL 129.68
Langley Mill
HABDs 129.27

Miles from St Pancras via Leicester & Toton

14A : to Toton

ALFRETON 136.07
Blackwell South Jn 136.10
Blackwell SDG 135.50
Alfreton Tunnel (840 yards) 135.11
9 APB LMS : Mid

Morton Jn 139.09
400 ft

DOWN EREWASH
UP EREWASH
UP & DN BLACKWELL SLOW

Tibshelf & Blackwell Branch Jn 137.16

Blackwell South Jn 135.50

SUTTON PARKWAY 137.11
Sleights (CCTV) 134.76
Pinxton (CCTV) 135.46
M1
135.63
Upper Portland Farm (UWC) 136.29
Lower Portland Farm (UWC)
Sowters (UWC) 137.67
Upper Portland (AHBC) 136.71

Sutton Forest (AHBC) 138.30
Kings Mill No.1 (BW) 139.22
Break-Hills Hermitage Mill Viaduct 139.33-38
Sutton (UWC) 138.83

Controlled by East Midlands CC
(KS)(MS)(PK)(TC)
(located at Derby)

PBS 1 [LN 3273]
Pye Bridge & Kirkby
PINXTON BRANCH
LMS : Mid

RAC [LN 3255] NR/LNE: GC/GN
"ROBIN HOOD LINE"

Grives Lane (AHBC) 138
138 – Kirkby South (AHBC)
Kirkby Summit Jn
Kirkby Lane End 138.31 137.60
COM 137.11
1 PBS 2 [LN 3273]

KIRKBY-IN-ASHFIELD 138.38
136.04 136.66
* former Kirkby Jn
138.50 via Pinxton
136.55 via Newstead and former Midland Line

(KS) UP DN MFLD

Kirkby Tunnel (198 yds) 135.49-57
135.75 via Pinxton
135.31 (Warren)
135.00
NEWSTEAD 134.20 via Mansfield
Hardstaffs 132.76 over 132.09 (UWC)
Linby Station (ASCU) former GC over 132.76
(MS)(KS)
4

13D : to Hucknall & Nottingham

"ROBIN HOOD LINE"
Miles from St Pancras via Corby & Newstead and former Midland Line

Derby EMCC [LN 768] (MANSFIELD and WORKSOP)

SHIREBROOK 145.06
Shirebrook Jn 144.69
3 PBS PSE
[LN 3273]
McKenzies (UWC) 142.79
Littlewood Viaduct 143.43-47
Sheepwash Viaduct 144.64-65
DOWN MAIN
UP MAIN
EM LINE
(SJ)

MANSFIELD WOODHOUSE
Mansfield Woodhouse Jn 142.17
3 PBS [LN 3273]
142.05 142.13

MANSFIELD
140.44 Mansfield 140.52-65
140.40 South Mansfield Stn
2 PBS [LN 3273]
7
5

Miles from St Pancras via Corby & Newstead and former Midland Line

Book 2 : to Worksop

B

STEEPLE GRANGE LIGHT RAILWAY 1' 6" gauge
Wirksworth
Loading Sdg

STEEPLEHOUSE JUNCTION 0.00
Workshop
Traverser
Engine House
Dark Porter Lane 0.10
RECREATION GROUND 0.25
Sandy Hill
Lawson's Loop
KILLER'S DALE HALT 0.12
DARK LANE 0.12
STEEPLEHOUSE QUARRY 0.07
MIDDLETON* WHARF 0.44
Geoff Coat's Sdg

* probable name (under construction)
On the trackbed of the former "Killer's Branch" of the Cromford & High Peak Railway

= Geoff Coat's Sdg
These tracks are mixed gauge 1' 6" & 2' 0"

12

December 2018

A

Controlled by East Midlands CC
(located at Derby)

Controlled by East Midlands CC (NN)
(located at Derby)

EREWASH VALLEY LINE
Long Eaton Town (CCTV)

NOTTINGHAM Platforms

RADFORD and TROWELL LINE

NOTTINGHAM and MANSFIELD LINE

DERBY and NOTTINGHAM LINE   Controlled by East Midlands CC (TN)

Miles from St. Pancras via Corby

LMS : Mid   LMS : Mid : Nottingham & Trent

13B

Eastcroft Depot :
East Midlands Trains
Nottingham TMD (NM)
Eastcroft Engrs

NET overbridge (former GCR alignment) 123.43

Nottingham East Jn 123.27

Carrington Street overbridge 123.48

NOTTINGHAM 123.39

Nottingham West Jn 123.52

Miles from St. Pancras via Corby and Plumtree

DERBY and NOTTINGHAM LINE

Mansfield Jn (mileage meet)

Lenton South Jn 125.27

LMS : Mid

14A : to Toton GDS

11B : to Derby   11A : to Loughborough

B

Controlled by East Midlands CC (NN)   NOTTINGHAM and LINCOLN LINE   Controlled by East Midlands CC (GN)

DERBYSHIRE EXTENSION BRANCH

NOTTINGHAM BRANCH

Book 2 : to Lincoln

ECM 1   Book 2 : to Retford

NEWARK CASTLE 17.02

NEWARK CROSSING CURVE

Book 2 : to Grantham via Newark North Gate

Doncaster (D)

BOTTESFORD 112.68

ELTON & ORSTON 115.34

ASLOCKTON 117.22

BINGHAM 119.39

THURGARTON

BLEASBY

LOWDHAM 7.31

ROLLESTON 12.46

FISKERTON 12.03

RADCLIFFE (Notts) 123.08

CARLTON

NETHERFIELD 125.13

Netherfield Jn 2.35

Book 2 : to Sleaford

Miles from Kings Cross

Controlled by East Midlands CC (GN)

13A

LNE : GN

C

Trent & Mersey Canal

(Chellaston W. Jn)(Chellaston E. Jn)

SSJ 2   MSJ 1   SSJ 1

Stenson Jn

Miles from St. Pancras via Leicester

LMS : Mid : Stenson & Weston / Sawley & Weston / Derby and Melbourne

Segro Logistics Park
East Midlands Gateway
(Kegworth) Rail Freight Terminal
(under construction)

Castle Donington
Marks & Spencer
Distribution Depot

EMCC (SS)   EMCC (DY)

River Trent Viaduct

M1

A50   A46

26C : to Peartree & Derby   26C : to N. Stafford Jn & Burton-on-Trent

D

12A : to Kirkby-in-Ashfield

"ROBIN HOOD LINE"

NOTTINGHAM EXPRESS TRANSIT (NET) 750dc Line 1
Alongside Network Rail
(see 49 for full detail)

NR Controlled by East Midlands CC (MS)

Book 2 : to Grantham   BR   ACD

Allington (AL)   ABE   North Jn

East Midlands   ROC

HUCKNALL 131.65

BULWELL 128.76

Bulwell South Jn 128.65

Bestwood Park Jn 130.21

Wilkinson St Overbridge 126.65

River Leen 127.07

Linby Colliery (ABCL) 132.24

Bulwell Forest Crossing (CCTV) 129.35

LMS : Mid : Nottingham & Mansfield

Miles from St Pancras via Corby

© Copyright TRACKmaps. No reproduction without permission

December 2018

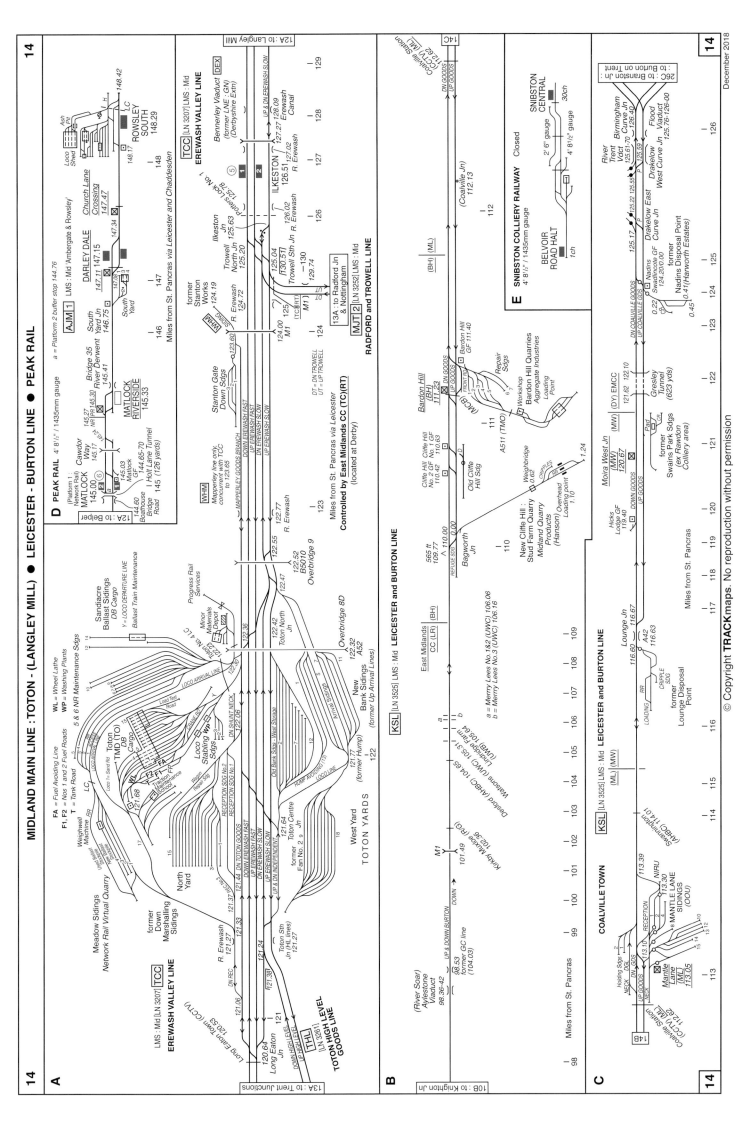

CHILTERN LINE : LONDON MARYLEBONE - AYLESBURY - (CLAYDON) ● BUCKINGHAMSHIRE RAILWAY CENTRE

A

Marylebone IECC Control Codes

(ME) Marylebone
(OB) Oxford - Bletchley

Platforms
1 (11) 4 (5)
2, 3 (12) 5 (10)
6 (10)

WALL SIDING
IECC 205.77
LONDON MARYLEBONE 205.77

Miles from Manchester (London Road) via former GCR line
London Underground distances, in kilometres from former Ongar Station

Regent's Canal
205.48
205.42
TUNNEL SDG UP SDG 205.44
205.33

LEC 1

St. John's Wood Tunnel (1606 yards)

205.22 TUNNEL SDG
UP MAIN
DOWN MAIN
204.40
204.37
2.29

MCJ 1

MCJ 1 [MD 701] LNE : GC

1 : to Euston
1 : to Willesden Junction

Hampstead Tunnel (694 yards)
204.35
204.03

Book 5 : LUL to Baker St.

8A : to Gospel Oak

FINCHLEY ROAD (203.79) 50.140

WEST HAMPSTEAD (203.51) 50.750

All NR lines from / to Marylebone controlled by Marylebone IECC
LUL Metropolitan lines controlled from Baker Street Signalling and Control Centre
LUL Metropolitan lines controlled by Transmission Based Train Control (TBTC) from Neasden Signalling Centre

205
204
203
202
201
200
199
198

KILBURN (202.17) 51.840
Kilburn Viaduct 203.32
203.21
203.09

BOK 3

WILLESDEN GREEN 53.030

NJN

8B : to Cricklewood

CAW [EA 1360] LMS : Mid

DOLLIS HILL 54.240

NJN [MD 715] LNE : GC
Territory Bdy on NJN
6.56 7.03
Neasden Junction (NJ)
6.51 LNW
201.09

1 : to Acton Wells Jn
1 : to Willesden Junction

Book 5 : LUL Metropolitan Line to Chesham

NEASDEN 55.090 (200.76)
LUL Neasden Depot

WEMBLEY PARK (199.41) 57.380 (6.59 from Baker Street)
(de-commissioned) Wembley Park Sdgs

MCJ 1 [MD 710] LNE : GC

NORTHWICK PARK 60.490 (198.50)
PRESTON ROAD 58.840

NR lines controlled by Marylebone IECC (ME) to 197.05

2B : To Euston West Coast Mainline (6 tracks)

MCJ 1 [MD 710] LNE : GC

200.15 River Brent
5.64
5.60
5.05 5.00
4.61

Great Central Way Jn

WEMBLEY STADIUM

South Sdgs
North Sdgs
Chiltern Rlys Wembley LMD
Mantles Wood Network Rail / LUL Boundary

MCJ 2 [MD 712]

16A : to West Ruislip

B

LUL Metropolitan and LNE : GC 197.05

HARROW-ON-THE-HILL 61.780 (9.13)

South 9.18 LUL Harrow South Jn (limit of electrification from the west)

2 MCJ 1 COM

NB MAIN 62.830 SB MAIN
SB LOCAL
Harrow 10.08 North Jn

15A

Book 5 : LUL Metropolitan Line to Uxbridge

NORTH HARROW 63.770 (10.57)
PINNER 65.250 (11.52)
NORTHWOOD HILLS 67.330 (12.76)
NORTHWOOD 68.950 (13.78)
MOOR PARK 71.160 (15.28)

METROPOLITAN LINE NB LOCAL
METROPOLITAN LINE SB LOCAL

Spur Road
River Gade
Watford North Curve

Book 5 : LUL Metropolitan Line to Watford

Watford North Jn 73.350
Watford South Jn 73.100
73.260 Watford East Jn

16.28
16.45
16.57
72.770

South Sdgs

RICKMANSWORTH 74.520 (17.36)
North Sdgs

CHORLEYWOOD 78.030 (19.53)

M25
76.630 (18.60)

CHALFONT AND LATIMER 81.580 (21.67)

AMERSHAM 84.850 (23.70)
Highest station on London Underground - 147 metres above Sea Level

10, 11, 12, 13, 14, 15, 16, 17, 18, 19, 20, 21, 22, 23, 24, 25, 26, 27, 28

LUL Metropolitan Line NB
SB

Southern Stabling
Neasden South Sdgs
Neasden South Wembley Aggregate Industries
Neasden Freight Term.

NAJ 1 [MD 701]

Miles from Baker Street (Metropolitan)
Kilometres from Ongar in brackets ()

C

158, 159, 160, 161

Ditchburns (UWC) 159.33
159.10
(Grendon Underwood Jn)

3 MCJ 2 (Quainton Jn) COM LNE : GC LT(Met) & LNE (GC) Jt
161.50 161.57 44.48
1 DN 44.22

QUAINTON ROAD 44.22 (Buckinghamshire Railway Centre see 15D)

*Platform 1 at Quainton Road is usable by services on Network Rail Infrastructure

[MD 725]

17A : to Claydon L& NE Jn

MCJ 2 (Quainton Jn) COM

WADDESDON 42.77

AYLESBURY VALE 'AYLESBURY VALE'
AYLESBURY VALE PARKWAY 40.38
River Thame
40.05 UP
Aylesbury Vale Jn 40.26

Miles from Baker Street (Metropolitan)

41, 42, 43, 44

16A : to Princes Risborough

GREAT MISSENDEN 29.00
WENDOVER 33.43
STOKE MANDEVILLE 35.75

UP MAIN
DOWN MAIN

MCJ 2 [MD 712]
LT (Metropolitan) and LNE : GC Joint

28.77

29, 30, 31, 32, 33, 34, 35, 36, 37, 38, 39, 40

Miles from Baker Street (Metropolitan)

AYLESBURY Platforms 1 (10) 2, 3 (9)
38.08
38.13
38.38
38.43
Aylesbury Jn
Aylesbury North Goods Loop
Carriage Sidings
CET
★ = Underframe Cleaning Shop
38.21 Servicing Depot
Chiltern Railways Aylesbury Maintenance Depot (AL)
Chiltern Depot

[MD 725] [MD 710]

PRA [MD 720]
GW & LNE (GC) Jt
37.62
48

Miles from Manchester (London Road) via former GC main line
Controlled by Marylebone IECC (ME)

D

BUCKINGHAMSHIRE RAILWAY CENTRE (Quainton Railway Society Ltd)
4' 8½" / 1435mm gauge

REWLEY ROAD STATION

Traverser

44.25
44.22
44.16
44.18
44.01
43.64
44.63
44.29

Up Yard
Down Yard
QUAINTON ROAD
NETWORK RAIL
Museum

Miles from Baker Street (Met.) 44

15C

15B

December 2018

© Copyright TRACKmaps. No reproduction without permission

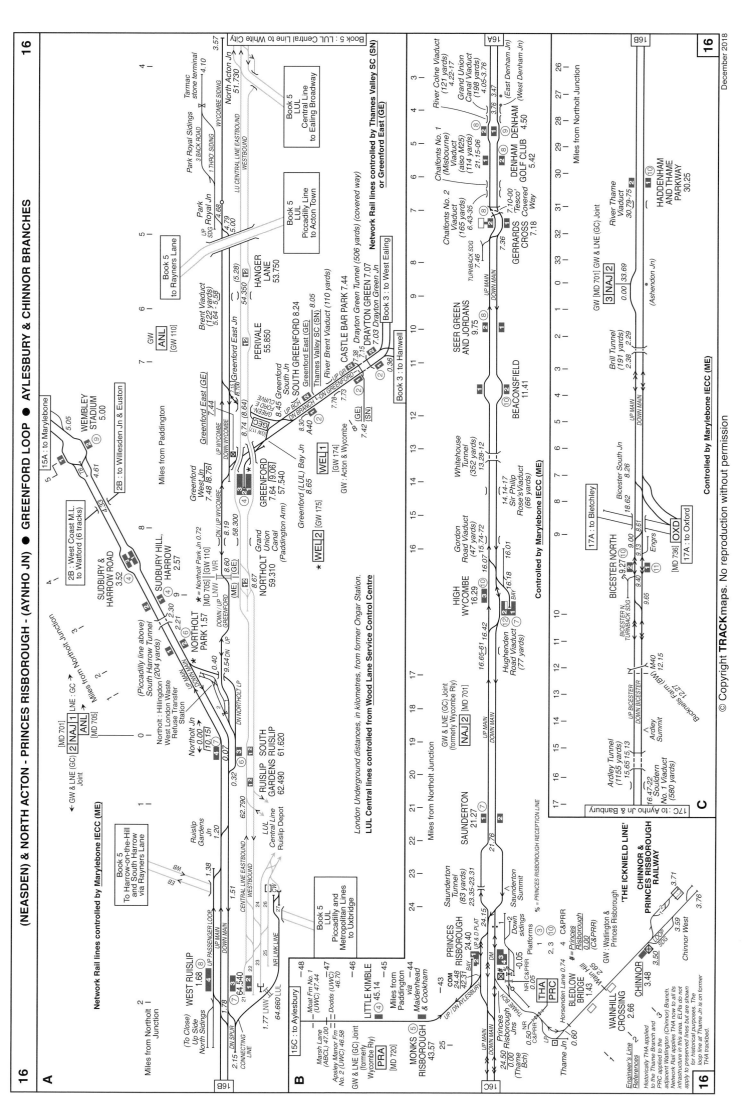

(NEASDEN) & NORTH ACTON - PRINCES RISBOROUGH - (AYNHO JN) ● GREENFORD LOOP ● AYLESBURY & CHINNOR BRANCHES

December 2018

© Copyright TRACKmaps. No reproduction without permission

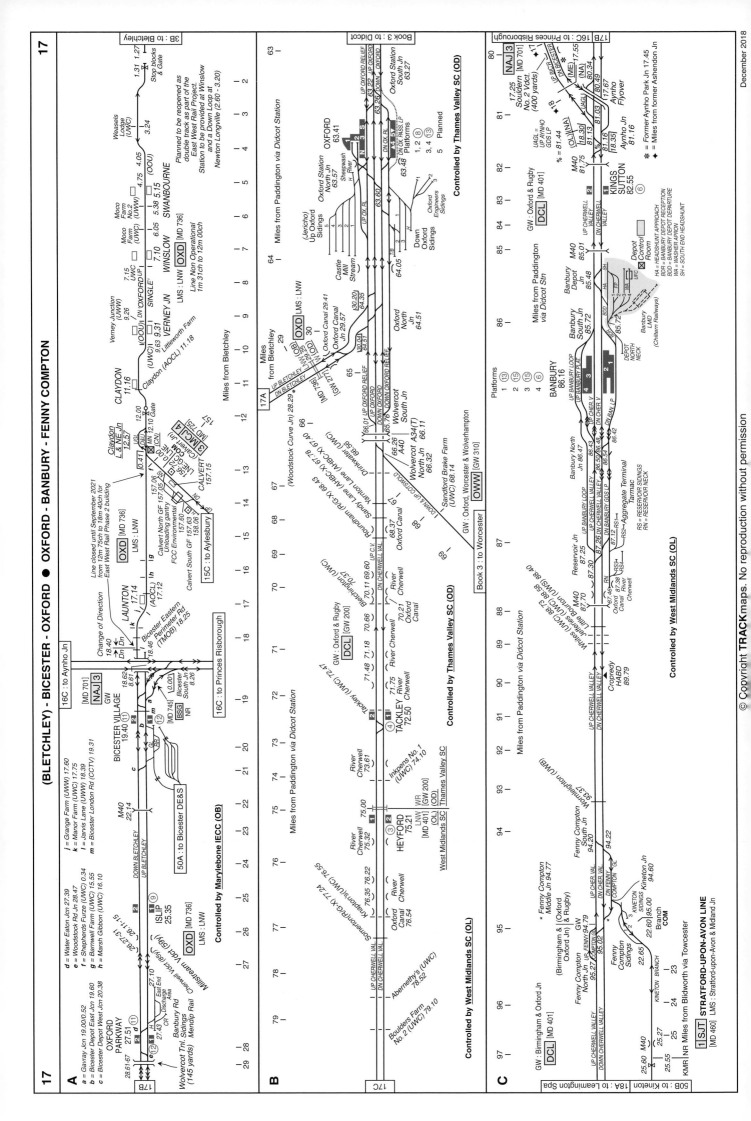

December 2018

(FENNY COMPTON) - LEAMINGTON - WARWICK ● LEAMINGTON - COVENTRY ● (RUGBY) - COVENTRY - STECHFORD ● COVENTRY - (NUNEATON)

A

Controlled by West Midlands SC (LC) (LJ) (LN) (OL)
(located at Saltley)

GW : Birmingham & Oxford Jn
DIDCOT to CHESTER LINE

19A : to Hatton
17C : to Banbury

River Avon Viaduct 107.15-18
WARWICK 108.02
#108.15
107.72 # Foot of Hatton Bank
B4115 1.61-63

106.73 Grand Union Canal (Aquaduct) 1.00
Milverton Jn 0.10
West Midlands SC
COM
KENILWORTH 107.00 0.00 UP & DN 1.13-22

(LN) (LJ)
WMSC
[MD 405]
1 LSC 2
DCL
[MD 401]

Milverton Viaduct
LEAMINGTON NEW JUNCTION LINE (BR)

DN KENILWORTH
UP KENILWORTH
106.55 106.40 DOWN DORRIDGE 106.52
106.32
Leamington Spa North Jn 106.26
Foundary Wood 106.44
Foundary Wood Jn 106.39
Leamington Spa South Jn 105.78

LEAMINGTON DEPOT SDG
DN LEAMINGTON BAY
DN LEAMINGTON PLATFORM
DOWN
DN CHERWELL VAL
UP CHER VAL
UP LEAM PLAT 106.11
UP LEAMINGTON BAY

LEAMINGTON SPA 106.07
Leamington Viaduct
Grand Union Canal 105.49
Neilson Street Viaduct 105.53-63
Emergency Crossover 105.30

Platforms 1 ⑦ 3 ⑪
2 ⑮ 4 ⑤

(OL) (LN)
(OL) (LN)
WMSC

DIDCOT to CHESTER LINE

DOWN CHERWELL VALLEY
UP CHERWELL VALLEY

Harbury Tunnel (70 yards) 100.49-52

Miles from Paddington via Didcot

DCL [MD 401]

B

COVENTRY and LEAMINGTON LINE
LMS : LNW

18C

Controlled by West Midlands SC (CB) (CN) (LC) (RC)
(located at Saltley)

Beechwood Tunnel (300 yds) 98.28-42
98.45 310 feet

TILE HILL 97.45 ⑧

CANLEY 95.37 ⑧
A45 95.66

COVENTRY and NUNEATON LINE
LMS : LNW

CNN [MD 410] LMS · LNW

Three Spires Jn 3.08 (0.00)
West Midlands SC (CN) Rugby SCC (CN)
Coundon Road (CCTV) 1.04
0.63
DOWN BEDWORTH
UP BEDWORTH 3.69
Hen Lane Bridge (N'n bdy) 0.38
Wheelwright Lane 1.13
4.15 River Sowe
COVENTRY ARENA 3.56 ④
PROLOGIS PARK

Limit of Electrification 0.45 0.47

RUGBY and BIRMINGHAM LINE
LMS : LNW (London & Birmingham)
RBS 1 [MD 301]

Coventry North Jn 94.19/0.00
Coventry North Yard
North Neck
South Neck
Coventry/Spon End Viaduct (River Sherbourne)
Coventry South Jn 93.71

COVENTRY 93.79

UP & DN SLOW
DOWN FAST
UP FAST
UP SLOW
94.33 94.40 94.25 94.14

Carriage Sidings
8.57 8.45 8.25 8.20
Limit of Electrification

Platforms 1 ⑯ 2,3 ⑰ 4 ⑫

(CB)
(LC)
(RC)
(CB)
(RC)

DOWN KENILWORTH
UP KENILWORTH
DN KENILWORTH

LSC 2 [MD 405]
6.15
Gibbet Hill Jn

COVENTRY and LEAMINGTON LINE

Sherbourne Viaduct 92.76-93.00
A4082 92.09
91.64-68 Sowe Viaduct
91.18
A46 90.69

Milburn (UWC) 5.62 Grange

Kenilworth 4.21-23 Stoneleigh Road Viaduct
Finham Brook Viaduct 4.27-30
Kenilworth North Jn 4.47
Kenilworth South Jn 3.75
KENILWORTH 3.49 ⑤
Kenilworth By Pass 2.25-30
A46
A452 100.25

U&D LP
DOWN KENILWORTH
UP KENILWORTH

DCL [MD 401]

Miles from Milverton Jn

Rugby SCC WMSC (RC)
Brandon HABD 89.05
Brandon (Avon) Viaduct 88.69-74
90.35

RUGBY and BIRMINGHAM LINE
LMS : LNW (London & Birmingham)
RBS 1 [MD 301]

Long Lawford Jn
84.25 84.33 84.30

DOWN COVENTRY
UP COVENTRY
DOWN MAIN
UP MAIN

Miles from Euston via Kilsby

5A : to Rugby
18A

C

LMS : LNW (London & Birmingham)
RUGBY and BIRMINGHAM LINE
RBS 1 [MD 301]

20 : to Birmingham New Street
20 : to Aston

ADDERLEY PARK 110.79 ④
DOWN GRAND JN
UP GRAND JN
DOWN COV
UP COV

STECHFORD and ASTON LINE
LMS : LNW
SAS [MD 315]

STECHFORD 109.08 (-0.08)
Stechford North Jn 109.12
Stechford North Jn Stechford Viaduct 110.79
Stechford South Jn 108.66
River Cole Viaduct 109.28-30
109.17 0.11-13
-0.30

(CB)
(SB)
(CB)(SB)

RBS 1 SAS 109.16 0.00
COM

LEA HALL 108.00 ⑨ 1
MARSTON GREEN 106.33 ⑧ 2
UP COVENTRY 104.70
DOWN COVENTRY 104.70

Birmingham International North Jn 105.09

BIRMINGHAM AIRPORT TERMINAL 1 0.585
Birmingham International Airport Air-Rail link Cable propelled
RAIL STATION 0.000

BIRMINGHAM INTERNATIONAL 104.55 ⑮
Birmingham International South Jn 104.36
104.20
104.63
103.62 104.13
M42
A45
'a' end 'b' end
1 2 3 4 5 6

Platforms 1 2 3 4 5 6

Blythe or Hampton-in-Arden Viaduct 101.75-78
HAMPTON-IN-ARDEN 102.61 ⑨
101.14 Bradnocks Marsh HABD

BERKSWELL 99.38 ⑧
99.39
DRS

Miles from Euston via Kilsby

DOWN MAIN
UP MAIN

Controlled by West Midlands Signalling Centre (CB)

5B : to Nuneaton
18B
18B

December 2018

© Copyright TRACKmaps. No reproduction without permission

December 2018

A

Miles from Honeybourne

SPRING ROAD 0.56 ⑥

HALL GREEN 1.22

Covered Way 0.66 ⑦
Covered Way 0.60

Stratford-upon-Avon Canal

UP N WAR
DOWN NORTH WARWICK
UP NORTH WARWICK

YARDLEY WOOD 2.48 ⑦

SHIRLEY 3.66

ACOCKS GREEN 125.08 ⑦
125.50

WHITLOCKS END 4.60

Stratford-upon-Avon Canal 4.36

WYTHALL 5.59 ⑥

River Cole 6.19

EARLSWOOD (West Midlands) 6.65

River Cole 5.14

THE LAKES 7.50
M42 8.21

OLTON 124.11 ⑤

Beanmont (UWC) 8.62
Wood End Tunnel (173 yds) ④ 8.70

WOOD END 8.56 ⑥

DANZEY 10.43 ⑦

SOLIHULL 122.25 ⑦

WIDNEY MANOR 120.66 ⑦
M42 120.44

Bentley Heath (CCTV) 119.43

UP DORRIDGE
DOWN DORRIDGE

DN D SPUR 119.31
DN DORR
UP DORR

HENLEY-IN-ARDEN 13.41

DORRIDGE North Jn 119.38

DORRIDGE 118.75 ⑨

Dorridge South Jn 118.53

WOOTTON WAWEN 15.22
River Alne 15.78

DIDCOT and CHESTER LINE
DCL [MD 401]
GW (Birmingham & Oxford Jn)

LAPWORTH 116.31 ⑨ ②

Stratford-upon-Avon Canal 115.72 ⑥

BEARLEY 13.19
Edstone Aqueduct 17.14

STRATFORD-UPON-AVON BRANCH

Songar Grange Farm (UWC) 14.38

Edstone Hall No. 1 (UWW) 14.06

Park Farm No. 1 (UWC) 16.00
Burnham Bros (UWC) 16.20

CLAVERDON 16.38 ⑥

DN & UP CLAVERDON

Miles from Paddington via Didcot

Park Farm No. 2 (UWC) 15.48

Bearley Jn 17.71
Stratford-upon-Avon Canal 17.40

GW [MD 415] HSA

★ = Hatton West Jn 17.62

Hatton North Jn 112.57/18.25

M40 alongside
UP DORRIDGE
DOWN DORRIDGE

DCL [MD 401]
DIDCOT and CHESTER LINE
GW (Birmingham & Oxford Jn)

WARWICK PARKWAY 109.26 ⑩

Grange Farm (UWC) 109.71
Budbrooke Jn

Hatton Station Jn 112.18/18.12

HATTON 112.14 ⑥

[MD 415] HSA

Hatton Bank (summit) 112.59

Hatton Bank 111.76
Hatton Bank (foot) 108.15

18A : to Leamington Spa

H 8.63

STRATFORD-UPON-AVON 8.77 ⑧
9.13 [MD 415] HSA
9.01
9.20

UP NTH WARWICK
DN NTH WARWICK

STRATFORD-UPON-AVON PARKWAY 9.78 (UWC)s

Burton Farm No. 2 10.10
No. 1 10.05 (UWC)s

WILMCOTE 11.49 ⑥
11.66
Stratford-upon-Avon Canal 12.72

New Tree 12.23 (UWC)
12.48

12.18/18.12

B

20 : to Stourbridge Jn

BIRMINGHAM MOOR STREET 128.66 ⑩
128.72
128.56
128.50

New Street Tunnel (under) 128.69-128.70 see map 20

Snow Hill Tunnel (635 yds)

MOOR ST SDG 1
MOOR ST SDG 2

Midland Metro Eastside Extension, due to open in 2022

High Street Deritend

MSL

DN SNOW HILL
UP SNOW HILL

Bordesley Viaduct

Meriden Street

20 : Midland Metro

Controlled by West Midlands SC (LJ)

Duddeston Viaduct to former Curzon Street Line never opened 128.24
128.40
128.24

23B : to Kings Norton

Corporation Yard Viaduct 128.12
128.03

Grand Union Canal

Bordesley Neck 127.72-128.00

BORDESLEY 128.03 ⑦
DCL [MD 435]

LMS : Mid SKN [MD 570]

UP CAMP HILL 41.68
DOWN CAMP HILL

Bordesley Jn 128
Lawden Road Viaduct 41.44

Bordesley South Jn 127.57

GW / LMS (LL)
(LJ)

128.11

20 : to Saltley & Grand Jn

Aggregates Terminal Tarmac

Caledonia Yard

Bordesley Down Yard

Controlled by West Midlands SC (HS) (LJ) (TB) (WM)
(located at Saltley)

UDDGL = UP & DN DORRIDGE GOODS LOOP
UDDPL = UP & DN DORRIDGE PASSENGER LOOP
UDDPL = UP DORRIDGE PASSENGER LOOP

BORDESLEY JN BRANCH
BCV [MD 401]

Miles from Paddington via Didcot

Main Lines Controlled by West Midlands SC (LJ)

DIDCOT and CHESTER LINE
DCL [MD 435]
GW (Birmingham & Oxford Jn)

Small Heath North Jn 127.14

SMALL HEATH 127.04 ⑦

Small Heath South Jn 126.67
126.65
126.59
126.59

Grand Union Canal 126.53

River Cole 126.44

TYSELEY LOCOMOTIVE WORKS (TM)
Vintage Trains Trust (formerly Birmingham Railway Museum)
4' 8½" / 1435mm gauge

Tyseley Depot (TS)
West Midlands Railways

NR boundary

Diesel Shed

Turntable
Work Shed (28 roads)

Carriage Shed

TYSELEY WARWICK ROAD 126.14

Former Oil Discharge Sdgs
Former Scrap Sidings

Ø Derailer
Tyseley Yard Line
Tyseley No. 1 (TY1) 126.44
126.40

DN THROUGH SDGS
UP THROUGH SDGS

TYSELEY ON THROUGH SDGS
TYSELEY UP THROUGH SDGS

DOWN SNOW HILL
UP SNOW HILL
DOWN BORDESLEY
UP BORDESLEY

WASH ROAD

FUEL

Carriage Stabling Sdgs

Tyseley North Junction 126.26
126.23
126.22

TYSELEY 126.05 ⑦
126.04

DCL [MD 401]

Tyseley Carriage Neck

0.00

Tyseley South Junction 125.73
TSB [MD 425] DCL [MD 401] BCV

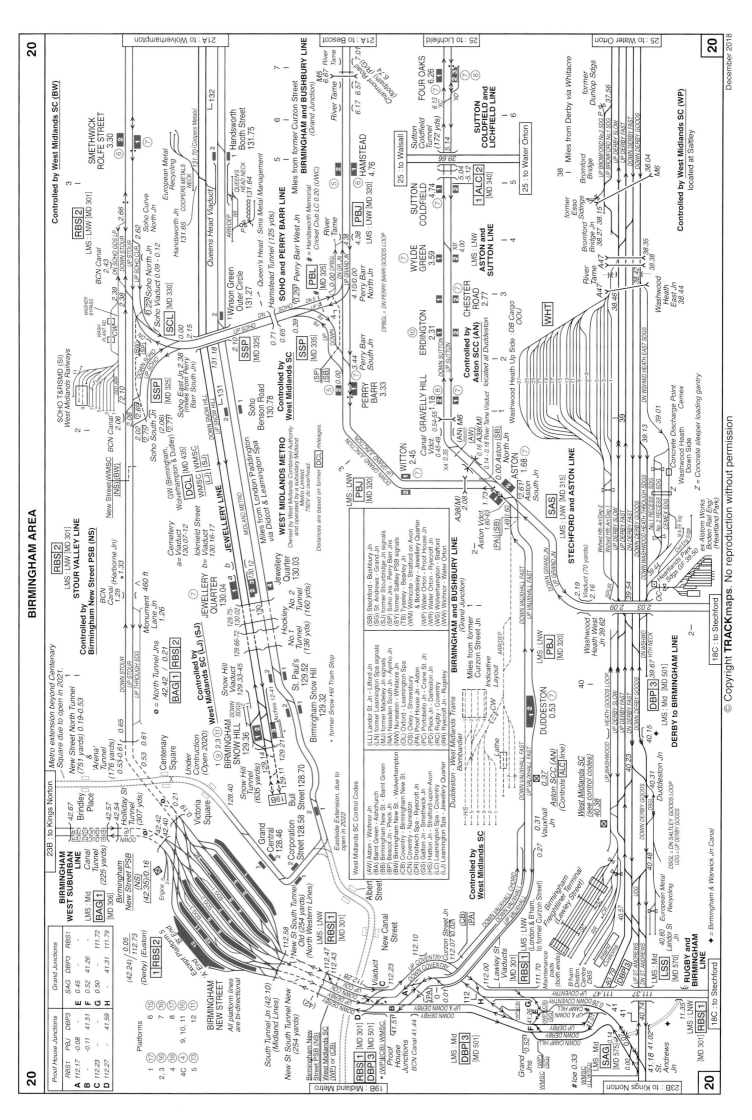

BIRMINGHAM AREA

A
24C : to Stourbridge Junction

GW
(Stourbridge Rly
Extn.) 2 GSJ
[MD 435]
— 135
Miles from Paddington
via Snow Hill

Langley Green
West (CCTV)
134.60

**HANDSWORTH JN to
STOURBRIDGE JN LINE**

LANGLEY GREEN 134.47

Wolverhampton St. George's

Platforms	
1	13
2	13
3	12
4	14
5	4
6	6

13

Piper's Row
141.67

The Royal
141.35

Bilston St
141.60

141.68

Wolverhampton 142.10

Wolverhampton St Jn
Crane St 142.14

WOLVERHAMPTON
[BW] (WS)

Under construction

*12.25-12.28
Peto/Betts Vdct
12.36-12.42
Wolverhampton
Viaducts
12.45
Wryley & Essington
Canal
12.48-12.60
Crane Street
Viaduct

@=(PC)(BW)
WMSC

22A : to Penkridge

2 RBS
[MD 301]
LMS : LNW
12.75

**WATER ORTON, WALSALL and
WOLVERHAMPTON LINE
Controlled by
West Midlands SC (PC)**

Monmore Green Jn
0.00
11.62

Wishbone Bridge

Bilston Road

BCN Canal

DOWN STOUR
UP STOUR

BCN Canal 10.61

BCN Canal 10.09

**Controlled by
West Midland Signalling Centre (BW)**

[MD 301] RBS 2

STOUR VALLEY LINE

Priestfield 2
140.33

The Crescent 139.45

Bilston Central 139.23

Loxdale 138.58

Bradley Lane2
138.20

Wednesbury Parkway
137.03

Wednesbury Great Western Street
3.27 Wednesbury Town Jn

WEDNESBURY TOWN

Pound Lane
3.26
3.24

136.51

136.59

COSELEY 9.46

TIPTON 8.16

Dudley Port

B   BLACK COUNTRY LIVING MUSEUM *

3' 6" gauge tramway
overhead electric
570 yards

Colliery
path LC's
Village
Entrance
Road Transport
Shed (no trams)
Depot

WEST MIDLANDS METRO (formerly DCL)

There are no distance posts, mileages are based on BR to Priestfield and by extension to Wolverhampton (BR mileages are from Oxford).

DEPOT & Control Room "Metro Centre"

Washer

Wheel Lathe

**OXFORD, WORCESTER and
WOLVERHAMPTON LINE**

OWW GW
DPJ LMS

Dudley Tunnel (944 yards)

Site for proposed 'Very Light Rail Innovation Centre'

Museum

Eagle Crossing 2.23

Trackbed planned for use by an extension to the Midlands Metro from Wednesday to Brierley Hill via Dudley Town Centre

DUDLEY 4 PORT 7.29

Swan Village Hill Top Tunnel (412 yards)

Swan Lane 135.18

135.74
135.55
135.26

Black Lake 135.26

Dudley Street Guns Village 134.70

Dartmouth Street 134.44

Lodge Road West Bromwich Town Hall 134.22

West Bromwich Central 134.05

Trinity Way 133.49

Kenrick Park 133.05

SOUTH STAFFORDSHIRE LINE (OOU)

LMS : LNW DPJ

Albion Canal BCN 5.73

SANDWELL & DUDLEY 5.28

Rood End Yard (OOU)

HSJ Smethwick Jn

SMETHWICK WEST

SMETHWICK GALTON BRIDGE 133.21 (High Level)
4.05 (Low Level)

[MD 301] RBS 2 HSJ
LGSJ 2 HSJ

Galton Tunnel (164 yds)
Galton Jn

THE HAWTHORNS 132.41

The Hawthorns 132.44

20 : to Birmingham Snow Hill
20 : to Birmingham New St

BIRMINGHAM and BUSHBURY LINE

PORTOBELLO and HEATH TOWN JN LINE

Heath Town Jn [HTW] over
(former Heath Town to Lichfield Rd Jn)
Wednesfield Heath Tunnel (179 yards)

PBJ [MD 365]

Portobello Jn 12.64

13.65
13.73 DOWN GRAND JUNCTION
UP GRAND JUNCTION

LMS : LNW Mid
Wolverhampton Logistics Centre DB Cargo
(Heath Town Jn) 1.29
(53.24 from Derby via Water Orton)

WILLENHALL (proposed) 11.55

Walsall Canal (Aqueduct) 10.23

James Bridge Jn 10.04/0.00

DARLASTON (proposed) 10.04
Darlaston Jn

0.15
0.33 M6

River Tame 0.27

9.65 9.46

WDJ [MD 360] LMS : LNW

PBJ [MD 320]

**Controlled by
West Midlands SC (SB)**

DPJ [MD 370] LMS : LNW

WALSALL 6.29

Walsall North Jn 6.40

6.40

6.34

Walsall South Jn 6.18

6.21

Ryecroft 6.76

47.48 [MD 345] LMS : Mid

**WALSALL and
CANNOCK LINE**

BJW 2 RRN 1
BJW 3
(formerly to Lichfield City)

RN 1 [FRN1]
LNW 47

THE CHASE LINE

UP SUTTON PARK a
DOWN SUTTON PARK 46.18
Daw End Aqueduct

25 : to Water Orton

Wryley & Essington Canal Aqueduct 0.66
6.79 0.00
COM

**WATER ORTON, WALSALL and
WOLVERHAMPTON LINE**

Miles from Derby

22B : to Bloxwich

Network Rail Training Centre

UP WALSALL SLOW
DOWN WALSALL SLOW
UP WALSALL FAST
DOWN WALSALL FAST

Midland Yard

Express Freight Platform

Tasker Street

Cement Loading Breedon

Walsall Pleck Jn 5.45
1.16

5.74

5.52

5.42
0.65 1 BJW 2

DPJ BJW 1 [MD 345] LMS : LNW

0.61

0.65

River Tame 0.33 M6

UP DARLASTON
DOWN DARLASTON

SOUTH STAFFORDSHIRE LINE

BJW 2 [MD 345] LMS : Mid 6.40

CBR [MD 565] LMS : Mid

a = (Lichfield Road Jn) 46.73

Miles from Dudley Jn

DOWN WALSALL
UP WALSALL

PLECK CURVE

BJW 1 [MD 345] LMS : LNW

DOWN G JN 4.72
UP G JN 4.63

(Bescot Curve Jn)
0.00/4.73

DN DUDLEY SDGS
UP DUDLEY SDGS

UP G & DOWN G JN
9.00

4.65

River Tame 8.65
River Tame 8.64
8.60

River Tame M6 0.07
0.10
0.11
0.07

PBJ [MD 320]

BESCOT YARDS

BSD 5 Bescot Depot (BS) DB Cargo

Down Storage Sidings (1-5)

Down Sorting Sdgs (1-20)

BSD 4

BSD 3

Down Sorting Sdgs (1-4)

Down Reception Sdgs (1-4)

Down Local Sorting Sidings (1-10)

BSD 2

BSD 1

ENGINE NECK

SOUTH NECK

SHUNTING LINE

UP GRAND JUNCTION
DOWN GRAND JUNCTION
UP BESCOT UP GOODS

Bescot Jn 8.28
8.25
8.43

Bescot Middle 8.17

New Ballast Sidings 8.47
Virtual Quarry

Up Yard

UP Bescot

BESCOT STADIUM 4

BSD 7

BSD 6

Newton Jn 7.59

TAME BRIDGE PARKWAY 7.48

7.42 Tame Valley

7.44 Tame Canal (Aqueduct)

Used Ballast Pile

Maintenance Apron

**Controlled by
WMSC (SB)**
located at Saltley

[MD 320] PBJ
LMS : LNW

BIRMINGHAM and BUSHBURY LINE
(Grand Junction)

BSD 6

Up Sorting (or Brook) Sidings
DB Cargo

20 : to Aston

	(BP)	(PD)	(SB)
(DR)	(RR)	(WR)	

Controlled by West Midlands SC located at Saltley

Miles from Birmingham New Street

22   22

22 (WALSALL) - CANNOCK - (RUGELEY) ● (WOLVERHAMPTON) - (TELFORD)/(STAFFORD) ● IRONBRIDGE BRANCH ● CHASEWATER RAILWAY ● TELFORD STEAM RAILWAY

A

MADELEY BRANCH

Madeley South Jn 156.51

22C   27A : to Telford

A464 156.01

156.19   Madeley Jn

1 WSJ 2

156

DIDCOT and CHESTER LINE

GW : Shrewsbury & Birmingham

MD 801 WSJ 2

SHIFNAL 154.24 154.28- 154.38
Shifnal Viaduct (194 yds)

River Worfe 152.08-12
Ruckley Viaduct (90 yds)

COSFORD 150.69 150.75
Tamper Sdg

ALBRIGHTON 149.38
151.23

Miles from Paddington via Oxford & Birmingham Snow Hill

Controlled by West Midlands SC (MJ)

BILBROOK 145.66   CODSALL 146.41   146.27

145.38

WMSC 145.42 (OS) (MJ)

Site of proposed 'West Midlands Interchange' (Intermodal Freight Terminal)

Oxley South Yard Shunters Cabin (CS)
Main Carriage shed
Lift shed
OXLEY T&RSMD (OY) Midland Traincare Centre
Alstom UK for Virgin West Coast
Roads 8-18 Oxley Down Sidings
Roads 5-7 Oxley Down Through Roads
Roads 1-4 Oxley Down Wash Roads
a = Oxley No.1 Shunting Spur
b = Oxley No.2 Shunting Spur

143.65-67 Stafford & Worcester Canal
143.49 LoE 143.65

Oxley Down Goods Loop / Down Wellington
Oxley Up Goods Loop / Up Wellington
Oxley Up Sidings

Controlled by West Midlands SC (OS)

Oxley Viaduct (188 yds)

Oxley, Stafford Road Jn 142.79 143.02

MD 805 OXC BR

MD 301 RBS 3 PBJ 2

Bushbury V. 14.04   Bushbury Jn 14.43
15.42 (WS) (SB)
Bushbury (Oxley) Jn

OXLEY CHORD
OXLEY CHORD UP / DOWN 0.57
13.66 0.00
15.32 15.23 (WS) (SB)

BIRMINGHAM and BUSHBURY LINE

VICTORIA BASIN BRANCH
WSJ 1 MD BR
MD 810 UP BR

13.52
13.32 Wolverhampton North Jn
13.26 BCN Canal

1 WSJ 2 COM
MD 801

DN STOUR / UP STOUR
RBS 2 STOUR VALLEY LINE
MD 301 LMS : LNW

BCN GRAND JUNCTION 0.55
DN GRAND 320 (MD) LMS : LNW
PBJ 2

Controlled by West Midlands SC

21A : to Bescot / 21A : to Wolverhampton

B

Controlled by West Midland Signalling Centre (WS)

BUSHBURY to STAFFORD LINE (Grand Junction)

West Midlands Signalling Centre (WS)

Miles from Birmingham (former Curzon Street) via Bescot

22.50

6B : to Stafford
Stafford Trent Valley Jn No. 1 28.50
POLSD1
Rickerscote Jn 27.55
6B : to Rugeley LEC
DOWN BIRMINGHAM / UP FAST BIR
UP SLOW BIR / BIRMINGHAM

Controlled by Rugby ROC (WS)

M6 26.38
DOWN / UP

Panriott's No. 1 (UWG) 25.27
Penkridge Up HABD 25.20
Penkridge Down HABD 23.52- 23.56

PENKRIDGE 23.32 23.56
23.30 23.50 Viaduct (River Penk)
RBS 3 MD 301 NW 1002
LMS : LNW

Miles from Paddington via Oxford & Birmingham Snow Hill

M54 17.32
DOWN PENKRIDGE / UP PENKRIDGE

Four Ashes 19.71 20.20
18.61 Stafford & Worcester Canal

M6 Toll 6.15
Mid Cannock Jn 6.30
Mid Cannock Sdgs (OOU)

Controlled by West Midlands SC (RR) located at Saltley

'THE CHASE LINE'
MD 345 1 RRN 2 LMS : LNW

CANNOCK 7.16
7.20

Hednesford Jn 8.62
HEDNESFORD 9.05

Miles from Ryecroft Junction

West Midlands Signalling Centre (WS)

CANNOCK BRANCH
WYRLEY & CHESLYN HAY 5.67
LANDYWOOD 5.12

BLOXWICH NORTH 3.01
BLOXWICH 2.32

21A : to Walsall

C

CANNOCK and RUGELEY LINE

6A : to Rugeley

RRN 2 NW 1004 (RR) (CH)
MD 345 LMS : LNW

RUGELEY TOWN 14.00 14.05
13.70
13.62 Trent & Mersey Canal
13.27

Rugeley Power Stn Jn
Power Station Control Room
6A : to Rugeley 'B' Power Station

Miles from Paddington via Oxford & Stourport (Severn Valley) and reversing at former Buildwas East Jn 160.01 (Buildwas East Jn)

NR Power Station 160.29
End of running line 160.16
160.01
1 MJ SVB COM
No.2 RECEPTION WB HH WB
No.1 DEPARTURE / No.1 RECEPTION
OIL SDG
Tare Gross
RUN ROUND (160.61)
160.41

IRONBRIDGE 'B' POWER STATION
Uniper CLOSED

Controlled by West Midlands SC (MJ)

Albert Edward Viaduct 160.29 160.34

KETLEY BRANCH
161.37-161.25 Coalbrookdale Viaduct (275 yards)
Otunes (UWG)(MJ) 160.59

UP DN / UP DN BRANCH
161

MADELEY BRANCH
MADELEY 160.15 162.25 (Lightmoor Jn)
MD 810 1 MJ 2 COM
MADELEY 159.10
22E 160

Trackbed towards Doseley (Telford Steam Railway)

Madeley South Jn 156.51
22A

157 158 159

D CHASEWATER RAILWAY   4' 8½" / 1435mm gauge

Great Crane Brook
Willow Vale Bridge
NORTON LAKESIDE 1.41
Silver Birch 0.27 / Crossing 0.48
Causeway 1.00 / 0.66
0.11

CHASEWATER HEATHS 1.38
1.61
CHASETOWN (CHURCH ST) 1.65

Loco shed
Heritage Centre
Dock
BROWNHILLS WEST 0.07
0.00

E TELFORD STEAM RAILWAY   4' 8½" / 1435mm gauge

22C
DOSELEY 163.00 (Proposed)
163.20 163.38 163.20

HORSEHAY & DAWLEY 163.75
passenger limit
164
164.07
LC 163.70
SPRING VILLAGE 163.75

Heath Hill Tunnel (59 yds)
LAWLEY VILLAGE 164.45 164.30 164.33
164.48
MJ 2
towards Ketley

Steam Tramway 2' 0" gauge 210 yards

December 2018

22

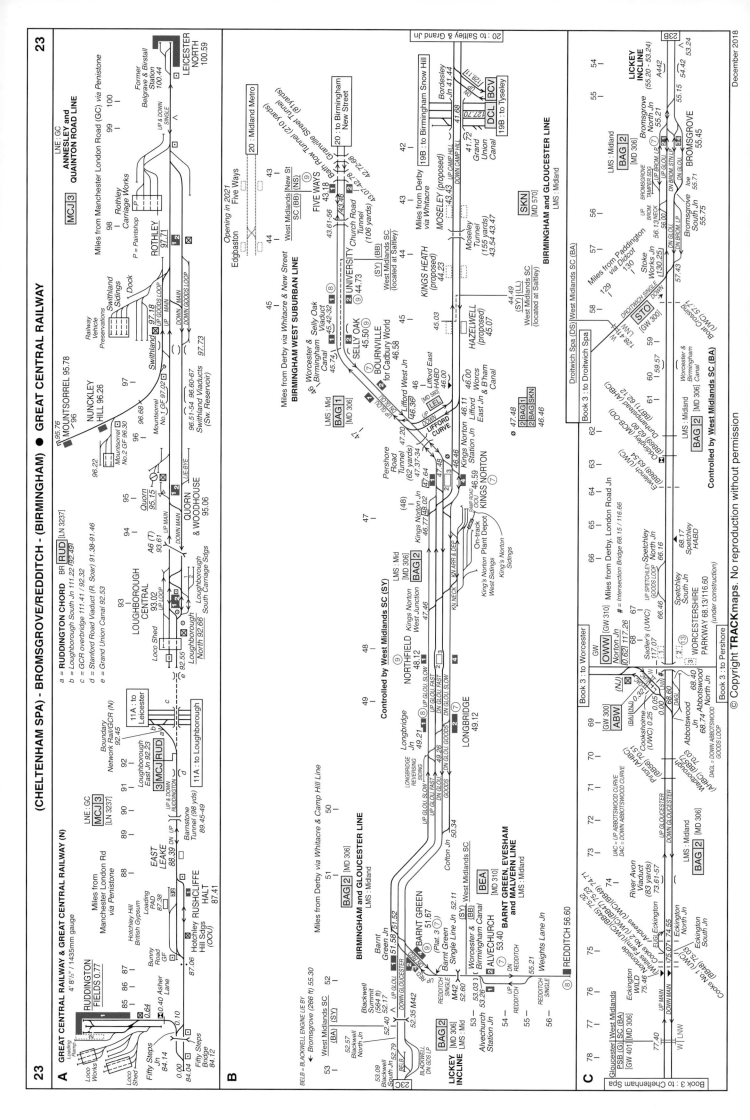

A — SEVERN VALLEY RAILWAY PLC

4' 8½" / 1435mm gauge

Bridgnorth Cliff Railway
3' 8" gauge
201 ft long
1 in 1.8

Loco shed
Boiler shop
150.09
150
C3
149.76
BRIDGNORTH 149.72
Castle Hill
Oldbury Viaduct (87 yards) 149.28-32
149.05-06
Knowlesands Tunnel (44 yards)
149
148

EARDINGTON 147.59
147
146

145.72 Sterns
HAMPTON LOADE 145.33
145.31
COUNTRY PARK HALT 144.07
Miles from Paddington via Worcester & Stourport
145
144

HIGHLEY 143.20
Engine House Museum
142.34
143
142

Borle Viaduct (43 yards) 142.28-30
ARLEY 140.74
140.76
141
140

Victoria Bridge (River Severn) 140.33-38
NORTHWOOD HALT 138.77
(AOCL) 138.75
139

Bewdley North 137.43
Witribbenhall (Bewdley) Viaduct 137.33-38
137.32
BEWDLEY 137.28
Bewdley South 137.12
COM 137.10 SVB
138.24 BYK
Carriage shed
Sandbourne Viaduct 138.14-19
138
Diesel depot
KIDDERMINSTER TOWN (SVR) (KR) 135.40
135.46
(miles from Paddington via Worcester)
Kidderminster Jn
¶ = Reversal of mileage 135.20
* = Kidderminster Stn (SVR) (KR) 135.27
Car. CW
P.W. Sidings
135.40
135.15 135.28
135.30
134.59 135.24
Bewdley Tunnel (486 yards)
Falling Sands (Kidderminster) Viaduct 136.69-137.11
Foley Park GF 136.10
(132 yards) River Stour & Canal 135.78-136.04
(Foley Park GF) 136.10
135.40 UK & CW MN

= SVR EXCHANGE LINE
Kidderminster/Hoobrook Viaduct (371 yards) 134.36-53
DKGL = DOWN KIDDERMINSTER GOODS LOOP
KTB = KIDDERMINSTER TURNBACK SIDINGS
OXFORD, WORCESTER and WOLVERHAMPTON LINE
OWW GW [MD 430]
DN KIDDERMINSTER
UP KIDDERMINSTER
(DR) (KR)
DKGL
KTB
135
134

Hartlebury (CCTV) 131.72
131.68
LNW WR
Cutnall Green 130.40
[GW 370]
133 132 131 130

Book 3: to Droitwich Spa

B — CRICH TRAMWAY VILLAGE

Crich, Derbyshire   Electrified 600v DC
4' 8½" / 1435mm gauge

Traverser
Exhibition Hall
Depot
Work-shop
Exhibition
18
13
12
6
3
Town End
0
Pick up
Set down
Car Park
Bowes-Lyon Bridge (interlaced tracks)
LC
14
26
Wakebridge
43
Glory Mine
65
68

Distances in chains

(Lower right — Stourbridge area)

21A : to Walsall
21A : to Smethwick
Book 3: to Droitwich Spa

KINGSWINFORD BRANCH (OOU)
Pensnett 146.30
NR limit 145.60
145.73
DOWN/UP BRANCH
KWD GW [MD 455]
146 145

Kingswinford Jn GF 144.56 (OOU)
Kingswinford Jn 144.31
Brierley Hill Terminal (OOU) Stone Stockpile
DISCHARGE RD
RUN ROUND
Tata Steel Europe
Round Oak Steel Terminal
ROS1 ROS2 ROS3 = ROUND OAK SDG 3
RONH = ROUND OAK NORTH HEADSHUNT
RON4
ROS3 = ROUND OAK SDG 1
Stop Blocks
146.16
Rowley Regis 136.14
ROWLEY REGIS 136.14
Old Hill (or Blackheath) Tunnel (896 yards) 137.30
OLD HILL [MD 435]
GSJ 2 [MD 435]
GW
Stourbridge Railway | Stourbridge Railway Extension
URRGL = Up Rowley Regis Goods Loop
DRRGL = Down Rowley Regis Goods Loop
M5
135.62 135.61-58
136.07
136.40
137.01
137
138
139
145 144

DOWN ROUND OAK SDG 1
UP ROUND OAK SDG 2
UP DUDLEY
DOWN DUDLEY
144.40
144.08

STOURBRIDGE TOWN 142.78
SNW = STOURBRIDGE NORTH NECK
SDS = STOURBRIDGE DOWN SIDING
SDTS = STOURBRIDGE DOWN THROUGH SIDINGS
SDGL = STOURBRIDGE DOWN GOODS LOOP
GF Front Yard LMD
142.24
* = Stourbridge Middle Jn 142.25
Chiltern Railways
(SJ) (DR) Dudley Canal 144.08
142.68-77
SJS GW [MD 445]
Stourbridge Junction 142.16
Stourbridge Viaduct (190 yards)
Stourbridge North Jn 142.51
OWW OWW [MD 450]
GSJ 2 [MD 435]
141.06
PMOL Depot Pre Metro Operations Ltd
(DR) (SJ)
142 141 140

River Stour 138.85 (CCTV)
CRADLEY HEATH 138.70
139.04
LYE 140.14
140.29
HAGLEY 140.29
OWW GW [MD 430]
BLAKEDOWN 138.54
Blakedown (or Churchill) Viaduct (173 yards)
138.17-25
Blakedown (CCTV) 138.51
140 139 138 137 136

Miles from Paddington via Didcot, Oxford & Worcester
Miles from Paddington via Worcester & Kidderminster
Miles from Paddington via Oxford & B. (Snow Hill)
OXFORD, WORCESTER and WOLVERHAMPTON LINE
DN KIDDERMINSTER
UP KIDDERMINSTER
Controlled by West Midlands SC (DR) (SJ)

A

26C : to Burton-on-Trent

Miles from Derby

Central Rivers Depot
see below

(15.20)
14.55
14.50 Barton
Barton North Jn
South Jn
15.65
Wichnor
22.65-78
16.22 15.73
23.33 15.65
UP TAM
DOWN TAM

DBP 1
[LN 3501]
LMS : Mid

DERBY to BIRMINGHAM LINE

Controlled by East Midlands Control Centre (DY)

Wichnor Viaduct 22.65-78 (DY)
Wichnor Viaduct (Rivers Tame & Trent) 16.79-58

22.12
Little Wichnor Viaduct (R. Trent) 22.53-54

LICHFIELD SINGLE (AS)
Alrewas (AS) 22.09
22.09

SOUTH STAFFORDSHIRE LINE
LMS : LNW
BJW 3
[MD 340] [LN 3340]
LNW EM
18.74 19.00
WMSC EMCC
(WW) (EM)

Miles from Dudley Jn 19

Elford GF 19.40
Elford Loop
20.17
EGL = ELFORD GOODS LOOP

Brookhay (AHBC) 19.4
Frog Lane (MCG) 20.52
Padstge (MCG) 21.16 20.13
Watery Gate (UWC) 20.13

Coventry Canal

BIRCH COPPICE

VW Group Logistics

LC
Travelling Cranes
Birmingham Intermodal Freight Terminal (BIFT)
Maritime Group

Tamworth HABD 22.30
Tamworth or Kettlebrook Viaduct (River Anker) 24.16-05
3.06 H
3

Exchange Sidings

Hollinds (Shrewley) 18.41
Corks Farm Jn 18.74
Miles from Derby
UP MAIN
DOWN MAIN
DN LICHFIELD
UP LICHFIELD
THROUGH LINE
UP TAMWORTH
DOWN TAMWORTH

22 23

CENTRAL RIVERS DEPOT (CZ)
Bombardier Transportation for CrossCountry Trains
B

Wheel Lathe
Heavy Maintenance
Stores
Light Maintenance
Servicing
UC = Underframe Cleaning
Cleaning
Platforms
Refuelling points
NORTH ARRIVAL ROAD
NR limit
CW
NR
SOUTH ARRIVAL ROAD
NR limit
Barton SD
Barton South Jn
15.65
15.73
= Push button control point

KINGSBURY BRANCH
Hall End Jn 2.26
KBC

Kingsbury SF (KY)
KINGSBURY
Warwickshire Oil Storage Co.
European Metal Recycling
Kingsbury 28.26/0.03

Oil Sdgs
Down Sidings
0.35 DOWN
SHUNTING
UP DERBY 28.33 -0.00
Kingsbury Branch Jn 28.33
28.40

Kingsbury Jn 29.27
LMS : Mid
KJW
[MD 545]

DERBY to BIRMINGHAM LINE
Controlled by WMSC (WW)

TAMWORTH (HIGH LEVEL) 23.58
TAMWORTH (LOW LEVEL) 110.01
23.30
23.35
23.55
5B : to Nuneaton
LNN
[LN 3501]
[MD 501]

WILNECOTE 24.52
25.47 4

M42 27.63

Coventry Canal 24.52

Lichfield TV Chord
Lichfield TV Jn 0.22/18.13
[MD 365] LTV
Lichfield TV HLJn (TV) 18.15
A4.38 18.24
Lichfield TV Jn
18.05 (TV)
Lichfield TRENT VALLEY (HL) 18.05/18.19 (LL)
116.19 (LL)

Lichfield Chord Jn
-116.28/0.02
Up Sidings
Lichfield Chord (LS) (TV)
LC
WEST COAST MAIN LINE
6A : to Rugeley
18.04
Aston (AN) 18.05

Controlled by Aston SSC (AN)
located at Duddeston

LICHFIELD CITY
16.70
Engineers' Sdg
STABLING
13.37 (11)
(7)

Lichfield City 3 Jn
11.47 A5
11.38 M6 (Toll)
11.00 Shenstone Viaduct 10.75
SHENSTONE 10.53

BLAKE STREET 8.15

BUTLERS LANE 7.27

FOUR OAKS 6.26
6.13
6

Aldridge Jn 44.73
46 45 44 43 42 41
(OOU)
21A : to Walsall
12.15
12.34
12.64
12.66 M6 (Toll)

Anglesea Sidings
Quattro Group Lichfield Depot

SOUTH STAFFORDSHIRE LINE
Fosseway (AHBC) 15.32
BJW 3 [MD 350]
SUTTON COLDFIELD and LICHFIELD LINE
MS : LNW
[MD 340]
Miles from Aston North Jn
8.03

Controlled by Aston SSC (AN)

KINGSBURY to WATER ORTON LINE
LMS : Mid DBP 2 [MD 501]
Controlled by WMSC (WW)

HAMS HALL
National Distribution Park
Associated British Ports
Adam Dales Viaduct 30.64-62
TRANSFER LINE
Hams Hall Control (HH) (33.05)
Loading Pad
E. ARR
W. ARR
DEP R/R
Coleshill East Jn 33.04
Coleshill West Jn 33.16
32.15
32.37 32.54
32.40
COLESHILL PARKWAY 6
33.10
H 32.00
31.69/0.00
Whitacre West Jn 31.69/0.00
DBP 3 KJW NWO
[MD 555]
(WW) (NW)

29.39
Whitacre East Jn 0.28
31
30
32.03
Hams Hall Jn 32.03
DAGL = DOWN ARLEY GOODS LOOP
# = Hams Hall Jn

WHITACRE and NUNEATON LINE
Controlled by West Midlands SC (NW)
located at Saltley

5B : to Nuneaton
9.28
Coventry Canal
8.71 8.34
WMSC Rugby SCC (NW) (Stockingford)
[NW]
Arley Tunnel (709 yards)
6.22 6.55
Daw Mill Arley HABD 5.60
Windridge 3.03
Daw Mill East Jn 2.36
Daw Mill West Jn 2.05
NWO [MD 555] LMS : Mid
Whitacre West Jn 32.03

Closed Daw Mill Colliery Harworth Estates
Loading Pad
Reception/ Departure
2.07

UP ARLEY
DOWN ARLEY
UP UNEATON
DOWN UNEATON
UP WHITACRE
DOWN WHITACRE
UP NUNEATON

DBP KJW
1 2

WATER ORTON, WALSALL and WOLVERHAMPTON LINE
LMS : Mid CBR 2 [MD 565]
Controlled by WMSC (WR)

Water Orton Curve
36 CBR 1 [MD 560] WOP
36.04
35.10 35.15
35.37 R. Tame
Water Orton East Jn 34.54
Water Orton West Jn 34.43
33.33 34.54 5
COM
2 DBP 3
WP (WW)

River Tame Flood Arches
M6 Toll
M6 Toll 33.74
COLESHILL
32.40
Coleshill West Jn 33.16
Castle Bromwich Jn
Castle Bromwich Curve
Park Lane Jn 36.15
UP SUTTON PARK
DOWN SUTTON PARK
UP WR
DN WR
UP DBY FAST
UP DBY SLOW
Park Hall Viaduct (River Tame) 35.43-40
36.22 36.08
36.12
36.04/34.00
CBR 2 [MD 565]
Castle Bromwich 0.55

Miles from Derby via Whitacre 36.47

Birmingham & Fazeley Canal 36.47

DERBY to BIRMINGHAM LINE
[MD 501] DBP 3 LMS : Mid
Controlled by WMSC (WP)

Jaguar Terminal
37.10 Ramps
Heartlands Power Station
Oil Discharge Sdg
(OOU)

SUTTON PARK 40.09
Sutton Coldfield Tunnel (172 yds)
39.55 5.14
5.12
5.04 4.74
SUTTON COLDFIELD (7)
20 : to Aston
20 : to Saltley

UP DERBY SLOW
UP DERBY FAST
DOWN DERBY FAST
DOWN DERBY GOODS

Miles from Derby via Whitacre 37
38 39
Miles from Dudley Junction

DERBY to BIRMINGHAM LINE
[MD 501] DBP 3 LMS : Mid
Controlled by WMSC (WP)

13 14 15 16 17 18 19 20 21 22 23 24 25 26 27 28 29 30 31 32 33 34 35 36 37

© Copyright TRACKmaps. No reproduction without permission

December 2018

A FOXFIELD RAILWAY 4' 8½" / 1435mm gauge

Ipstones RR 4.27 4.38 4.45
Apesford (MG) 3.20 3.69
Bradnop Tunnel 1.54 2.17-19

WATERHOUSES BRANCH
(leased to Moorland & City Railways Ltd.
operated by Churnet Valley Railway)

[NW 5010] SCQ 3 LMS : NS 4.07

DOWN 6.65/0.00/17.56 COM
417.51 NR/CVR Boundary
GF 17.50

LEEK LINE
LMS : NS SCQ 2 [NW 5010]

River Churnet 17.63
6.67/17.58
Leekbrook Jn 6.59/17.50 (OOU)
Leekbrook Jn 17.44
LEEK BROOK 17.44
17.29
17.05 — 17 UP Carriage Shed
RR LS

13.32 Banshall (AHBC-X)
13.57 Veterans Lane (UWC)
14.11 Loxley Crossing (UWC)
14.50 Stallians (OMSL)
13.71 Bakers 15.27

Non operational
(leased to Moorland &
City Railways Ltd)

Cheddleton Tunnel (531 yds)
CHEDDLETON (TMO) 16.45
16.42 16.39 16.39
Carriage Shed 16.42

CHURNET VALLEY RAILWAY
4' 8½" / 1435mm gauge

CVL
CONSALL 14.17 14.19
Miles from Uttoxeter
Upper Leigh (AHBC-X) 9.57
Leigh (AHBC-X) 10.06 (CL) 10.24
Colliers (UWC) 9.39
Bailey's (UWC)
Newton (UWC)
5.74 Jacksons (CL)
6.07 Bennetts (UWC)
6.76 Cresswell (AHBC)
6.45 Critchlows (UWC)

KINGSLEY & FROGHALL 11.72 12.17 Froghall Jn 12.23
GF
Stock Sdg with road access 11.35

DERBY LINE

NSS [LN 3505] LMS : NS

LEEK LINE

Stockton Brook Tunnel (72 yds)
2.09-2.12
0.40 (Milton)
Change of mileage

Abbey (TMO) 3.20

SCQ (Milton Jn) 0.00 3.51
(ELR origin at -0.22)
Exton (ACE) 3.11

LMS : NS [NW 5010] SCQ 2
LMS : NS SCQ 1

River Trent

BIDDULPH VALLEY LINE
Non operational
Fenton Manor Tunnel (106 yds)
(SOT) (FY) 0.68 0.63

BLYTHE BRIDGE 5.23 26A 5.23
5.19

Stallington (CL)
4.58 DOWN (SMM) 4.58
4.59
4.54
26C
4.13
Meir Tunnel (814 yds)
3.49
3.12
Caverleigh Farm (UWC)

LONGTON 1.71
(FY) Longton Vdct
Foley Crossing A50(T) 1.56
1.75-2.05
1.40 LNW EM [LN 3505]
NSS [NW 5012] LMS : NS

Stoke/Seven Arches Viaduct 20.22 - 20.26
6D : to Wedgwood
20.36 Stoke Jn
20.10 Glebe Street Jn
20.33

STOKE-ON-TRENT 19.78
N 1 S
SCC 19.60
Stoke-on-Trent SCC
Stoke North Jn 19.61
BAY 3 2
[NW 5009] CMD 2 LMS : NS

19.45 Trent & Mersey Canal
19.44 UP MAIN
19.35 Newcastle Jn
19.12 Cliffe Vale Jn

MACCLESFIELD and COLWICH LINE
London North Western Yard
Cockshute Sdgs
Cliff Vale Terminal
Imerys Minerals
Miles from Macclesfield

Controlled by Stoke-on-Trent SCC (SOT)

26B
(CCTV) 5.19 NR

B

Stoke-on-Trent SCC Control Codes
(SOT) Stoke-on-Trent
(CH) former Colwich SB signals

Controlled by (SOT)

2.60 2.22 1.73

FOXFIELD RAILWAY 4' 8½" / 1435mm gauge

BLYTHE BRIDGE (CAVERSWALL ROAD)

Hegarty's or Blakeley-bank Wood
Foxfield Bank 1/31, 1/25, 1/19, 1/28
0.62 0.56 0.69
DILHORNE PARK

FOXFIELD COLLIERY 0.05 0.00

Cresswell Ford 2.06 1.60
Cash Heath Jn 2.54
Forsbrook Road 2.55

Loco Shed
Running Shed

2.63 2.69
3.20 3 3.23
BLYTHE BRIDGE
Blythe Bridge West
DOWN

All level crossing are "open"

C 26C

DERBY LINE

NSS [LN 3505] LMS : NS

Hilton (MCG) 27.08
Egginton (AHBC-X) 27.50
26.67 UP STOKE DN STOKE
28 28.58
27
Egginton Jn (EN) 26.69
26.66 Marston-on-Dove (AHBC)
25.45 Hayside (UWC)
25.28 Rowes (UWC)
24.57 Rowes (UWC)
Miles from Stoke Jn

Willington (AHBC) 29.19
Findern (AHBC-X) 29.49
Trent & M. Canal Jn
Stenson
(EN) A38
(DY)
6.01 Willington Down HABD 6.03
WILLINGTON
29.51

5.14 North Stafford Jn
4.58 [132.18]
4.56

STENSON BRANCH
SSJ 2 [LN 3520] LMS : Mid
4.25 4.16 Stenson Haynes (UWC)
4.06 A50
UP Chellaston
DN Chellaston

13C : to Sheet Stores Jn

Controlled by East Midlands Control Centre (DY)

DERBY to BIRMINGHAM LINE
DBP 1 LMS : Mid [LN 3501]

Sunny Hill 2.34 (DY) (DW) SINFIN NORTH 130.73
2.08 (UP TAMWTH) UP SUNNY HILL LP
Melbourne Jn 131.13 131.27
PEARTREE 1.16
1.44 1.31 1.72
L & NW Jn 0.60

DERBY to MELBOURNE LINE

11B : to Derby

Controlled by East Midlands Control Centre (DW)

UP TAMWORTH FAST
DN TAM. F.
DN TAM SLOW

DERBY CENTRAL 130.37
130.52 130.69
130.20 (Oil Terminal) SINFIN SDG
SINFIN CENTRAL 130.37
Rolls Royce Ltd
EMCC
= SINFIN ARR/DEP
129.79 St. Pancras
-131

LMS : Mid [LN 3515] MJS 1

C

DERBY to BIRMINGHAM LINE
DBP 1 LMS : Mid [LN 3501]

Tibbury Crossing (LT) 22.73
Tamworth (UWC)
Barton & Walton (UWC)
22.75 Scropton Mill (UWC)
23.43 West Lane (UWC)
22.53 Scropton (SM) 22.53
22.41 Archers No. 1 (UWC)
22.15 Archers (UWC)
21.47 Leathersley (UWC)
21.20 Nashs (UWC)

TUTBURY & HATTON 24.13
9.51 9.42
9.46 9.51
9.60 Wetmore Jn
Depot Nemesis Rail (BO)
New Wetmore Sdgs
Horninglow Sdgs
Maurice Hill Transport Ltd
East Yard
West Yard
DEP ARR

Horninglow Bridge Jn 10.33
10.25
BURTON ON TRENT 10.67
11.02
11.17
NIRU
Mosley Street Sdgs
Cambridge Street (UWC) 126.60
Branston Jn 126.40

Sudbury (LSV) 20.67
Sudbury Vdct 21.15-19
River Dove 21 Dove 21.84
19.62 Doveleighs (RG)
Marchington Old Stn (UWC) 19.01
Marchington No. 1 (UWC) 21.20 Dumsells (UWC)
MARCHINGTON 18.78
17.75 Langhills No. 2 (UWC)
17.20 Tumncliffs No. 1 (UWC)
Leicester Jn 11.17 127.00
Birmingham Curve Jn 126.40

Controlled by East Midlands Control Centre (DY)

BIRMINGHAM CURVE
BCJ LMS : Mid [LN 3535]

14C : to Coalville

LEICESTER and BURTON LINE

KSL LMS : Mid [LN 3525]

Branston (OOU) 127.13
127.19
127.25

Miles from Derby, London Road Jn

DERBY to BIRMINGHAM LINE
DBP 1 LMS : Mid [LN 3501]

Hockley (CCTV) 15.91
DGL
Uttoxeter Old Stn (UWC)
13.31 Dumsells (UWC)
13.44 Uttoxeter (UWC)
Pinfold (MCB) 16.00
Bridge St Vdct 16.17
UTTOXETER (T) 16.29
A518
Engrs 16.26
Uttoxeter Racecourse (UWC) 16.39
Uttoxeter (UWC) 16.17

25 : to Wichnor Jn & Tamworth

Branston Up HABD
Bourtons (UWC) 12.47
Boultons (UWC)
UP TAM DOWN TAM

26B

Controlled by East Midlands Control Centre (DY)

© Copyright **TRACKmaps**. No reproduction without permission

December 2018

26

A

Controlled by West Midlands SC (MJ)

WSJ2 [MD 801]

GW & LMS (LNW) Joint : Shrewsbury & Birmingham
GW : Shrewsbury & Birmingham

Book 3 : to Craven Arms & Welshpool

0.28 English Bridge Jn

GW & LMS (LNW) Joint
AFE [GW 732]
GW & LMS (LNW) Joint
WSJ2 [GW 731]
[MD 801] [GW 731]
LNW WA

Abbey Foregate Jn 171.13

SHL zero 171.49
H = Hereford
W = Wolverhampton
SHL 171.49
SHL [GW 730]
SHL 0.20-0.07
WSJ2 171.41-44

Severn Viaduct (286 yards)
SHREWSBURY 171.46
(GW & LMS (LNW) Joint)
Crewe Junction 171.57
32.251

Platforms
3 13
4
5,6 6
7 15

DIDCOT and CHESTER LINE
GW : Shrewsbury & Chester

(MJ) (AF)
166.57
River Tern
167.41
Belvedere Viaduct
(River Severn)
169.79-170.02
170.46
170.68
171.08
171.30
171.33
Severn Bridge Jn (SBJ) 171.33
Abbey Foregate LMD
West Midlands Railways
S = Shropshire Carriage Sdgs
Cattle Pens Vdct
32.20
32.26

WELLINGTON (Shropshire) 161.27
x = WELLINGTON BAY
6 = DOWN WELLINGTON PLATFORM
z = UP WELLINGTON PLATFORM

Miles from Paddington via Oxford & Birmingham Snow Hill

161.36
160.73
160.76
161.10 0.00 161.02
(Ketley Jn) (Stafford Jn)
160.22
NR Donnington Jn
* = Donnington Sdg

TIRFT 0.44

OAKENGATES 158.31

Hereford Storage Sdg
163.70
Allscott GF

Telford International Railfreight Terminal (TIRFT)

TELFORD CENTRAL 157.40 13
156.74 157.45 157.76-158.17
Oakengates Tunnel (468 yards)
M54
2.68

22A : to Shifnal

B

Controlled by Wales ROC (FH)

Book 3 : to Holyhead

Miles from Euston

CHESTER and HOLYHEAD LINE
LMS : LNW
CNH 3 [NW 3001]

Beeches Farm (UWG)
184.03
183.35-32 Hawarden Aerodrome Flight path

SHOTTON HIGH LEVEL 13.00
A494 (T) 186.03
SHOTTON (5)
186.74

SHOTTON LOW LEVEL 186.77
39C : to Bidston
13.08
WDB 27C

188.58
(CR) Chester PSB
Wales ROC (FH)
WA LNW
188.40
187.57
(FH) (CR)

Pentre Sea Wall
189.51-47
Rockcliffe Hall Tunnel (99 yards)
190.60-189.60
Flint Jn 191.00
Pentre (190.65)

FFLINT 191.47

Bagillt 193.52
BAGILLT 193.51

Fishpool Farm (UWG)
194.61

Maesteg (UWG) 195.24
HOLYWELL JUNCTION 195.71

Stolyn Lodge (UWG)
Bradford (UWG) 196.09
196.35

UP HOLYHEAD
DOWN HOLYHEAD

Book 3 : to Holyhead

C

Book 3 : to Wrexham & Chester

Hencote Bank

GW : Shrewsbury & Chester
DIDCOT and CHESTER LINE
WSJ2 [GW 731]

172
172.40
DOWN MAIN LOOP
UP MAIN

Coton Hill Yard
Coton Hill North
Coton Hill SB 31.79
Coton Hill South
- 32
Coal Concentration Depot
(Crewe Bank SB)
31.47

Controlled by Wales ROC (SC)
(located at Cardiff)
CREWE and SHREWSBURY LINE
SYC
LMS : LNW [GW 735]

Book 3 : to Nantwich & Crewe

28A : to Chester
32.10 (SC) Wales ROC
(CJ)

UP GOODS LOOP
UP MAIN CREWE 32.08
DOWN MAIN CREWE 32.05
NEW YARD
LIVERPOOL SDG
DOWN SIDING

39C : to Bidston

27B CNH
SHOTTON LOW LEVEL (5) 186.77
River Dee
186.74
11.59
A494 10.64
11.59
13.24 14.15
COM (mileage meet)
13.37
13.33 181.03
Saltney Jn 181.03
1 WDB 2
27B CNH
SHOTTON HIGH LEVEL 13.00
(PENARLÂG) HAWARDEN
2 6
28A : to Chester
212.10
Green Lane (AHBC) 211.01
Balderton Tunnel (53 yards) 209.49-51
210.08
Balderton (AHBC) 209.67
A55

Controlled by Chester PSB (CR)

Penyfford
(Padeswood Hall Works)
Hanson Cement Discharge Area
I Hope Exchange 7.67
HOPE EXCHANGE 7.64
8.08
PENYFFORD 7.39
WB

WREXHAM, MOLD and CONNAH'S QUAY LINE 'BORDERLANDS LINE'
LNE : GC
WDB 1 [NW 3007]

(PD)
7.41
(UWC)
BUCKLEY (BWCLE) 8.68

Miles from Wrexham Central

CAERGWRLE 4.73
HOPE (Flintshire) (YR HOB) 5.44
5.04 R. Alun

CEFN-Y-BEDD 4.20
Cefn-y-Bedd Viaduct 4.09-4.13

GWERSYLLT 2.29

WRECSAM CYFFREDINOL
WREXHAM GENERAL 201.66
Wrexham Exchange
0.49
A483
WDB 1 [NW 3007]

former MDH 1

Rossett (R/G) 206.49
Rossett Jn R. Alun 206.48
Pulford (AHBC) 208.12
208.73
Broad Oak (AHBC) 207.37
206.42 A483
(CN) WA LNW
202.60
A483 Gresford Bank
204.09 A483
Gresford 202.57
Wrexham North Jn 202.40 A483
202.49 (CR)
UP BIDSTON
DOWN MAIN
UP MAIN
DIDCOT and CHESTER LINE
GW : Shrewsbury & Chester
WSJ2 [NW 3005]
Miles from Paddington via Oxford

Controlled by Chester PSB (CR)

[WRECSAM CANOLOG]
WREXHAM CENTRAL 0.16
0.19
0.43
201.62
201.49
Up Bay Sdgs
[WRECSAM CANOLOG]
NECK
Croes Newydd (CN) North Fork
LNE : GC [MC]
DOWN MAIN
UP MAIN
201.43
Watery Road GF 201.17
WREXHAM and ELLESMERE BRANCH

Ruabon Road Tunnel (64 yards) 200.43-46
200.65 River Clywedog

WSJ1 [GW 731] [NW 3005]
199.00
199.45 A483
DIDCOT and CHESTER LINE
GW : Shrewsbury & Chester

Book 3 : to Shrewsbury

December 2018

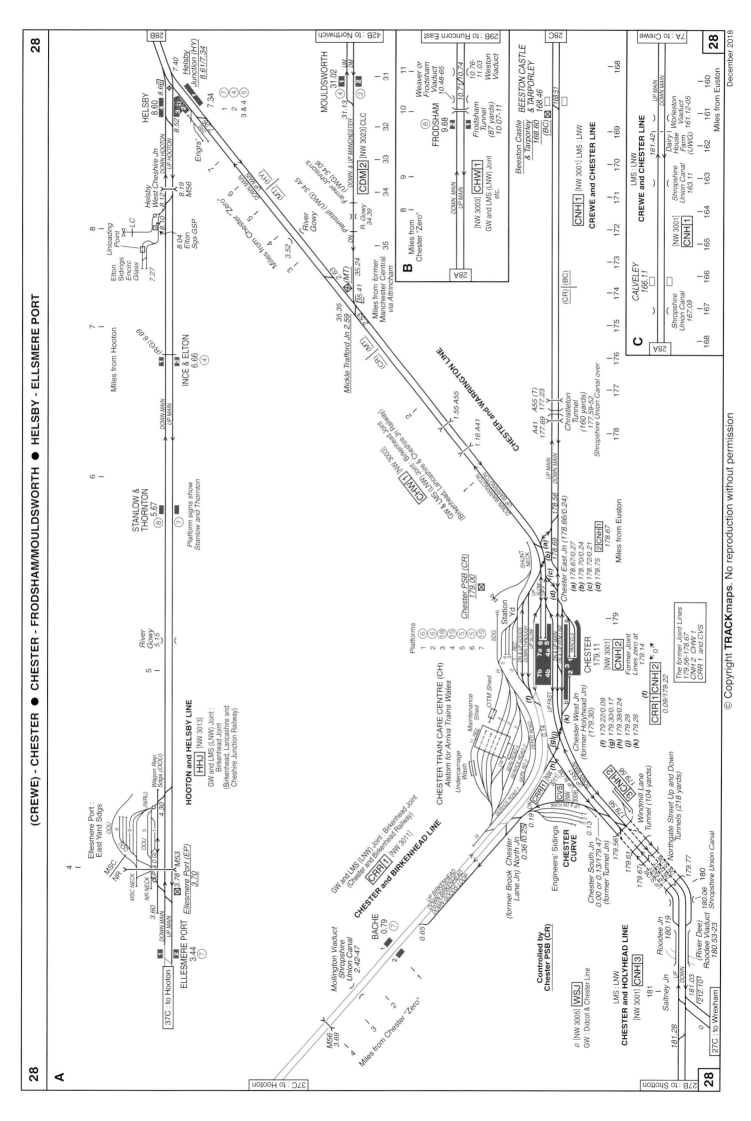

WEST COAST MAIN LINE : (CREWE) - WARRINGTON - BAMFURLONG

A

RUNCORN BRANCH

Preston Brook HABD 176.39
M56 177.03
DM
Preston Brook Tunnel (78 yds) 176.00
(flyover)
Birdswood (WD) (WN)
175.58
175.43-176.04-07
175.44
174.70 DN DITTON
174.70

29B

[WN 2001] LMS : LNW

29B

[LT]
LMS : LNW

1 CGJ 2 [NW 1001] LMS : LNW

BIRDSWOOD and WARRINGTON LINE

Weaver Jn Up174.53 Dn 174.70
174.65 174.70
Weaver 174.53
Emergency Facing Crossover

(River Weaver) Dutton Viaduct 173.76-174.18

Acton Bridge Jn 172.49 172.19

6 ⑥

ACTON BRIDGE 172.38
7 ⑦ 9 ⑨

CREWE and BIRDSWOOD LINE (Grand Junction)

Controlled by Winsford (WD)

DOWN FAST / DOWN SLOW / UP FAST / UP SLOW

Hartford Jn 170.56 170.07
170.65 170.70
170.43 170.47
170.19 170.16
(former LNW Jn) (WD) (GK) HCM [NW 3037] LMS : LNW
0.44 Limit of electrification
DB = DOWN BRANCH UB = UP BRANCH
0.72

23.11
Hartford CLC Jn
42B : to Northwich
CDM2 [NW 3023]

CLC [NW 3023] ALTRINCHAM and CHESTER LINE

42B : to Mouldsworth

HARTFORD 169.64 A556 169.40
12 ⑫
2 1

Vale Royal Viaduct (River Weaver) 168.66-168.72

Winsford South Jn 165.11
WINSFORD 165.41
Winsford (WD) 166.66
2
4 ④
Winsford HABD 166.38
166.33 Middlewich Canal 164.33 (CY) (WD) 164.56

[NW 1001] CGJ 1
LMS : LNW

CREWE and BIRDSWOOD LINE (Grand Junction)

161.17 (Coppenhall Jn)

160.04 (CY) (WD)

159
LEC 5 CGJ 1 [NW 2001]
LMS : LNW

7A : to Crewe

Miles from Euston

B

29C

Dallam WILD 153.68

Dallam Freight Depot - DB Cargo (OOU)
Dallam Royal Mail Terminal 183.40
183.56 183.52

DOWN SLOW / DOWN FAST / UP SLOW / UP FAST
183.15 182.78

CGJ 3 [NW 1001] LMS : LNW

Dallam Jn 182.67

183

38B : to Widnes

MAJ

38B : to Warrington Central

182.40
182.60
Warrington N. Jn 182.25
182.11
Bank Quay Sdgs
WARRINGTON BANK QUAY 182.11

CLC - LIVERPOOL and MANCHESTER LINE

Lever Bros. OOU
Litton's Mill LCF
Crosfield's Crossing (CCTV)11.35 (MGC)11.45

37B : to Widnes & Ditton

SDJ 2 [NW 2009] LMS : LNW

182
181.76
181.62
CGJ 3
2 CHW 2
17.76
Warrington South Jn

WS = Warrington South Jn

WALTON JN to EARLESTOWN LINE (Grand Junction)

Lines controlled by Warrington PSB (WN)

River Mersey

181.25 LMS : LNW
Walton Old Jn 17.23
Walton Old Jn Sdgs
1 CHW 2 [NW 1019]
DOWN HELSBY / UP HELSBY
17.57 17.16

Canal Sidings MSC Holding Sdgs

BIRDSWOOD and WARRINGTON LINE

Lines controlled by Warrington PSB (WN)

Summit 180.40 180.35 180.30
Acton Grange Jns 180.26 180.24 180.21
180.20 180.19 180.16
Manchester Ship Canal
Acton Grange Viaducts (Bridge 77) [CHW 1]

CGJ 2 [NW 1001] LMS : LNW
Miles from Euston

RUNCORN VIADUCT 13.74-13.76
Norton (R/G-X) (bridleway) 177.40
CHW 1 [NW 3003]
178.11 177.11
Norton 14.06
(WN) (WD)
CHESTER and WARRINGTON LINE (Grand Junction)
Bridgewater Canal
M56 177.03 177.08
M56 13.33 13.06
Sutton Tunnel (1m. 154yds) 11.63-12.70
Norton Jn 13.17

Controlled by Manchester ROC (WE)

Halton Jn 179.24 LMS : LNW
WJL 1 [NW 2001]

RUNCORN BRANCH

FJH [NW 3021]
FRODSHAM BRANCH
LMS : LNW

Frodsham Jn 178 (FJ)
11.09/11.50 11.60
HALTON 11.34
M56 11.17
Frodsham 0.37 (WE)
Halton (WE) A5126
179
GSP 177.32
177.35 177.02
Sutton Weaver
Manchester ROC (WE) / Winsford (WD)
1.17 11.31 11.04
UGL
11.54
176

28B : to Frodsham

29A : to Weaver Jn

28B : to Runcorn

37A : to Runcorn

C

30A : to Wigan

Miles from former Timperley Junction

SDJ 2 [NW 2009] LMS : LNW

TIMPERLEY and GARSTON LINE

Arpley Junction (AJ) 11.02
Arpley Jn South
Arpley Junction 0.00/11.03
10.76 10.66 River Mersey
10.60 10.11 Latchford
11.16 Slutchers Lane (FP)
DN LATCHFORD SDG
UP LATCHFORD SDG
MAIN LINE SDG
FOOTBALL FIELD SDG (Former MSC)
Down Sdgs
Arpley
Holding Sdgs
Arpley Grid Iron Jn Nth
Arpley Grid Iron Jn South
Arpley Shunting Necks
Arpley Grid Iron
1.06
0.66 0.68 0.62 0.63
0.00 0.05
WOAT [NW 2011]
(AJ)
(WN)
G
E
A
UTS
WS
DB Cargo
The Hole
OF 3 4
1 2
DPL
OOU
NEW FORD OUT SDG

41B : to Ince Moss Jn

Bamfurlong Sdgs Jn 4.43
DN GOODS
Bamfurlong Jn 4.26
Haydock Branch 4.17
4.56
0.18

NORTH UNION LINE
CGJ 5 [NW 1001] LMS : LNW

Miles from Newton-le-Willows Jn
Newton-le-Willows Jn
(Leigh Bch) Leeds/Liverpool Canal
Ashton-in-Makerfield 0.53 Hanson 0.53
(WN)
3
2.42
2
No.2 ARR/ UNLOAD
No.1 RTN
HAYDOCK BRANCH
HOB 2 [NW 1023]
0.00 0.32 0.03
0.71
Golborne Jn 187.76
4 CGJ 5 [NW 1021] [NW 2019] LMS : LNW
A580 1.07
187.40
187.19
LOWTON Jn 0.48 0.05 0.28
Lowton 0.26 0.36
NGJ [NW 1021]
PJL [NW 2019]
M6
(NGJ)

WINWICK and GOLBORNE LINE

Controlled by Warrington PSB (WN)

43C : to Patricroft

M6 16.17
Newton-le-Willows 16.37
Huskisson Memorial ●
Parkside Jn 16.56
16.19

LIVERPOOL and MANCHESTER LINE

NEWTON-LE WILLOWS 15.60
15.78 15.63
15.55- 15.57
DSE [NW 2015] LMS : LNW
(Newton Viaduct) ⑤
Earlestown East Jn 15.75 -15 -16
Miles from Liverpool Lime Street
DSE [NW 2015]
EARLESTOWN 187.14/14.51
Earlestown West Jn 187.05/14.58
WEE [NW 1021] LMS : LNW
Earlestown South Jn 187.03 186.74
UP EARLESTOWN / DOWN EARLESTOWN
WEE
DSE
2 3 1
Platforms 1 ⑧ 2,3,5 4 ⑦ 5 ⑤
41B : to Huyton

EARLESTOWN LINES
Controlled by Warrington PSB (WN)
LMS : LNW [NW 1021]

DN CHAT MOSS / UP CHAT MOSS 16.00
DOWN MAIN / UP MAIN
Winwick Jn
186
185.49 185.40
CGJ 4 [NW 1001]
185.37
3
WALTON JN to EARLESTOWN LINE (Grand Junction)
LMS : LNW [NW 2015]

185
DOWN SLOW / DOWN FAST / UP FAST / UP SLOW
M62 184.58

26B

WINWICK and GOLBORNE LINE

PARKSIDE WEST CURVE NGJ [NW 1021]
PARKSIDE EAST CURVE PJL [NW 2019]
both LMS : LNW

UTS = Arpley Up Through Sdg
Platforms
1 ⑫
3 ⑬
4 ⑫

A = Arpley Extension Sidings
E = Old Side Exchange
G = Grid Iron Feeding 0.21

December 2018

© Copyright **TRACKmaps**. No reproduction without permission

30

WEST COAST MAIN LINE : BAMFURLONG - WIGAN - PRESTON ● INCE - WIGAN - ORRELL ● CHORLEY - EUXTON JN ● RIBBLE STEAM RAILWAY

A

41A : to Southport

WIGAN and SOUTHPORT LINE
LMS : L&Y   [NW 6009]   [WBS] 3

Miles from Manchester Victoria

Miles from Newton-le-Willows Jn

LOSTOCK JN to PEMBERTON LINE
LMS : L&Y   [WKL] 1

Adam Viaduct (R. Douglas)
18.48-47

Wigan Wallgate (WW) 18.09
Wigan Wallgate Jn 18.04
Wigan North 6.60
WESTERN

PEMBERTON 19.23
Pemberton Tunnel (40 yds)
19.29-27

COM (Pemberton Jn)
19.09 19.48 19
2 WKL 1

ORRELL 20.77
M6 20.40

40A : to Kirkby

LANCASHIRE UNION LINE
LMS : LNW   SBH 3   [NW 2023]
Controlled by Warrington PSB (WN)

Ince Moss Jn 12.10 [0.78]
*0.60
IMG
LMS : LNW [NW 1025]

INCE MOSS CHORD

Bamfurlong Sidings
[0.00] 0.18/4.43

Bamfurlong Jn 4.26
4.17

Leeds & Liverpool Canal 4.24

41B : to St. Helens

12 Miles from Huyton Jn

CGJ 5   LMS : LNW [NW 1001]

29C : to Warrington Bank Quay & Newton-le-Willows

B

WIGAN NORTH WESTERN
Platforms 1 6 9 4 12 13

Station arches 6.45-49
WKL 1
2 WBS 3

Springs Branch (Slow Lines) Jn 5.57
Springs Branch Jn [12.54]

Wigan, Springs Branch Component Recovery & Distribution Centre (SP)
DB Cargo

EMU Stabling (June 2019)
CW SERVICE SDG 1
CRDC BAY
LOADING
NECK

SBH 3   LMS : LNW [NW 2023]
BIK
BICKERSHAW HEADSHUNT 1 0.31

EUXTON BALSHAW LANE 14.77
Balshaw Lane Jn 14.02

R. Yarrow Viaduct 14.50-55
Chorley Tunnel (124 yds)

CHORLEY 22 20.20

BUCKSHAW PARKWAY
Buckshaw Parkway Jn 24.24
MVE 2   LMS : L&Y [NW 6001]
Euxton Jn 25.31
Flying Arches 23.40-44
BOLTON to EUXTON JUNCTION LINE 23.25-20

Yarrow Viaduct 21.29-35

CGJ 5   LMS : LNW [NW 1001]
Miles from Manchester Victoria

46C : to Chorley

NORTH UNION LINE
LMS : LNW   CGJ 5   [NW 1001]
Controlled by Warrington PSB (WN)

Wigan South Jn 6.04
Leeds & Liverpool Canal 6.18

INCE 16.70
Wigan Station Jn 17.44
LOSTOCK JN to PEMBERTON LINE
WBS 2   LMS : L&Y [NW 6009]

46C : to Hindley

47B : to Ormskirk
Miles from former Liverpool Exchange

WALTON JN to PRESTON LINE (Farington Curve)
LMS : L & W   FCO   [NW 7007]

C

47A : to Kirkham
31A : to Lancaster

PRESTON : RIBBLE BRANCH
LMS : North Union / Corporation of Preston
* LMS : L&Y and LNW Jt (Preston & Wyre Jn)
$ LMS : L&Y and LNW Joint (Preston & Longridge)

Preston PSB (PN) ⊠   (Croft Street)
PBN   [NW 4005]

RIVERSIDE 2.13
Navigation Way, Ashton Swing Bridge (Combined Rail & Road) 0.66
Maritime Way 1.55
RSR Bay
Museum
Preston Council 2.30
Ribble Steam Railway

Exchange Sidings
Fishergate Tunnel (140 yards)
RIBBLE BRANCH   1 PSR 2   [NW 1027]

PRESTON 21.57/0.00 (Centre of station)
Preston Fylde Jn (0.33)
Preston North Jn (0.21)
Preston South Jn 21.39
Carriage Sdgs
Dock St Sdgs

CGJ 6   [NW 4001]
CGJ 5   [NW 1001]
PDB   LMS : L&Y & LNW Joint (Preston & Longridge)

PRESTON and LONGRIDGE LINE (OOU)
Deepdale Jn 0.00/1.31
Skeffington Road (TMO) 1.33
Preston (Deepdale) 1.59
Deepdale Tunnels No. 2/3 (272+384 yds)   No. 1 (162 yds)

Platforms 1 & 2, 3, 3C & 4C, 5, 6
From former Liverpool Exchange 28.60

Ribble Viaduct
Preston Ribble Jn (21.13)
Skew Bridge 20.34
Skew Bridge Jn 20.41

NORTH UNION LINE
LMS : LNW & L&Y Joint   CGJ 5   [NW 1001]
Controlled by Preston PSB (PN)

Farington Curve Jn (East Lancs) 0.06 [25.64]
Farington Curve Jn 20.08

LOSTOCK HALL CONNECTING LINE

WALTON JN to PRESTON LINE
FHR 2   LMS : L&Y [NW 7009]
LOSTOCK HALL 1.20
FHR   FHR

Engine Shed Jn 0.64
Farington Jn 0.00

LOSTOCK HALL LINES (FARINGTON OLD CURVE)
LHL   [NW 7011]

1.42 Lostock Hall
46A : to Blackburn

Lancashire Enterprises Sdgs 19 (Arriva Rail North)
DMU servicing

LEYLAND 17.54

CGJ 5   LMS : LNW & L&Y Joint (North Union) [NW 1001]

30B

December 2018
© Copyright TRACKmaps. No reproduction without permission

30

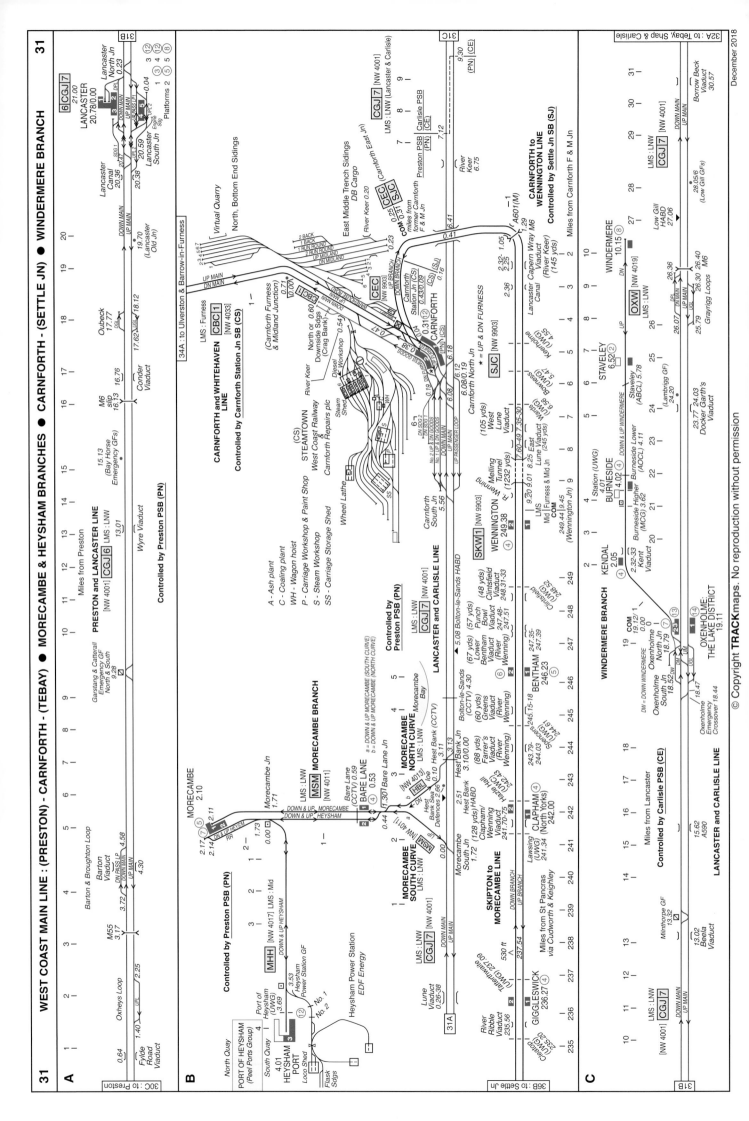

WEST COAST MAIN LINE : (PRESTON) - CARNFORTH - (TEBAY) ● MORECAMBE & HEYSHAM BRANCHES ● CARNFORTH - (SETTLE JN) ● WINDERMERE BRANCH

© Copyright TRACKmaps. No reproduction without permission

December 2018

WEST COAST MAIN LINE : TEBAY - CARLISLE

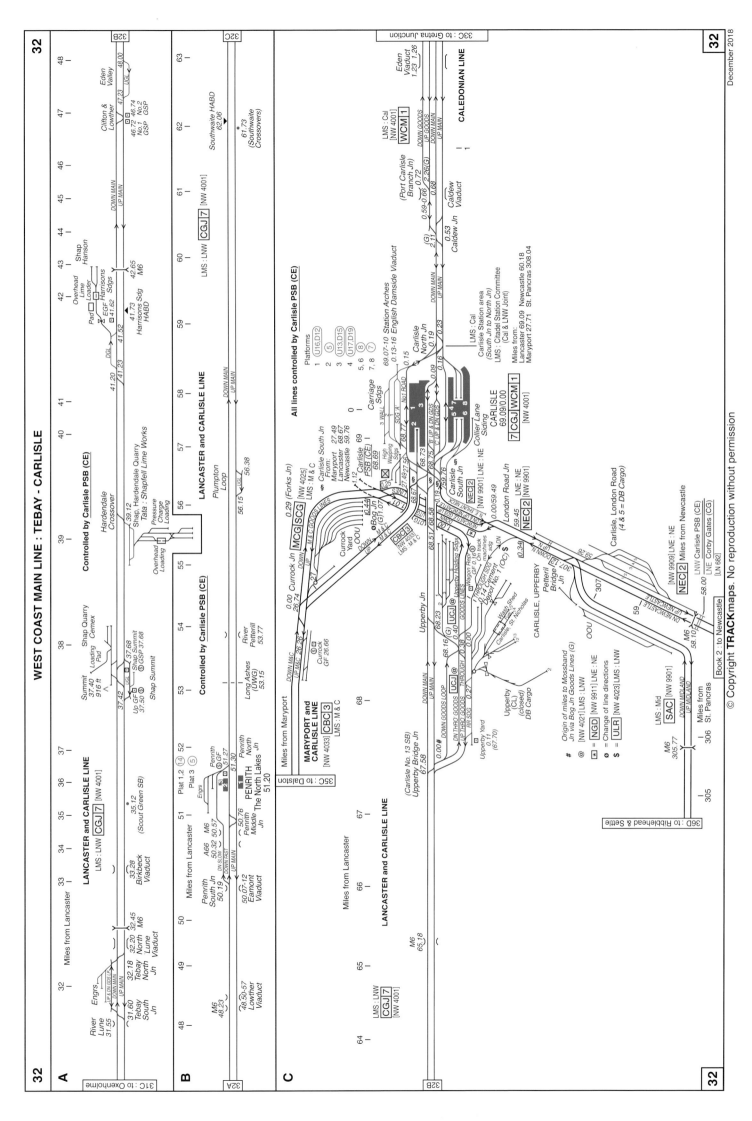

December 2018

WEST COAST MAIN LINE : KINGMOOR - SCOTLAND ● LONGTOWN BRANCH ● RAVENGLASS & ESKDALE RAILWAY

A

MAIN LINES   CALEDONIAN LINE   WCM 1   LMS : Cal [NW 4001]

GOODS LINE   KMG 2

33D

Controlled by Carlisle PSB (CE)

Esk Viaduct 6.51-6.58

Floriston 8 (G) (CCTV)
Floriston HABD's
7 (G)   6.05
7.44 (G)   6.07
7.47 (G)
7.48 (G)

DN DEP DN GDS
DOWN MAIN
UP MAIN
UP AVOIDING ARRIVAL

33C

Miles on Goods Lines (G) via former Bog Jn/Rome Street route to Mossband Jn

Admiralty Sdgs Jn (7.23)
7.18
Admiralty Sdg GF (OOU) 8.69 (G)
M6
33D

Miles From Carlisle Station 8

Mossband Jn 7.57
7.64

DOWN MAIN
UP MAIN
UP GOODS
9 (G)
9 (G)
3.02

former regional boundary LMR / Sc (1948-92) 8.00

Gretna Jn 116.09
T 16.13
8.55-8.57
Sark Viaduct (England/Scotland border)
Quintinshill 10.13
Old box 10.19
GSP 10.33
Loop Jn 9.72
Loop Jn 10.30
10.36
DPL
DN
UP
UPL

A74(M) 115.38
116
A74(M) 12.47

Carlisle PSB (CE) LNW
Motherwell PSB (SC) [SC 001]
Carlisle PSB (CE) LNW [NW 4031]
WCM 1 LMS : Cal

115.40
Carlisle PSB Dumfries SB [NW 4031] [SC 031]
GSW (CE) (DE)
LMS : GSW
GRETNA GREEN
115.12 (5)
2 DOWN DUMFRIES
T
115
Kirtle Water Viaduct 113.47
114
A75   113.18 (G)
113 13.10 (UWE)
112

Miles from former Bridge Street Station via Dalry & Kilmarnock

Book 1 : to Annan, Dumfries & Glasgow

Book 1 : to Lockerbie & Glasgow

B RAVENGLASS AND ESKDALE RAILWAY 15" gauge

RAVENGLASS (NR) for Eskdale

Railway Museum
Workshop
Joinery and paint shop
Carriage Shed
Diesel Shed
Loco Shed

2 3
1
0.10
0.08

34C   0.00

MUNCASTER MILL 1.12

MITESIDE HALT 1.55
Miteside Loop 1.70

Murthwaite Sdg (Per. Way Store) 2.42
MURTHWAITE HALT 2.65
Murthwaite GF

1   2   3   4

Control Is by 'Radio-controlled Train Order' except at Ravenglass

Eskdale Green 4.65 (OPEN)
IRTON ROAD 4.18
THE GREEN 4.69
Fisherground Loop 5.39
FISHERGROUND HALT 5.47

5   6

R. Esk
BECKFOOT 6.40
6.43 (OPEN)
DALEGARTH for Boot 6.75
6.77

D

NW 4029   GJH

LONGTOWN SIDING

33A   33A

N1RU emergency connection

a = Bush-on-Esk No. 4 (OC) 1.79
b = Bush-on-Esk No. 2 (AOCL) 1.07
c = Bush-on-Esk No. 1 0.65

a
b   West Jn 1.06
Bush-on-Esk
c   East Jn 0.69

DE&S LONGTOWN
Ministry of Defence (Defence Munitions)

Solway 1
Solway 2
Solway 3

Y1
Y2
Y7

Stabling Area
Road Rail Transfer Platform
Gaitle Yard
Y9

Loco Shed
FP
CR

Exchange Sidings

4.22
0.24
0.67
(n00)

Formerly connection to MOD Smalmstown (now closed, all track lifted) Zero at former NR Bdy +0.24
Longtown Branch Jn 88.46 (Edinburgh)

C

CALEDONIAN LINE   WCM 1   [NW 4001]

Kingmoor Virtual Quarry LC 4.79
Virtual Quarry LOADING SDG
BSW Timber
Virtual Quarry 'B' Group GF GF 4.47(G)
'B' Group GF 4.48(G)

Carlisle : B Group Sidings- former Down Departure Sdgs

DOWN DEPARTURE

Timber Loading Sdgs
Rail Recovery Train

RR
31
30
25
24
23
21
19
13
6

Used Ballast Stockpile (former Up Sorting Sdgs)
UNLOADING SDG
UP AVOIDING/ARRIVAL

1 KMG 2

UP AVOIDING/ARRIVAL
5.70 (G)
5.61 (G)
4.25
4.31
4.04(G)
4.43/(G)

CALEDONIAN LINE

DOWN MAIN   LMS : Cal
UP MAIN

CARLISLE (KINGMOOR) YARD

Up Departure Sdgs
Up Reception Sdgs
RR
11
7
6
3
1

LC 4.29

Brunthill Branch (0.66) DOWN ARRIVAL/DEPARTURE
Brunthill Branch 4.04(G)
BSN [NW 4027] BR
KMG1
Down Recess Sdgs
No 2 UP DEP
No 2 DN DEP
No 1 UP DEP
4 (G)
WCM 1 [NW 4001] LMS : Cal

2.11
2.16   A689

Harker : Kingstown Carlisle Warehousing Limited
95.00

LNE : NB   ETC   [NW 4027]
NR limit 95.06

EDINBURGH to CARLISLE LINE (NB)

Miles from Edinburgh Waverley via Portobello Jn

Kingmoor Maintenance TMD (KM) Direct Rail Services

Stainton Crossing 96.09
Stainton Jn 95.67
95.02
95.39
ETC [NW 4027]
Kingmoor Jn
3.36(G)
3.53(G)
3.42(G)
3.42(G)
2.03
1.79

N5
a = BREAKDN TRAIN
RR
FP
DOWN GOODS
DOWN MAIN
UP MAIN
UP GOODS
UP PASSENGER LOOP
UP THROUGH SIDING

Etterby / Exchange Sidings (OOU)
1.64
1.59
1.50
1.40
1.33
1.32
1.23   1.26   2.70

Eden Viaduct 1.23-1.26

32C : to Carlisle

Miles on Goods Lines (G) from Upperby Bridge Jn via former Bog Jn/Rome Street route to Mossband Jn.
Miles on Main Line from Carlisle Stn

5
6(G)
4

1 KMG 2
WCM 1 [NW 4001] LMS : Cal

33A

December 2018

© Copyright TRACKmaps. No reproduction without permission

Miles on Goods Lines (G) from Upperby Bridge Jn via former Bog Jn/Rome Street route to Mossband Jn

CUMBRIAN COAST LINE : (CARNFORTH) - BARROW - BRAYSTONES ● LAKESIDE AND HAVERTHWAITE RAILWAY

A

Miles from Carnforth

31B : to Carnforth

Silverdale Quarry (UWG) 4.14
Waterslack (UWG) 4.57
Black Dyke (AOCL-B) 5.12
Leeming (UWG) 4.25
SILVERDALE 3.55
Silverdale (AOCL) 3.11

Sea Defence Works

Kent/Arnside Viaduct 6.49-72
ARNSIDE (AE) 6.29
6.21

CARNFORTH and WHITEHAVEN LINE
LMS : Furness   CBC 1   [NW 4033]

8.09 River Winster

GRANGE-OVER-SANDS (GS) 9.31   9.43
Bathing Pool 10.20

Cart Lane (UWB) 10.59
KENTS BANK (UWB) 11.30   11.27

CARK & CARTMEL ● 13.59
station signs carry Cark only.

Crook Wheel (UWG)(GS) 14.24

Sea Defence Works

Wraysholme (AOCL-B) 12.42

16.57-17.01
Leven/Plumpton Viaduct
17.62 (Plumpton Jn)
(0.00 LKD to Haverthwaite)

Ulverston Canal Viaduct 18.38-43
ULVERSTON 19.28

Certas energy
(NIRU)

19.47 (UN)

Lindal Tunnel (439 yards)
22.53-22.73

Dalton Tunnel (225 yards)
24.01-11
DALTON 23.67

31B

CARNFORTH and WHITEHAVEN LINE
LMS : Furness   CBC 1   [NW 4033]

UP MAIN
DOWN MAIN

SEA DEFENCE WORKS   E = Embankment

1.34-1.67 Warton Sands E.
2.04-2.50 Warton Sands E.
2.68-2.70 Quicksands Pool Bridge
6.33-6.33 Arnside Station E.
6.47-7.66 Kent Viaduct Approach
7.66-8.00 Meathop March E.
8.09-9.18 Meathop Fell E.
9.18-9.34 Grange Goods Yard
9.34-9.66 Grange Station

9.77-10.19 Pitching & Prom.
10.32-10.66 Cart Lane E.
10.66-11.51 Kents Bank Pitching
11.27-11.78 Kents Bank E.
11.67-11.78 Kirk Head E.
11.21-16.49 Capes Head E.
16.49-16.49 Leven Viaduct
17.01-17.05 Approaches
17.05-17.24 Threadow Point E.

B

PORT OF BARROW

DEVONSHIRE DOCK
BUCCLEUCH DOCK
CAVENDISH DOCK
RAMSDEN DOCK

International Nuclear Services
ABP
NR
(Buccleuch Jn) 28.10
LC 28.19
27.57

Salthouse Jn 27.59
Salthouse Viaduct
28.03 28.10

Dukes Sdgs
Fuel Point
Carriage Sdgs (BW)
29.28
29.05 (BF)
BARROW-IN-FURNESS 28.76
28.58

Arriva Rail North
Barrow Depot

LAKESIDE and HAVERTHWAITE RAILWAY
D
4' 8½" / 1435mm gauge

LAKESIDE 7.74
7.63   LKD

Stock shed
HAVERTHWAITE 4.70
4.59 4.67
4.56
5.02 5.06
Haverthwaite Works
Haverthwaite West Tunnel (165 yards)
Haverthwaite East Tunnel (87 yards)

Miles from former Plumpton Jn
NEWBY BRIDGE HALT 6.67
6.69 (path)

C

Miles from Carnforth

CARNFORTH and WHITEHAVEN LINE
LMS : Furness   CBC 1   [NW 4033]

ROOSE 27.13

Goldmire Quarry (UWG) 0.58
DOWN BRANCH
UP BRANCH
Park South Jn
Park South (PS) 33.06
Park North (PS) 33.05
32.77
(0.76)

Furness Abbey (BF) 25.31
Furness Abbey (UWG)(BF) 25.31
Furness Abbey Tunnel (76 yards)
25.41 25.44
26.08 Park House Farm (MWLO)

DAP [NW 4041]
LMS : Furness
DALTON LOOP
Dalton Jn 24.38/0.00
Dalton Jn 24.37 (DJ)

34A

Sandscale (finish) (AOCL)
Ceallpharque (AOCL)

AM 35.03
ASKAM 35.06
Johnson's No. 31 (UWG) 35.31
Dunnerholme (UWG) 36.27
Lidgate 35.24
KIRKBY-IN-FURNESS 38.19
Kirkby Viaduct

Skelly Crag (MCG) 38.75
Angerton Hall No. 2 (UWG)(F) 40.41
FOXFIELD 40.37
40.40
Duddon/Foxfield Viaduct (Approaches) 40.70-41.06 41.11-41.27

UP MAIN
DOWN MAIN

SEA DEFENCE WORKS   E = Embankment

35.59-36.00 Dunnerholme E.
36.48-36.53 Souter Gate
36.65-37.41 Souter Gate Marsh E.
37.41-37.57 Lidge Gate Wall
37.57-38.18 Sandside Marsh E.
38.18-38.50 Head Cragg Pitching
40.00-40.17 Angerton Marsh E.
40.25-40.41 Foxfield Marsh E.

Underhill (UWG) 43.12
Green Road Viaduct 42.20
GREEN ROAD 42.37
41.06-11
King (UWG) 42.34
(ABCL-X)
a = Angerton Hall (UWG)(F) 38.59
b = Ladyhall (UWG)(F) 41.28
c = Dodd's (UWG)(F) 42.19
d = Waltham Nurseries (UWG) 42.62
e = Stone Cabin (UWG)(M) 42.75

34B

Long Marsh No. 1 (UWG)(M) 43-56
Castle Farm (UWG)(M) 43.92
Slothouse No. 3 (UWG)(M) 44.22
Slothouse No. 1 (UWG)(M) 44.05
Slothouse No. 2 (UWG)(M) 44.46

MILLOM 45.01
45.07 (MM)
Moor Farm No. 1 (UWG)(M) 45.27
Haverigg (AHBC) 46.05
Hestham Hall (UWG) 46.32
Longthwaite (UWG) 46.32
Kirksanton (MCG) 47.08
Mill Dam (UWG) 47.27
Millers (UWG)(S) 47.43
Limestone Hall (MCG) 47.17
SILECROFT 48.16
48.12
Whitbeck (ABCL-X) 48.55
Stangroft Farm (UWG)(S) 50.27
Moss (Tip) (UWG)(S) 50.13

BOOTLE 53.34
Bootle Beck Viaduct 51.70
53.37 (BE)

Middleton Place (UWG)(S) 55.15
Eskmeals Viaduct 56.43-58

RAVENGLASS for ESKDALE 57.79

River Esk Pitching 56.59-56.73
Walls Bridge E. 57.24-57.37
River Mite Pitching 58.18-58.23
Seascale Foreshore 62.06-63.02

33B : to Ravenglass & Eskdale Railway

Ravenglass (UWG) 58.10-14 59.25
Ravenglass Viaduct (River Mite) 58.49
Hall Carleton (UWG) 59.25
DRIGG 60.02
59.52
Drigg Viaduct (River Irt) 59.79
Drigg : LLW Repository Ltd
60.42   (D)   (S)

SEASCALE 62.12

35A : to Whitehaven

CARNFORTH and WHITEHAVEN LINE
LMS : Furness   CBC 1   [NW 4033]

Miles from Carnforth via Barrow

Sea Defence Works

34A

© Copyright TRACKmaps. No reproduction without permission

December 2018

CUMBRIAN COAST LINE : NETHERTOWN - WHITEHAVEN - WORKINGTON - MARYPORT - (CARLISLE)

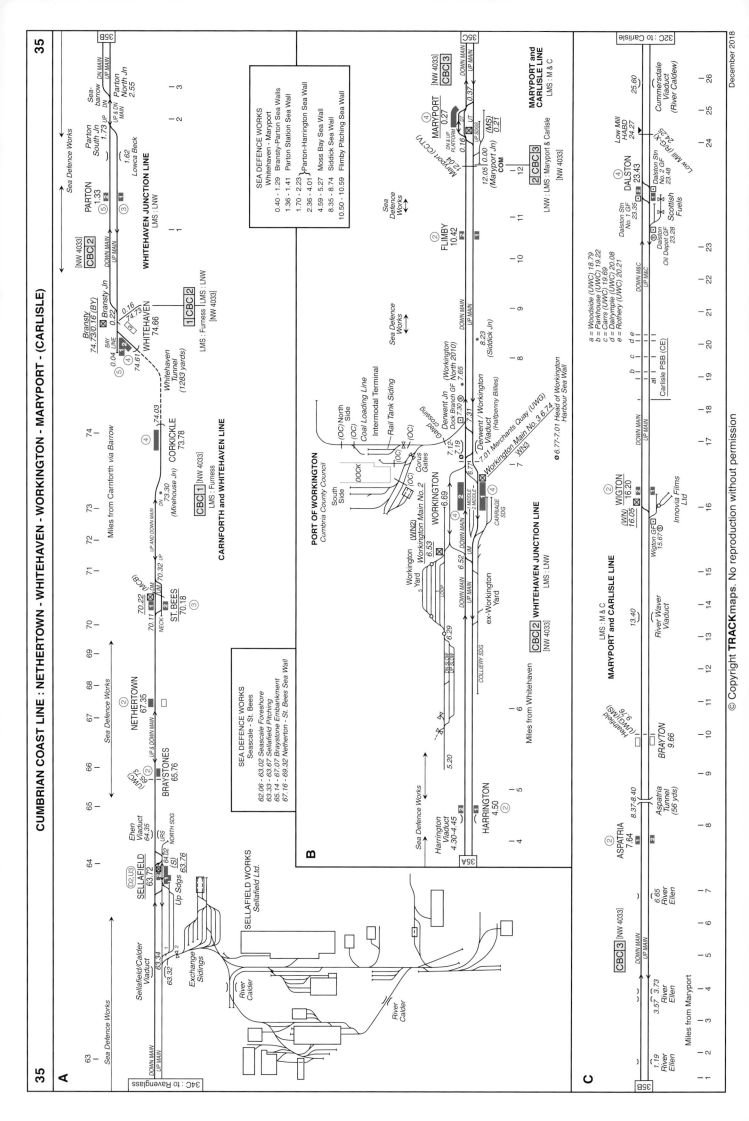

December 2018

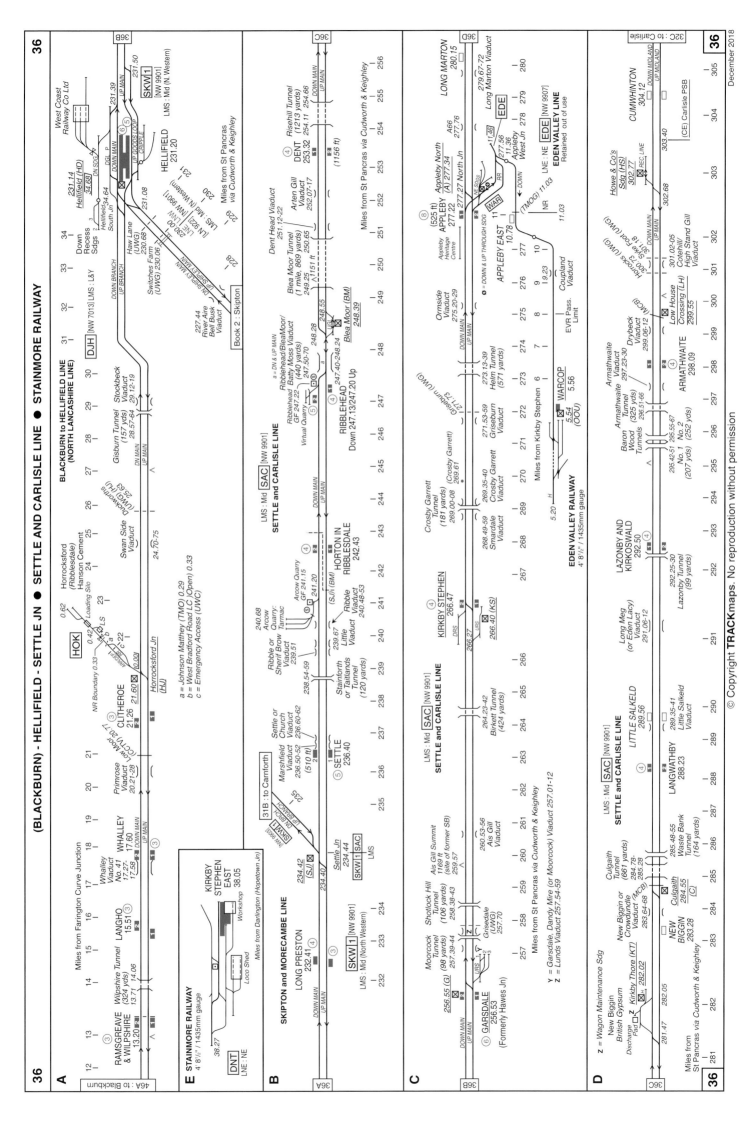

(BLACKBURN) - HELLIFIELD - SETTLE JN ● SETTLE AND CARLISLE LINE ● STAINMORE RAILWAY

December 2018

A

Controlled by Fiddlers Ferry (FF)

Carterhouse Jn (UWG) 16.27 16.32

UP GOODS
DN GOODS

to former Timperley Jn 16

WIDNES LOOP

SDJ 2 [NW 2009] LMS : LNW

WIDNES SOUTH

Viaduct 17.15 16.75
17.18

Miles from former Timperley Jn

17.50 (West Deviation)

*17.60
17.60

181.69 Ditton Viaduct

Spans Runcorn Viaduct North
(River Mersey: Spans 1-5)

(DN) (WE)
182.10

Controlled by Manchester ROC (DN)

RUNCORN BRANCH

WJL 1 LMS : LNW

Controlled by Manchester ROC (WE)

Halton Jn 179.24

UP DITTON
DOWN DITTON

FJH LMS : LNW [NW 3021]

FRODSHAM SINGLE

180

29B : to Frodsham/Acton Bridge

RUNCORN 180.40
Runcorn Jn 180.29
180.22

180.48

181.11

180.77 Manchester Ship Canal
180.52 Bridgewater Canal

RUNCORN BRIDGE
River Mersey 915 yards

Viaduct (WE) (DN)

The Queen Ethelfreda

0.25 A557(T)

DN (A up FOLLY LANE

0.69 NR boundary
0.72

FOLLY LANE
(Western Point)
Ineos Gantry Crane

Loading facility

1.21

RDB [NW 2003]

RUNCORN DOCK BRANCH
FOLLY LANE SINGLE

TIMPERLEY and GARSTON LINE

LMS : LNW WJL 2 [NW 2001]

2 WJL 1
SDJ 2

DITTON 182.79

DITTON
East Jn
182.67 18.55
182.60

UP DITTON FAST
DOWN DITTON FAST
UP DITTON SLOW
DOWN DITTON SLOW

183.30
183.22

West Jn 183.22

UP LATCHFORD GDS
DOWN LATCHFORD GDS

DITTON INTERMODAL TERMINAL

181.33
Spans
16 Spans
181.25

182

Widnes Intermodal Rail Depot
Stobart Group

* = Crane Pad

181

183

Ditton Reception Sdgs

Ditton Sidings GSP 183.06

Widnes Train Care Centre
Alstom

184 Miles from Euston

Manchester ROC
(WE) (DN)
186.56

3 WJL 2
Speke East Jn
186.72 (22.59)
186.57

SPEKE COMPOUND SDG
186.56

Garston
Car Terminal
Ford Motor Co.
/ Ansa Logistics

Ramps

187

38A : to Garston & Liverpool Lime Street

TIMPERLEY and GARSTON LINE
LMS : LNW WJL 2 [NW 2001]

A561
184.44

HALEWOOD E. NECK
184.45

Halewood East Jn 184.64

Halewood Exchange Sdgs

185.43

185.16 Halewood
HALEWOOD W. NECK
185.16
Halewood West Jn 185.16

Jaguar Land Rover 185

Car Ramps

186

B

29B : to Arpley Jn

TIMPERLEY and GARSTON LINE
SDJ 2 [NW 2009] LMS : LNW

Litton's Mill LCF (MCG) 11.45

Miles from former Timperley Jn

St Helens Canal

Monks Sdg (MS)
12.31 11.70
12

Fiddlers Ferry (CCTV) 14.09
Penketh Hall (UWG) 13.63 13.37
13

Marsh House (CCTV) 14.46
14

FIDDLERS FERRY POWER STATION
Scottish & Southern Energy

Control Building

Gypsum (FGD) Loading Plant

Fiddlers Ferry (FF)
Power Station 14.46

Coal Track Hoppers

0.33 0.00

15

UP GOODS
DOWN GOODS

HOPPER APPROACH TRACKS

37A

C

MANCHESTER SHIP CANAL
Ellesmere Port : West End Sidings

Ellesmere Port Docks
(Peel Ports Group)
(Quality Freight Ltd)

1.15

Dock 0.72

M53 0.63

Footpath 0.48 MSC 0.05
NR 0.00
Richard Lawson Transport
West End Sdgs

28A : to Helsby

3.37
3.44
ELLESMERE PORT

1.11

1.44 1.72

Manisty Wharf (Coal Loading)

DOWN MAIN
UP MAIN

OVERPOOL 2.28

Miles from Chester

LITTLE SUTTON 1.47

Chester PSB
(HN) (CR)

UP HELSBY
DOWN HELSBY

HOOTON and HELSBY LINE

GW & LMS (LNW) Joint :
(Birkenhead, Lancashire & Cheshire Jn Railway)

HHJ [NW 3013]

CAPENHURST 5.11

UP BIRKENHEAD
DOWN BIRKENHEAD

CHESTER and BIRKENHEAD LINE

CRR 1 GW & LMS (LNW) Joint :
(Chester & Birkenhead Railway)
[NW 3011]

28A : to Chester

2 HHJ
2 CRR 1

Hooton South Jn 0.02
HOOTON 8.08

BAY

Hooton North Jn 8.17

SIDING

CHESTER and BIRKENHEAD LINE

CRR 2 GW & LMS (LNW) Joint : Birkenhead Joint
[NW 8C13]

'Merseyrail Wirral Line'

BROMBOROUGH RAKE 10.38

BROMBOROUGH 9.71
9.41

Merseyrail (ML)

RR

DOWN CHESTER
UP CHESTER

EASTHAM RAKE 8.68
8.53 M53

Controlled by Chester (HN)

SPITAL 11.16

Controlled by Merseyrail (ML)
Located at Sandhills

DOWN SDG 11.42

Rock Ferry South Jn 13.30

PORT SUNLIGHT 11.61

BEBINGTON 12.36

39A : to Birkenhead

December 2018

© Copyright TRACKmaps. No reproduction without permission

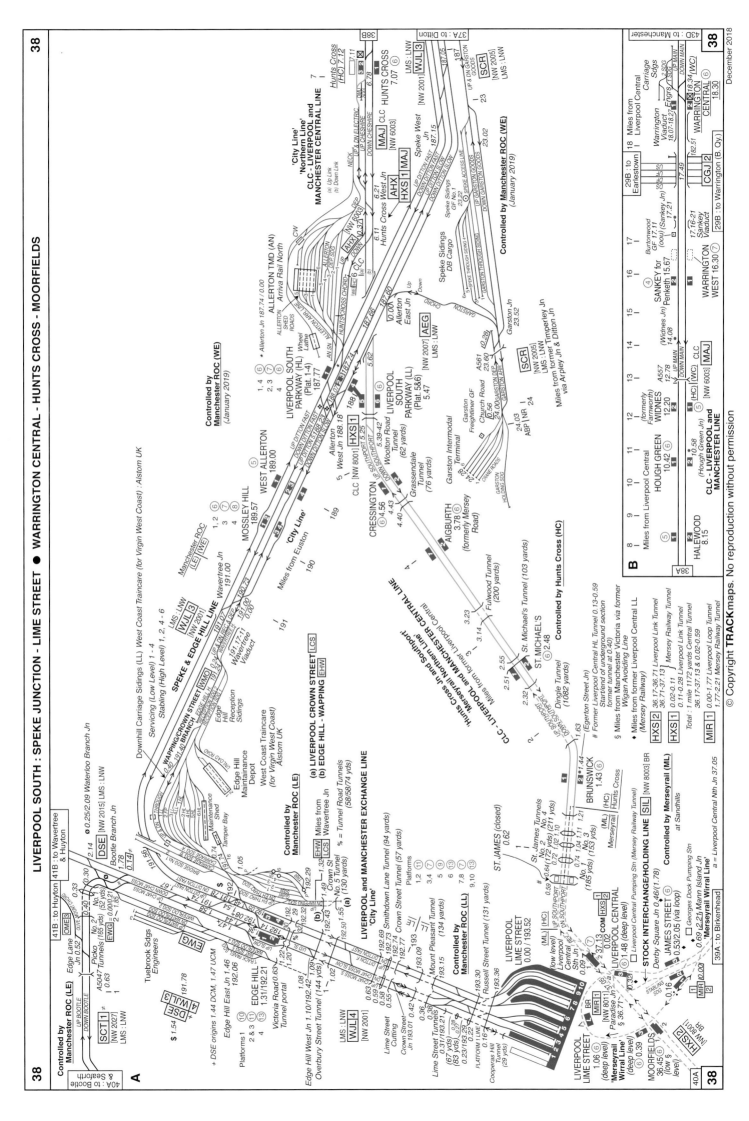

December 2018

A

Controlled by Merseyrail (ML)
Located at Sandhills

LMS : Wirral [BEN] [NW 8015]

BIRKENHEAD PARK and NEW BRIGHTON LINE
'Merseyrail Wirral Line'

NEW BRIGHTON 7.18
SDG 1
SDG 2
WALL SDG
7.01
DOWN NEW BRIGHTON
UP NEW BRIGHTON

WALLASEY GROVE ROAD 5.73
WALLASEY VILLAGE 5.48

5.01 - 5.05 Bidston Moss Viaduct M53

(Seacombe Jn) 4.62

Bidston Dock Thro' Sdg
0.00
4.40
Bidston East Jn
Bidston West Jn 4.71
UP W. KIRBY
DOWN W. KIRBY

[BDS] STABLING

BIDSTON 4.75
Bidston Dee Jn 4.78
0.08 A553
0.33 A553

UP WREXHAM
DN WREXHAM

UPTON 1.67
HESWALL 6.03
NESTON 8.55

3.73 M53

NORTH WALES and LIVERPOOL LINE
'Borderlands Line'

[WDB] 3 [NW 8007] LNE : GC

Miles from Bidston West Jn via former avoiding loop

39C
38B

B

Controlled by Merseyrail (ML)
Located at Sandhills

WEST KIRBY to SEACOMBE LINE
'Merseyrail Wirral Line'

[NW 8011] [CWK] 3 LMS : Wirral

Leasowe (CCTV) 5.60
LEASOWE 5.65
5.13 M53
MORETON (Merseyside) 6.29

Car Lane (UWG) 7.53
Melrose Avenue (UWG) 9.05
Sandringham Avenue (UWG) 8.59
Carr Lane (UWG) 8.66
Tolans (UWG) 9.00

HOYLAKE 9.27
MEOLS 8.11
MANOR ROAD 8.71

Elm Grove (UWG) 9.31
Station Road (CCTV) (ML) 9.31

WEST KIRBY 10.46
SDG 1
SDG 2
UP WEST KIRBY
DN WEST KIRBY

39A

D

WIRRAL TRANSPORT MUSEUM 'BIRKENHEAD TRAMWAY'
4' 8½'' / 1435mm gauge
Operated by Wirral Borough Council
600v DC overhead

Woodside Ferry 0.00
Shore Road Pumping Stn 0.08
Pacific Road 0.18
Pacific Road Arts & Exhibition Centre
Store
Taylor St Depot & Museum
Egerton Bridge 0.38
Old Colonial 0.47
Cars, M'bikes

a = Shore Road passing loop

38A : to Liverpool

LMS : Mersey [NW 8011]
[MIR] 2
Mersey Tunnel 0.69
Mann Island Jn
Canning St Jn
DOWN CHESTER
UP WEST KIRBY
DN WEST KIRBY

HAMILTON SQUARE 1.67 (platform 3 = 1.68)
Miles from former Liverpool Central LL.
(Grange Road/Green Lane Jn)
1.60
1.72
[CWK] 1

[CCS] 2 1
Carriage Sidings (Disused)
14.55
14.58

GREEN LANE to CATHCART STREET LINE (Chester & Birkenhead)
GW & LMS (LNW) Joint : Birkenhead Joint

[CCS] 1 [NW 8017]
14.15 (former Green Lane Jn)
(OOU) Line Closed
14.00
Miles from Chester
Mersey Railway diverges

[CCS] 1 [NW 8017]
[CRR] 2 [NW 8013]

Birkenhead Tramway (See 39D)
DN Hamilton Sq. Jn
UP WEST KIRBY
DOWN WEST KIRBY
14.64
14.60

UP CANNING STREET
DOWN CANNING STREET
DN & UP CANNING STREET

Canning Street North 15.29 (Derelict)
(OOU)
15.26
15.40
Line Closed

Lorne Street 2.09
Haymarket Tunnel (139 yards)
Line Closed on CCS
2.24

MD&HC
NR

CONWAY PARK 2.24

Hinderton Field Tunnel (497 yards)
2.39

BIRKENHEAD CENTRAL 2.30

11.234
2.24
2.61
2.64
2.66
2.69

GREEN LANE 2.64
Green Lane Tunnel (59 yards)
Viaduct 3.06

MERSEY RAILWAY
'Merseyrail Wirral Line'

[MIR] 2
[CRR] 2
[NW 8013]

Rock Ferry Wirral Line
3.27
3.35
UP CHESTER
DOWN CHESTER
Viaduct 3.35

ROCK FERRY 3.42/13.43
13.51
13.59
Rock Ferry North Jn
Rock Ferry South Jn 13.30
13.39
3.46

37C : to Hooton

Vittoria Dock
Stanton Grove Warehouses

MD & HC LINES

Duke Street

Condition of dock lines uncertain

MERSEY DOCKS and HARBOUR CO'S LINES

2 [CWK] 1 [NW 8011]
LMS : Wirral | LMS : Mersey

2.69
3.00
3.05
3.15
BIRKENHEAD PARK 3.05
Miles from former Liverpool Central Low Level

Cavendish Street Tunnel (71 yards)
3.19
3.45
Corporation Road Tunnel (64 yards)
3.48

Wallasey Bridge Road 0.43
0.36
NR MD&HC
0.20
0.00
Roads 3 to 6 have 'overhead rails' inside depot

BIRKENHEAD NORTH T&RSMD (BD)
Stadler / Merseyrail
BACK ROAD
UP L
UP W. KIRBY
DOWN W. KIRBY

BIRKENHEAD NORTH 3.75

3 [CWK] 2 [NW 8011]
[BEN]
LMS : Wirral

C

Controlled by Merseyrail (ML)
Located at Sandhills

BIRKENHEAD PARK and NEW BRIGHTON LINE
'Merseyrail Wirral Line'
(Operated by Merseyrail, an Abellio-Serco joint venture)

NORTH WALES and LIVERPOOL LINE
'Borderlands Line'

[NW 3007] [WDB] 3

LNE : GC
Miles from Bidston

39A

BURTON POINT 10.64
12.37
11.00
WA | LNW
DN WREXHAM
UP WREXHAM

Shotwick Shotton Paper Co. Ltd.
Shotwick GF 11.74
12.33 A548

11
12
13

Birkenhead Sidings

Deeside Titanium CLOSED

DEE MARSH Shotton Works (Summers) Tata Steel
15.00
15.23
14.47
14.38
14.10
13.70
13.40
Dee Marsh North Jn (formerly Birkenhead Jn)
13.23
13.11

Government Sdgs

3 Summers
CRIPPLE
WB
18
16
10
5
6

Dee Marsh Jn (DM) 13.77
14.07
2 [WDB] 3
(Dee Marsh Jn West or Wrexham Jn)
14.15
14.12

HAWARDEN BRIDGE 14.14
13.33 14.15
COM (mileage meet)
13.24
13.37
2
River Dee
1 [WDB] 2

27C : to Wrexham

© Copyright **TRACKmaps**. No reproduction without permission

December 2018

LIVERPOOL NORTH : (MOORFIELDS) - BIRKDALE / ORMSKIRK / ORRELL ● BOOTLE BRANCH

A

PEMBERTON to LIVERPOOL LINE
LMS : L&Y
WKL 2 [NW 6015]

Knowsley Freight Terminal
SITA UK
W H Bowker Ltd

Dukes Wood (UWG) 23.11
Upholland Tunnel (959 yards)
Rainford Jn (RJ) 24.35

ORRELL 20.77
UPHOLLAND 22.24
RAINFORD 24.30
24.39
AUGHTON PARK 10.78
TOWN GREEN 10.08
MAGHULL NORTH
MAGHULL 8.16
KIRKBY
WKL 2 WJK
29.41
29.40
M57 30.06
30.72

Dale Lane GSP
Warehouse 27.30
28.31
28.25
28.60

WALTON JN to PRESTON LINE
LMS : L&Y
SJO 2 [NW 8005]

FAZAKERLEY 31 / 31.31
Fazakerley (UWG) 31.16
RICE LANE 32.60
A4506
AINTREE 4.68 Aintree Station Jn
OLD ROAN 5.62
WATERLOO (Merseyside) 5.20
SEAFORTH & LITHERLAND 4.14
BLUNDELLSANDS AND CROSBY 6.28
HALL ROAD 7.14

ORMSKIRK 12.15 / 12.13
HXS 3 [NW 8001]

Controlled by Merseyrail (ML)
LIVERPOOL, CROSBY and SOUTHPORT LINE
LMS : L&Y

'Merseyrail Northern Line'
(Operated by Merseyrail, an
Abellio-Serco joint venture)

Miles from former Liverpool Exchange

Leeds & Liverpool Canal

B

Controlled by Merseyrail (ML)
LIVERPOOL, CROSBY AND SOUTHPORT LINE
(Hunts Cross and Southport)
LMS : L&Y

HIGHTOWN 9.09 at Sandhills
FORMBY 11.14
FRESHFIELD 12.03
AINSDALE 14.62
HILLSIDE 16.26
BIRKDALE 17.22
South Jn 18.13
River Alt 10.25
Hesketh (UWG) 9.61
Eccles (UWG) 10.79
Clover-le-Dale (UWG) 12.12
Fisherman Path (UWG) 12.46
Crescent Road (UWG) 16.76
Portland Street (UWG) 17.65
Ainsdale Wheelchex (WILD) 14.03

'Merseyrail Northern Line'
HXS 3 [NW 8001]

SPELLOW 3.74 (closed)
WALTON & ANFIELD 3.41 (closed)
Spellow No. 2 Tunnel (339 yards)
Spellow No. 1 Tunnel (62 yards)

BOOTLE BRANCH
SCT 1 [NW 2027] LMS : LNW

Controlled by Edge Hill (LE)

Miles from Bootle Branch Jn, Edge Hill

KIRKDALE 34.14 / 34.17
Kirkdale South Jn 34.48
Kirkdale North Jn
Walton Jn 33.16
Kirkdale No. 1 Tunnel (497 yards)
Kirkdale No. 2 Tunnel (210 yards)
WJK SJO 1
[NW 8009] [NW 8007]
LMS : L&Y

WALTON (Merseyside) 3.45
ORRELL PARK 3.75
AFL NMB [NW 8007]

WALTON JN to PRESTON LINE

Controlled by Merseyrail (ML)

38A : to Edge Hill

38A : to Liverpool Central

ø = Start/End of Underground Section
Leeds Street Portal 36.17
Central Tunnel (1mile 1172yds)

Miles from Manchester Victoria
via former Wigan Avoiding Line

ASC (ML) 34.75
SANDHILLS 35.03
Sandhills Jn 35.14
SJO 1 35.00
HXS 1 35.41
HXS 2
[NW 8001]
LMS : L&Y

Merseyrail (IECC) 36
Miles from Liverpool Exchange

HXS2 viaducts
aa 35.14 - 35.62 Spans 1 - 68B Liverpool Exchange Viaduct
bb 35.62 - 36.10 Spans 69 - 100 Great Howard Street Viaduct
cc 36.08-36.12 Great Howard Street Incline

Controlled by Merseyrail (ML)

Kirkdale Depot
Stadler Rail Services (KK)
Carriage Shed

Westminster Tunnel (288 yards)
Former Atlantic Dock Jn (to Canada Dock)
2.04 Canada Dock Tunnel Under
BANK HALL 2.06
Oriel Road Tunnel (288 yards)

Miles from former Liverpool Exchange

Controlled by Merseyrail (ML)

BOOTLE EXTENSION LINE
LMS : LNW
SCT 2 [NW 2027]

Alexandra Dock Tunnel (283 yds)
2.39 Bootle Jn
BOOTLE ORIEL ROAD 2.61
BOOTLE NEW STRAND 3.15
Marsh Lane Crossover 3.52
BSJ (Crossover only)

Regent Road (AOCL) 5.53
5.43 Stop board
Alexandra Dock Sidings
European Metal Recycling Ltd.

NORTH MERSEY BRANCH
LMS : L&Y
NMB NMM [North Mersey Jn]
NMM HXS
COM (Marsh Lane Jn)

NIRU (Engineering Trains only)

Miles from Manchester Victoria via Wigan

SEAFORTH & LITHERLAND
Seaforth Viaduct
Leeds and Liverpool Canal (33.68)

LIVERPOOL DOCKS
(Peel Ports Group)

Royal Seaforth Dock
Grain Terminal
Coal Loading Bunker
Biomass Loading
Liverpool Bulk Terminal
FREIGHTLINER DEAD END 7.22
Royal Seaforth Container Terminal
Gladstone Docks

No. 2 Bch
No. 3 Bch
Alexandra Docks

BP - BYPASS ROAD
CR - COAL ROAD
IM - INTERMODAL ROAD

*Also known as GLADSTONE DEAD END

© Copyright TRACKmaps. No reproduction without permission

30A : to Wigan Wallgate
40A
47B : to Preston
41A : to Southport
40B

December 2018

40

SOUTHPORT - (WIGAN) ● (EDGE HILL) - EARLESTOWN ● HUYTON - ST. HELENS - (WIGAN)

A

30A : to Wigan Wallgate

WIGAN and SOUTHPORT LINE
LMS : L&Y WBS 3 [NW 6009]

Leeds & Liverpool Canal 19.14

GATHURST 20.46
20.73 GATHURST
M6 20.71-68
(Leeds & Liverpool Canal under)
Gathurst Viaduct 20.71-68

Waste Sdg 22.38
APPLEY BRIDGE 22.30 ④
Wigan Wallgate (WW) (PD)

Chapel Lane (MCG) 24.06
UP MAIN
DOWN MAIN

MCB 24.49 (PD)
Ferrett Lane (UWG) 25.12
PARBOLD 24.53 ⑥
Dean Lane (AHBC-X) 25.77 ⑤

Frog Lane (UWG) 25.41
Four Lane Ends 26.07
Hoscar (AHBC-X) 26.08
HOSCAR 26.13 ⑧
Shaw's (R/G) 26.71

Leeds & Liverpool Canal 27.09
BURSCOUGH JUNCTION
27.31
BURSCOUGH BRIDGE 27.58 ⑥
Burscough Bridge Junction (BBJ) 27.50
UP MAIN DOWN

47B : to Preston
47B : to Ormskirk
15.21

WALTON JN to PRESTON LINE
LMS : L&Y FCO [NW 7007]

Crabtree 28.19
Crabtree 28.67
NEW LANE 28.73 ③
Martins Lane 29.70
(AHBC) 28.70

Pool Hey (AHBC) 32.44
BESCAR LANE 30.74 ③
30.79 (AHBC) 30.78
Wyke Cop (AHBC) 32.20

Burscough Bridge Jn (BB)
Merseyrail (ML)

MEOLS COP 34.02₁ ⑤

Miles from Manchester Victoria via Wigan

Goods Yard (ML)
GF (ML) 34.58
34.58
St. Luke's Jn 34.77
North Jn 35.08
35.16
BRADFORD SDG
UP WIGAN
DOWN WIGAN
South Jn 18.13
Located at Sandhills

SOUTHPORT 35.27
⑦ ⑨ ⑧ ⑫ ⑫
18.35

WIGAN and SOUTHPORT LINE
LMS : L&Y WBS 3 [NW 6009]
*Southport Station Jn 18.29/35.21

'Northern Line'
LMS : L&Y HXS 3 [NW 8001]

Carr Sdgs
Birkdale Sdgs
Stabling Sdgs
WALLSIDE SDG
DOWN SOUTHPORT

Controlled by Merseyrail (ML)

40B : to Birkdale

December 2018

B

30A : to Wigan

Leeds & Liverpool Canal 11.72
12.10
0.78
Ince Moss Jn

BRYN 10.22 ②
M6 9.66
GARSWOOD 9.00 ④

ST. HELENS and RAINFORD LINE
LANCASHIRE UNION LINE
LMS : LNW SBH 3 [NW 2023]

Oil Terminal

St. Helens, Cowley Hill
Pilkington Glass

8.11
(SH) (WN) Warrington
UP ST. HELENS 7.00
DOWN ST. HELENS
6.74-7.00 Carr Mill Viaduct
6.69 A580
LMS : LNW SRD [7.68]

Gerards Bridge Jn GF 5.66
Down Siding
5.64 former St. Helens Canal 5.66
SRD [NW 2025]
2 SBH 3
St. Helens Canal

SHS 1 [NW 2025]
(OOU) LMS : LNW
(Ravenhead Jn) 6.62
6.51
(7.03 former St. Helens Canal)
UP GDS 7.15
DOWN GDS

Peasley Cross RR Loop
SIDING RR
6.29
6.04 NR bdy
Sutton

Miles from Widnes
ST. HELENS JUNCTION 11.70 ①
Cutting ②

ST. HELENS CENTRAL 2
5.16 [7.20]
SBH 1
Controlled by Manchester ROC (SH)

(St. Helens Station Jn) 5.12
Pilkington Viaduct
former St. Helens Canal
4.71
4.54-60
A58 4.67
4.43
4.23
WHATTO HEATH 3.43 ④

Ravenhead Works
Pilkington Glass
Oil Sidings
St. Helens Sutton Oak
(ex-Hays Chemicals)

LEA GREEN 10.57 ②
10.57 ⑤
Lea Green (UWC) 9.41

'Merseyrail City Line'
HUYTON and ST. HELENS LINE
LMS : LNW SBH 1 [NW 2023]

ECCLESTON PARK 2.47 ④
3.30-3.34
Scholes Tunnel (80 yards)

WHISTON 7.52 ②
Whiston ⑤
Incline 6.75 M57
UP MAIN
DOWN MAIN

RAINHILL 8.72 ⑨

PRESCOT 1.53 ⑤
0.15 M57
UP ST. HELENS
DOWN ST. HELENS
Huyton Jn 5.73
COM 6.12/0.00

Controlled by Manchester ROC (LL)

Platforms
1 ⑦
2 ⑦
3 ⑥
4 ⑤
HUYTON 5.55

UP CM SLOW
UP CM FAST
DN CM SLOW
DN CM FAST
CM - CHAT MOSS

Platforms
1 ⑥
2 ⑦
3 ⑤
4 ⑤
ROBY 5.14

Roby Jn 4.60

BROAD GREEN 3.47 ⑥
3.34

Edge Hill (LE) DSE [NW 2015]
UP CHAT MOSS
DOWN CHAT MOSS

Miles from Liverpool Lime Street

Olive Mount Chord OME 3 [NW 2029]
Olive Mount Jn
2.54/0.10
-0.24 0.31 Olive Mount Tunnel (146 yds)

WAVERTREE TECHNOLOGY PARK 2.29 ⑤
2.64
2.33 Olive Mount Cutting

LIVERPOOL and MANCHESTER LINE
'Merseyrail City Line'
LMS : LNW (Liverpool & Manchester) DSE [NW 2015]

38A : to Edge Hill and Liverpool Lime Street
38A : to Bootle

29C : to Newton-le-Willows

Earlestown East 14.75
Earlestown East Jn [187.10]
187.03
WEE
EEE 186.74
187.15

Platforms
1 ⑧
2,3 ⑥
4 ⑦
5 ⑤
EARLESTOWN 14.58

Sankey Jn 14.20
14.22
DN & UP E.W.
14.07-16
14.51
Sankey Viaduct (150 yards)
Earlestown West Jn 187.15
29C : to Warrington Bank Quay
Earlestown S. Jn 14.51
Earlestown West 14.51

Parr Moss
DOWN CHAT MOSS
Miles from Liverpool Lime Street
DSE [NW 2015]

DN & UP E.W. = DN & UP EARLESTOWN WEST

© Copyright TRACKmaps. No reproduction without permission

A

(STOKE-ON-TRENT) / (CREWE) - CHEADLE HULME ● MOULDSWORTH - KNUTSFORD ● SANDBACH - NORTHWICH ● WILMSLOW - STYAL

MACCLESFIELD and COLWICH LINE
LMS : NS [NW 5009] CMD 1

2GB : to Stoke-on-Trent

former West Coast Mainline Project Depot

Granville Sidings

18.54 UP GDS

UP MAIN
DOWN MAIN
DOWN GOODS

SHUNT 2
LINES

former Shelton Works

18.20
18.17
Grange Jn

Miles from Macclesfield Hibel Road

MACCLESFIELD and COLWICH LINE
LMS : NS CMD 2 [NW 5009]

(LT)
Repair Works (Electro-Motive Diesel Ltd)
17.03

LOCO RELEASE

LONGPORT
16.71

Down Sidings
DB Cargo

Longport Jn
16.48

CR8

UP MAIN
16.31 UP GOODS LOOP
DOWN MAIN
DOWN SIDING

16.50

Up Sidings

Controlled by Stoke-on-Trent SC (SOT)

Esso Sdgs (Depot closed)
16.24

former Carless Solvents Sdg
16.20

Bradwell Jn
16.16

* CMD 3 was Old Harecastle Tunnel Line 13.70-16.20

1 CMD 2
COM 16.00/15.65

DOWN MAIN

16 *
(new)

ENGINE RR

former Chatterley Valley Disposal Point

16 (old)

Northwich Oakleigh Sidings

Harecastle Tunnel (310 yards)
HABD 14.09
Harecastle 14.69

Trent & Canal 13.69
13.68

Trent & Mersey Canal 13.52

(SOT) Stoke-on-Trent SC
(CE) Crewe

Coopers (UWG)
1.35

KIDSGROVE
13.60 0.05

Kidsgrove Jn 14.13-27
14 15

LMS : NS
KCS 1 [NW 1005]

ALSAGER
2.33
2.37
2.47
2.27

UP & DN GL
DOWN MAIN
1.72
1.70

CREWE BRANCH
2

Mow Cop 11.90 (CCTV)

Home Farm 3.01 (UWG)

RADWAY GREEN
4.03

(MD) (SOT) Stoke-on-Trent

Radway Green 4.07 (CCTV)

UP MAIN
DOWN MAIN

9 10 11 12 13

3 4

7A : to Crewe

42B

December 2018

B

ALTRINCHAM and CHESTER LINE
CLC CDM 2 [NW 3023]

[NW 3023] CDM 2 CLC (Cheshire Midland)

Woods Tenement Farm (UWG) 16.55

KNUTSFORD 14.40

UP MAIN
DOWN MAIN

M6 15.73

Field House Farm (UWG) 18.43

PLUMLEY 17.17

Plumley West (PY) 18.07

A556
18.56

LOSTOCK GRALAM 19.15

Trent & Mersey Canal
Shop Sdgs

UGL 19.48
19.45

Greenbank (GK)
(PY)

NORTHWICH 20.47
Northwich Station Jn 20.52

Northwich East Jn 19.77

Lostock Works (Tata Chemicals)

Underline discharge

LC

UP SDG
ADEP
UP REC

20.33

6 Dn Gp Sdgs

DN REC
DN
CARR

Northwich South Jn 8.37

UP & DN GOODS
UP & DN B
DN CHORD

Northwich West Jn 20.79
21.16

SNJ [NW 3029]
LMS : LNW

Northwich (or Leftwich) Viaduct (R. Weaver, R. Dane)
20.76

21.60 DOWN
21.57 UP

π HWG WEST GOODS LINE [NW 3035] CLC
¥ HEG EAST GOODS LINE [NW 3033] CLC
NSN [NW 3029] LNW

Hartford North Jn 22.10

21.67 Hartford East Jn

Hartford West Jn 22.28

22.18 GREENBANK
22.12

22.21 (GK) 0.36
0.11 DN
22 0.56

DEEP ABR

[NW 3035]
HNO CLC

Winnington Works Tata Chemicals

PFA Discharge Hopper
Concrete Pad
Wagon Repairs

Vale Royal

Hartford Jn 170.56 0.07

Hartford CLC Jn 23.11
23.06

LMS : LNW
HCN [NW 3037]
Winsfd (GK)

1.03
0.44 (limit of elect.)

(WD)
0.72

WINNINGTON BRANCH

WEST COAST MAIN LINE

29A : to Crewe
29A : to Warrington

Hartford (LNW Jn) 170.47 0.16

170.19

British Salt GF 1.73

Tata Chemicals Europe

MIDDLEWICH BRANCH

Goostrey Jn
167.78 GOOSTREY 168.35
166.51 HABD 167.07

166.37 166.51
Dane Viaduct

166.78-167.24

Chapel Viaduct

Dane Viaduct

R. Dane 4.69 (North Rode Jn)

Higher Delacre (UWG) 1.27

North Rode Viaduct
5.54-35

MIDDLEWICH LOOP 3.46
E. Jn
3.39

DN M.L = DOWN MIDDLEWICH LOOP
UP M.L = UP MIDDLEWICH LOOP

4.05 W. Jn
E. Jn = Middlewich Loop East Jn
W. Jn = Middlewich Loop West Jn

(MS)
[NW 3029]
SNJ
LMS : LNW

NORTHWICH BRANCH

Trent & Mersey Canal

6.23

CREWE and STOCKPORT LINE

Alderley Edge South Jn 175.12
175.42

Alderley Edge 175.79
A34

ALDERLEY EDGE 175.21

CHELFORD 172.17

Chelford Sth. Jn
172.07 Chelford Nth. Jn

Chelford Loops 171.18

River Dane 4.07

Holmes Chapel Jn 166.78-167.24

HOLMES CHAPEL
166.37 166.51

0.51 Elworth Jn

M6

165.01

North Rode Viaduct

SANDBACH 162.50
162.62

Sandbach North Jn 162.68
162.28 Sandbach South Jn

Forest House Farm (UWG) 26.14

DELAMERE 28.11

CUDDINGTON 25.15

Mickle Trafford (MT) (GK) Greenbank

Mouldsworth Jn 30.60

Miles from former Manchester Central

ALTRINCHAM and CHESTER LINE
CLC CDM 2 [NW 3023]

Higher Delacre (UWG) 1.27

Controlled by Manchester South SCC (MS)
(located at Stockport)

MI. = MANCHESTER INDEPENDENT

Miles from Euston

160 161 162 163 164 165 166 167 168 169 170 171 172 173 174 175 176

Congleton Viaduct

Macclesfield Canal

Trent & Mersey Canal 7.68-58 7.38
162.10

CONGLETON 8.12

Elton 161.05/161.52
Wheelock Viaduct

8.17 8.16
Macclesfield Canal

(MD)
(SOT) Stoke-on-Trent

UP WILMSLOW
DOWN WILMSLOW
UP MAIN
DOWN MAIN
DOWN ML
UP ML
DOWN WILMSLOW

LMS : LNW (Manchester & Birmingham)

CMP 1 [NW 5001]

2.28

River Bollin 0.25

MACCLESFIELD 0.25

UP & DN PL

A537

9.27-12

Macclesfield Hibel Road Tunnel (343 yards)
COM 0.00/9.37

Prestbury Tunnel (273 yards)

PRESTBURY 7.10
7.06 6.69-7.01

Manchester South (MS)

ADLINGTON (Cheshire) 5.15

POYNTON 2.79

A555

BRAMHALL 1.49

Macclesfield South

0.20 River Bollin
0.20 0.37

MCH LMS : LNW

0.00 9.37
COM

MACCLESFIELD BRANCH [NW 5009]

MACCLESFIELD BRANCH [NW 5009] MCH LMS : LNW

WILMSLOW Wilmslow Sth. Jn 176.53
176.34 176.71

177 Styal Jn
177.23
178 HANDFORTH
178.24 178.52

HANDFORTH 178.07

STYAL 180
1.79

DEAN Viaduct

LMS : LNW (Man & Bham)

179 CMP 1
179.49
A34

CHEADLE HULME 180.74
180.67 Cheadle Hulme
180.59
180.57/0.08

Wilmslow Viaduct (R. Bollin)
0.26-35

Handforth Viaduct 178.05-11

Wilmslow Platforms
1 DN
2 DN
3
4

x Wilmslow Viaduct (R. Bollin)
y Wilmslow Old Viaduct 176.79-177.08
z Handforth Viaduct 178.05-11

177 Styal (STY)
LMS 5009 (IMP)
0.65
0.18 0.40

UP STYAL
DN STYAL

DN REV

Prestbury 7.10

MACCLESFIELD 0.25

MACCLESFIELD and COLWICH LINE [NW 5009] CMD 1 LMS : NS

43F : to Altrincham

43S : to Gatley

43S : to Stockport
43S : to Stockport

STALYBRIDGE to Stockport

7A : to Crewe

42A

28A : to Mouldsworth

© Copyright **TRACKmaps.** No reproduction without permission

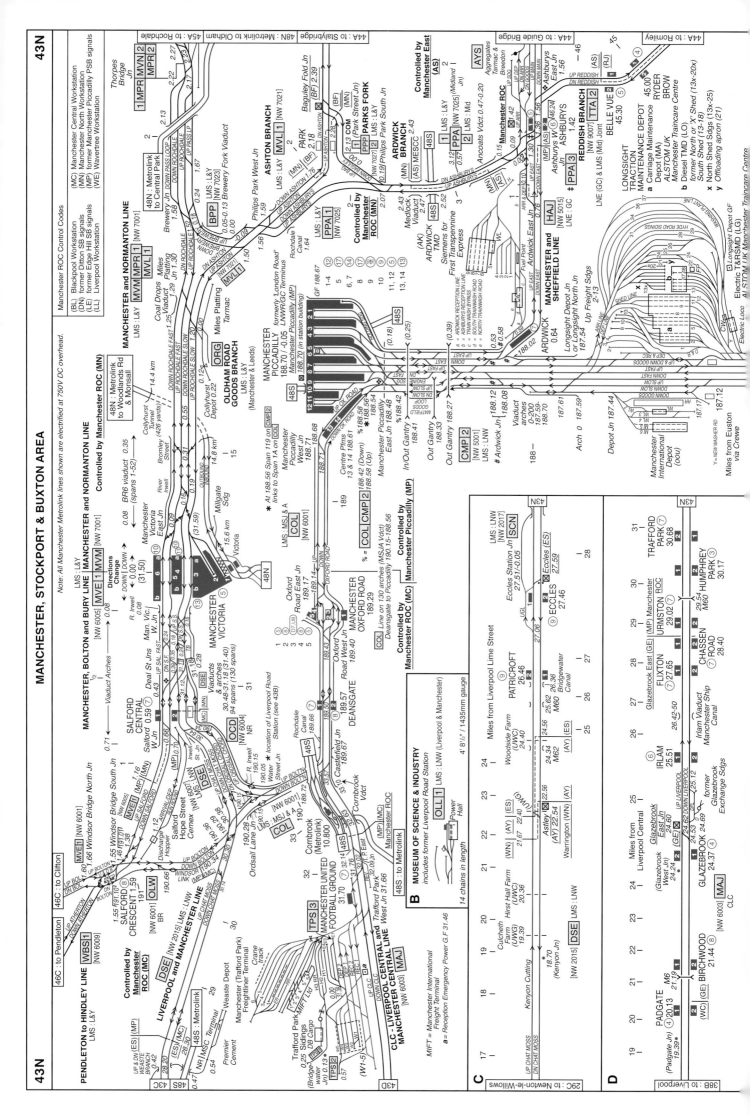

MANCHESTER, STOCKPORT & BUXTON AREA

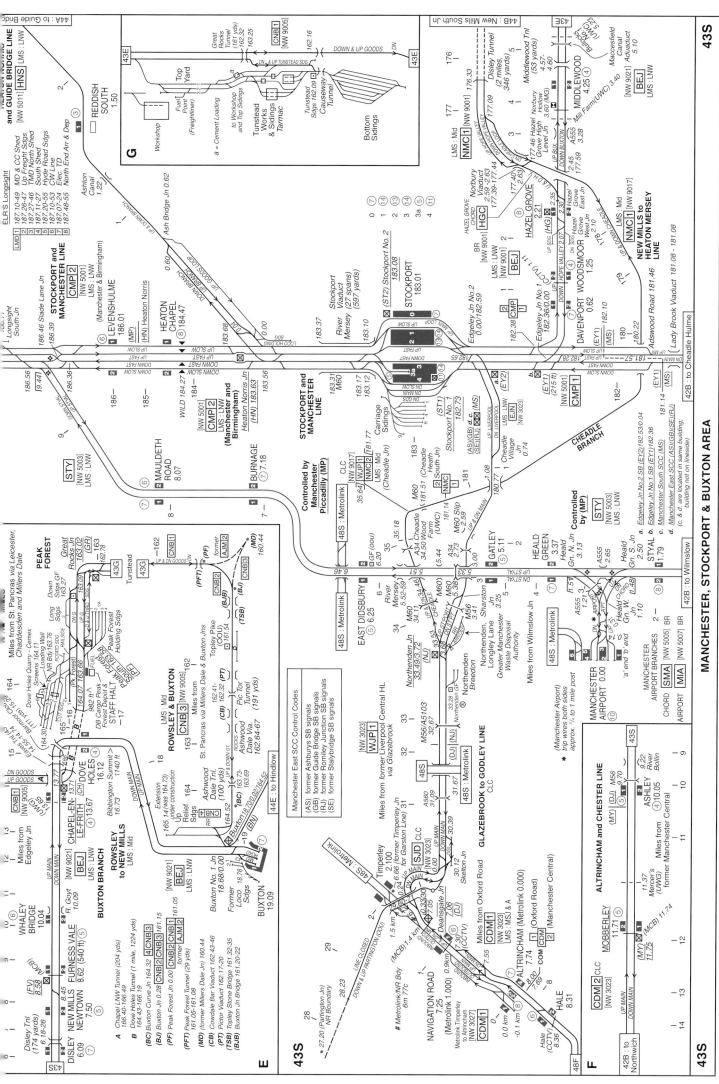

MANCHESTER, STOCKPORT & BUXTON AREA

December 2018

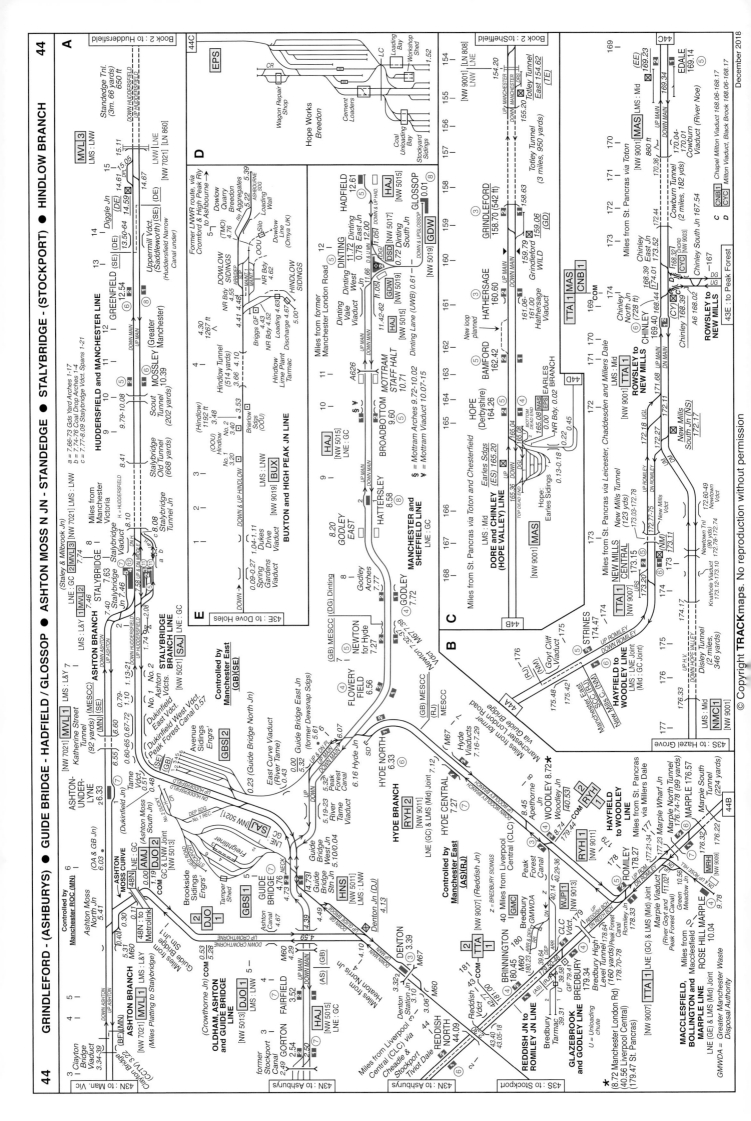

Key to Viaducts in Todmorden area
A Gauxholme No. 1 18.24-37
B Gauxholme No. 2 18.40
C Todmorden 19.20-27
D Lobb Mill 20.29-35
E Cockden 21.22
F Whitley 22.55
(R.Calder)

EAST LANCASHIRE LIGHT RAILWAY
4' 8½" / 1435mm gauge
The three single line sections named after intermediate points on each one:
"Up & Down Broadfield" (Bury-Heywood)
"Up & Down Summerseat" (Ramsbottom-Bury)
"Up & Down Irwell Vale" (Rawtenstall-Ramsbottom)

RAWTENSTALL 17.49
Rawtenstall West 17.28
(New Hall Hey Bridge (River Irwell)
Townsend Fold 17.00
16.20 EWOOD BRIDGE & EDENFIELD
Lower Ashen Bottom Viaduct
Hardsough Weir Viaduct (River Irwell) 15.61
IRWELL VALE 15.53
((Alderbottom) Viaduct No. 2 (River Irwell) 15.08)
STUBBINS 14.31
(Stubbins Jn) 14.25
Miles from Manchester Victoria via Whitefield
RAMSBOTTOM 13.43
Square River Bridge (River Irwell) 13.31
Nuttall Viaduct (River Irwell) 13.16
Nuttall Tunnel (115 yards) 12.73-12.78
Brooksbottom Tunnel (423 yards) 12.48-12.67
Brooksbottom Viaduct (River Irwell) 12.44-12.36
SUMMERSEAT 12.19
BURRS COUNTRY PARK 10.77
Burrs Viaduct 10.70-73
Calrows Viaduct 10.58-64
Buckley Wells Locomotive & Carriage Shed
Baron Street Locomotive Works (BQ)
BURY BOLTON STREET 9.48
Bury EL Tunnel (80 yards) 9.55-9.59
Roch 8.18 M66 Viaduct
Buckley Wells 9.23
Bury South 9.38
Bury South Jn 9.41
Metrolink Intersection Bridge 9.23
Bury Steam Locomotive Co. Ltd.
Bury Transport Museum
Castlecroft Yard
Castlecroft Diesel/Shed
ELR/Metrolink Bdy 8.74

CASTLETON to BOLTON LINE
HEYWOOD 5.35
Heywood GF 5.51
ELR NR (AOCL) 5.00/9.04
ELR GF (AOCL) 15.27
Hopwood GF 5.05
Miles from Manchester (Victoria) via Whitefield & Bury South Jn (reverse)
CASTLETON DEPOT Closed
Castleton East Jn (CE) 8.53
CASTLETON 8.69
Castleton North Jn 8.50
Castleton South Jn 8.21
Rochdale Canal
MILLS HILL 5.74
5.12 (Middleton Jn)
Vitriol Works 4.64 (VW)
MOSTON 4.00
M60 4.25
Newton Heath and Moston 5.850
NEWTON HEATH TMD (NH)
Dean Lane 3.05
Greater Manchester Waste plc 2.62
Arriva Rail North
Thorpes Bridge Jn 2.22
48N : to Man. Vic.

MANCHESTER & NORMANTON LINE

ROCHDALE 10.36
Rochdale West Jn (TH) 8.57
Rochdale East Jn 10.63
Rochdale Viaduct 6 span 10.47-50
Rochdale Rly Stn
RTMA = Rochdale Turnback / Metrolink access
Castleton East Jn (CE) 8.53 / 0.00
48N: Metrolink to Newbold

SMITHY BRIDGE 12.60
LITTLEBOROUGH 13.65
Littleboro Viaduct 13.69-73
Summit West Tunnel (55 yards) 16.05-15.08
Summit East Tunnel (41 yards) 16.65-67
Summit Tunnel (1 mile 1125 yards) 15.06-15.08
Dean Royd Tunnel (70 yds) 16.74-77
WALSDEN 17.70
Winterbutlee Tunnel (537 yards) 17.46-60
TODMORDEN 19.13
Todmorden Viaduct Jn 19.13
Hall Royd Jn 19.49
Millwood Tunnel (306 yards) 19.63-73
Stansfield Hall Jn 0.18/20.24
Horsfall Tunnel (274 yards) 20.44-56
Castle Hill Tunnel (194 yds) 20.07-16
Rochdale Canal
Book 2 : to Hebden Bridge

BLACKBURN to COLNE LINE
HAPTON 18.73
HUNCOAT 17.41
ACCRINGTON 15.41
Accrington Viaduct 15.72-
Church Viaduct 14.64-
CHURCH & OSWALDTWISTLE 14.76
RISHTON 13.26
Rishton Tunnel (68 yards) 12.76
Leeds & Liverpool Canal
ROSE GROVE 20.32
Rose Grove West Jn 20.05
GANNOW Jn 20.50
BURNLEY BARRACKS 21.38
BURNLEY CENTRAL 21.03
BURNLEY MANCHESTER ROAD 21.67
BRIERFIELD 24.20
Brierfield Trl (73 yards) 24.37-
NELSON 25.35
Marsden / Nelson Vdct
Colne Viaduct 27.22-27.29
COLNE 27.37, 27.41
Miles from Farington Curve Junction
48N: Metrolink to Failsworth

BURNLEY BRANCH
LMS : L&Y
Townley Tunnel (398 yards) 23.06-23.25
Towneley (MCB) 22.46
Holme Tunnel (265 yards) 26.20
Lydgate Viaduct 28.65-28.73
Kitson Wood Tunnel (290 yards) 29.10
Portsmouth (R/G) 27.30
DN E. LANCS / UP E. LANCS
Leeds & Liverpool Canal Bridges
a = 19.76 b = 20.08 c = 21.40 d = 22.73

Controlled by Preston PSB (PN)

D HEATON PARK TRAMWAY, Prestwich
4' 8½" / 1435mm gauge
Electrified 500v DC
Middleton Road 0
Depot 13
Lake Road 27
Lakeside 40
Depot 45
Distances in chains

December 2018

A

36A : to Hellifield
45C : to Burnley

BLACKBURN to COLNE LINE
BLACKBURN to COLNE LINE

[NW 7009]
LMS : L&Y
[FHR]5

Cobwall Viaduct 11.20
Daisyfield
Daisyfield Jn 11.09
[DS] (MCG) 11.30 11.36
(PN) (DS) 11.25 11.43
a = UP & DN HELLIFIELD
UP & DN HELLIFIELD
DN E. LANCS
UP E. LANCS
Blackburn East
[NW 7009]
LMS : L&Y
4 [FHR] 5

Blackburn Tunnel (435 yards) 10.55
Station Holding Sdgs
BBS 1
10.50

Platforms
1, 2 ⑪
3 ③
4 ⑤
BLACKBURN 10.42
UP & DN PASS LOOP
DN 2 UP THROUGH

$ Blackburn servicing point 9.55
DMU
Blackburn Bolton Jn 10.11/24.08
Blackburn West 10.28
(OOU) 10.30
10.17 10.21
Blackburn, Bolton Road
Galbraith Trainstore
BBS 3

Arriva Rail North
Blackburn, King Street 9.60
Taylor Street 9.60
MILL HILL (Lancs) 9.24 ④

Blackburn, Bolton Branch Jn 23.60
BOLTON to BLACKBURN LINE
LMS : L&Y
[NW 6011]
BBB

CHERRY TREE 8.50 ③
Cherry Tree GF 8.40

PLEASINGTON 7.43 ③
Hoghton Tower Viaduct 6.51-6.56
Pleasington Golf Club (UWE(X)) 5.27
Pleasington Viaduct (River Darwen)

River Darwen 6.77
Coppers (UWE) 3.70
Crams No. 2 (UWE) 3.52
Milhorne (CCTV) 4.49
Hoghton (AHBC(X)) 4.21
Coppas/UWE 3.70
Hospital (CCTV) 3.24
Crams No. 1 (UWE) 3.77
Bank Head (UWE) 2.40

M61 3.40
M6 2.61

Bamber Bridge Station GF 2.25 ④
Bamber Bridge Station 2.32
BAMBER BRIDGE 2.29
(MCG) 2.24
2.10 (Bamber Bridge Jn)
Whittle International GF 1.70 ⑤
Bamber Bridge W. H. Bowker
Down E. Lancs 1.73
UP E. LANCS
LMS : L&Y
[NW 7009]
FHR 3

PRESTON to BLACKBURN LINE
Controlled by Preston PSB (PN)

30C : to Preston
to Preston

B

46C

Bradshawgate Tunnel (88 yds) 10.68-10.72

Croal Viaduct 11.05-13

Astley Bridge Jn 11.66 11.64
Tonge Viaduct (72 spans) 11.30
HALL I'TH'WOOD 12.35 (12.32)
The O₄'s (UWE) (12.39) ④

BROMLEY CROSS 13.45 ⑤
Bromley Cross Jn 13.75
Bromley Cross (FP) 13.47 ②

ENTWISTLE 16.47 ⑥

Bradshaw Brook Viaduct 16.15-07

Sough Tunnel (1 mile, 255 yds) 737 ft
17.61
Darwen South 18.73
Darwen Jn 19.19

DARWEN 20.27 ④
BBB
[NW 6011]
UP DARWEN
DN DARWEN

Darwen North 21.25
21.55 (Hoddlesden Jn) M65
Raikes Viaduct 22.25-22
Blackrod Jn 17.34
BLACKROD 17.14 ⑤
BBB
[NW 6011]

Leeds-Liverpool Canal 23.26
Miles from Manchester Victoria

BOLTON to BLACKBURN LINE
LMS : L&Y

46A

C

43N : to Salford Crescent
43N : to Salford Crescent

Agecroft Tarmac
Brindle Heath Sidings 3
Agecroft South Jn 2.70
Agecroft North Jn 3.33
Cobden Street Waste Disposal Authority
Greater Manchester
MVE 1
[NW 6001]
3.38

CLIFTON 4.57 ④
(Clifton Jn) 4.51
5.40 M60

MANCHESTER, BOLTON and BURY LINE
Controlled by Manchester Piccadilly (MP)

Mileposts north of Manchester may be either side or both sides (unless missing)

FARNWORTH 8.31 ⑤
UP BOLTON
DN BOLTON
9.67
KEARSLEY 7.57 ⑤
Farnworth Tunnels (270 yds) 8.25-8.10
MOSES GATE 9.06 ④
9.74

Burnden Jn 10.09
Platforms
1 (Up Dn7)
2 (Up15,Dn11)
3 (Up15, Dn11)
4 ⑫
5 ⑭
10.10
10.18

Bolton East Jn 10.31
BOLTON 10.50
BBB
[NW 6011]

Bradshawgate Tunnel (88 yds) 10.68-10.72
ioe 10.65
loe 10.55
Bolton West Jn 10.55
DN & UP DARWEN

PLAT.5 10.40
BBB 10.40
2 MVE 1

Bolton ELR changes
BBB 10.40 10.31
MVE2 2MVE1 MVE1
BBB 10.55 10.31
MVE2 2MVE1 MVE1

Bullfields or Moor Lane Tunnels (77 yds) 11.05-11.01
10.70

BOLTON to BLACKBURN LINE
LMS : L&Y [NW 6011]

Miles from Manchester Victoria

LOSTOCK 13.52 ⑧
LMS : L&Y
Lostock Jn 13.39
ioe 14.14
ioe 14.14
4.49 M61

HORWICH PARKWAY 15.50 ⑦
M61 Link 15.20

WESTHOUGHTON 15.25 ⑤
UP HINDLEY BRANCH
DOWN HINDLEY BRANCH
[NW 6013]
LMS : L&Y
LCN
2
14

DAISY HILL 12.57 ⑤

HAG FOLD 11.59 ⑥

ATHERTON 11.01 ⑥

WALKDEN 7.42 ⑥
M60 6.32
7.32

MOORSIDE 5.61 ⑤

SWINTON 5.04 ⑤
former Fast line tunnel 5.04

BOLTON to EUXTON JUNCTION LINE
LMS : L&Y
[NW 6001]
MVE 2

ADLINGTON (Lancashire) 19.15 ⑥
(PN) (MP) 17.50
Blackrod Jn 17.34
17.18
Hyton Viaduct River Douglas
18.50 (MP)
Preston | Manchester Piccadilly
Leeds & Liverpool Canal
21.18

LOSTOCK JN to PEMBERTON LINE
LMS : L&Y [NW 6009]
WBS 2

HINDLEY 15.17 ⑤
WBS 2
Crow Nest Jn 14.64
LCN
2 WBS 1

1 INCE 16.70 ⑥
(WN) (MP)
Warrington PSB

Miles from Manchester Victoria (mileposts on both sides)

30B : to Euxton Jn
30A : to Wigan

PENDLETON to HINDLEY LINE
Controlled by Manchester Piccadilly (MP)
LMS : L&Y

43N : to Salford Crescent

Windsor Bridge Sdgs
MVE 1
[NW 6001]
Pendleton PENDLETON 2.21
Pendleton Viaduct 2.51-35
Pendleton Tunnels (52 yds) 2.27-25
2
UP ATHERTON
DOWN ATHERTON
Pendlebury Tunnels (201 yds) 4.34-4.43

Miles from Manchester Victoria via Walkden

December 2018

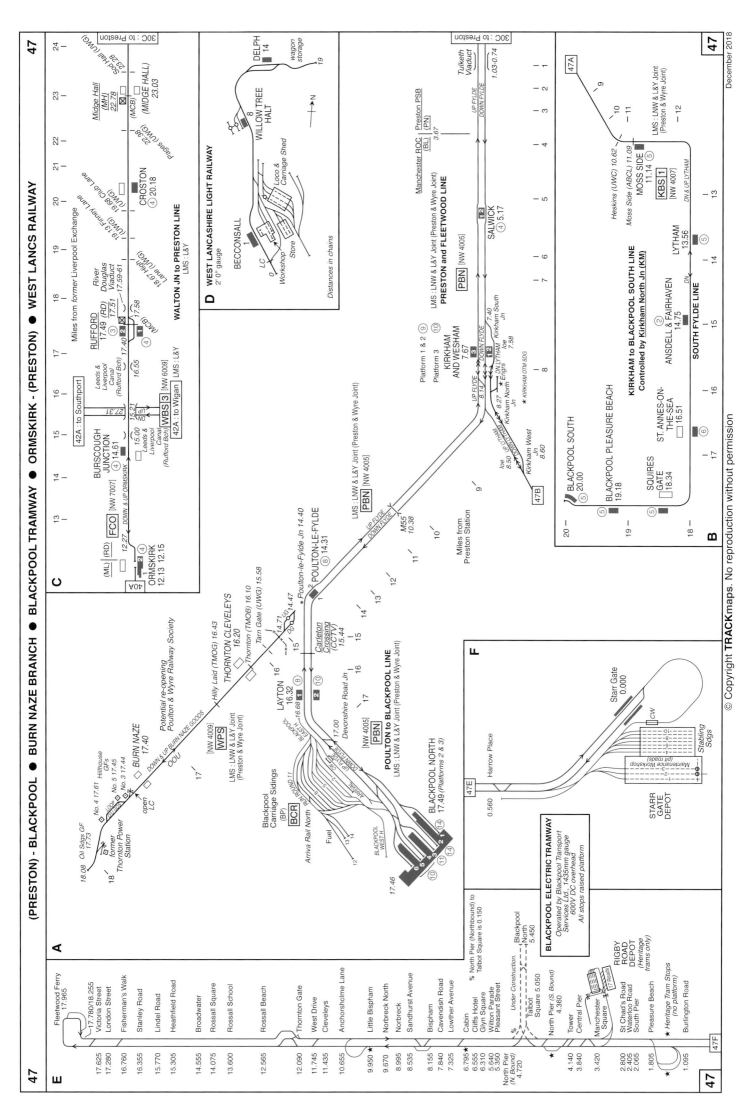

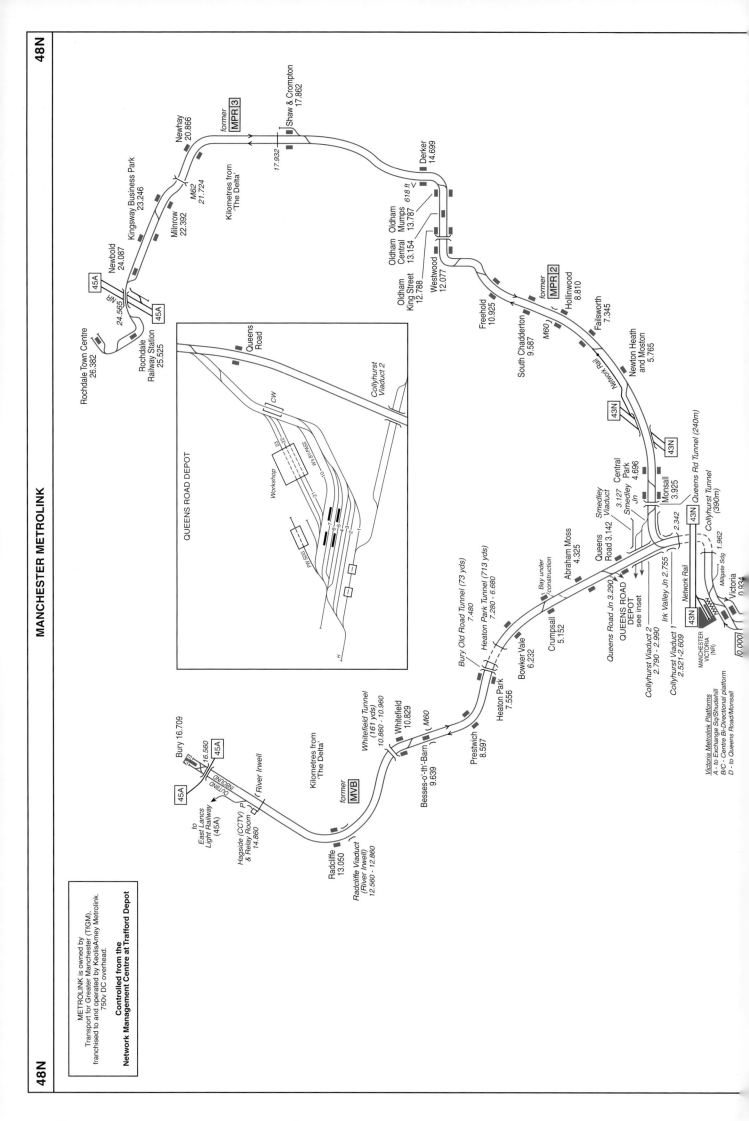

METROLINK is owned by
Transport for Greater Manchester (TfGM),
franchised to and operated by KeolisAmey Metrolink.
750v DC overhead.

**Controlled from the
Network Management Centre at Trafford Depot**

QUEENS ROAD DEPOT

Queens Road

CW

W's BYPASS

Workshop

Collyhurst
Viaduct 2

PW SDG

Rochdale Town Centre
26.382

Rochdale
Railway Station
25.525

45A

NR

24.565

45A

Newbold
24.087

Kingsway Business Park
23.246

Newhay
20.866

Milnrow
22.392

M62
21.724

former

MPR 3

Shaw & Crompton
17.862

17.932

Kilometres from
'The Delta'

Derker
14.699

618 ft

Oldham
Mumps
13.787

Oldham
Central
13.154

Oldham
King Street
12.788

Westwood
12.077

Freehold
10.925

South Chadderton
9.587

M60

former

MPR 2

Hollinwood
8.810

Failsworth
7.345

Newton Heath
and Moston
5.765

Network Rail

43N

43N

Central
Park
4.696

Monsall
3.925

Queens Rd Tunnel (240m)

Smedley
Viaduct
3.127

Smedley
Jn

Queens
Road 3.142

Queens Road Jn 3.290

QUEENS ROAD
DEPOT
see inset

Abraham Moss
4.325

Bay under
construction

Crumpsall
5.152

Bowker Vale
6.232

Heaton Park
7.556

Heaton Park Tunnel (713 yds)
7.280 - 6.680

Bury Old Road Tunnel (73 yds)
7.480

Prestwich
8.597

Besses-o'-th'-Barn
9.639

M60

Whitefield
10.829

Whitefield Tunnel
(161 yds)
10.860 - 10.960

Kilometres from
'The Delta'

former

MVB

Radcliffe
13.050

Radcliffe Viaduct
(River Irwell)
12.560 - 12.860

Hagside (CCTV) P
& Relay Room
14.860

River Irwell

to
East Lancs
Light Railway
(45A)

OUTBOUND

INBOUND

45A

45A

16.560

45A

Bury 16.709

Ink Valley Jn 2.755

Collyhurst Viaduct 2
2.790 - 2.990

Collyhurst Viaduct 1
2.521-2.609

2.342

43N

43N

Collyhurst Tunnel
(390m)

1.962

Millgate Sdg

0.934

Victoria

Network Rail

MANCHESTER
VICTORIA
(NR)

0.000

Victoria Metrolink Platforms
A - to Exchange Sq/Shudehill
B/C - Centre Bi-Directional platform
D - to Queens Road/Monsall

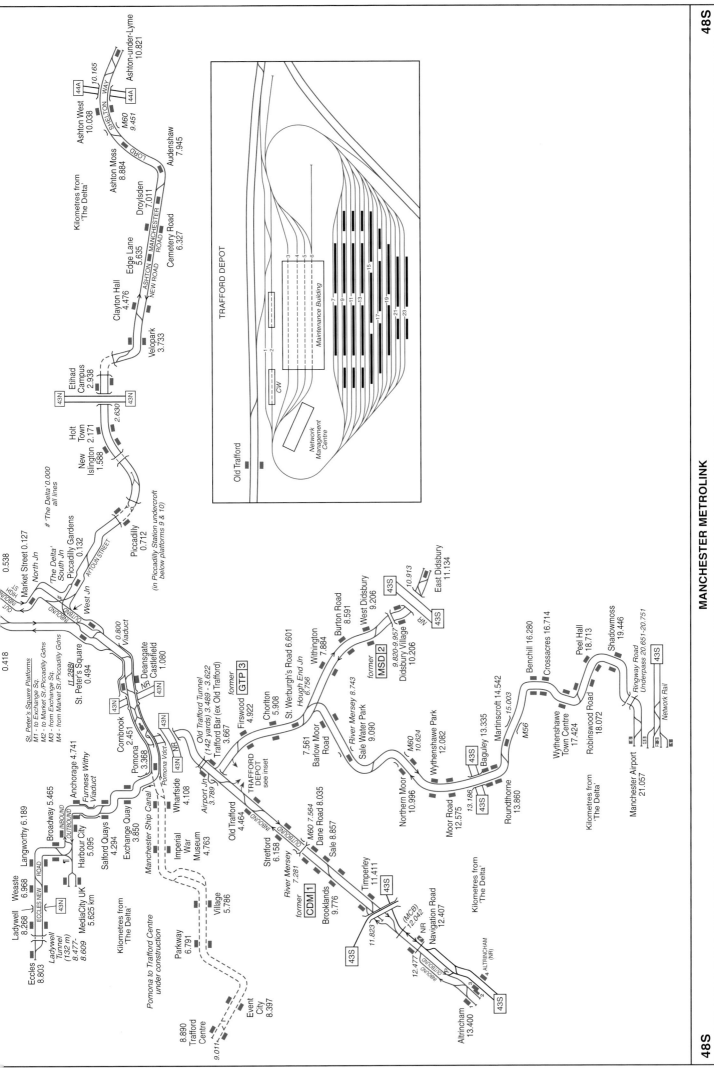

MANCHESTER METROLINK

NOTTINGHAM EXPRESS TRANSIT

A

Nottingham Express Transit (NET) is operated
Nottingham Trams Limited

750v DC overhead

Track gauge: 1435mm

Controlled from Wilkinson Street Depot

All distances are in kilometres

13A : to Grantham & Newark

Lace Market 11.731
Station Street 12.295
Nottingham Station 12.422
Jn
Sheriffs Way
Queens Walk 13.075
Meadows Embankment 13.542
(River Trent)
Wilford Village 13.941

Broadmarsh (proposed)
Old Market Square 11.365
Royal Centre 11.071
Nottingham Trent University 10.693
High School 10.024
The Forest (Park & Ride) 9.475 (9.429 via Noel St)
Gregory Boulevard
Noel Street 9.185
Beaconsfield Street 8.847
Shipstone Street 8.542
Depot (see 49C)
49A
River Leen
Wilkinson Street Overbridge
Wilkinson Street 8.216
Radford Road 8.648
Hyson Green Market 9.088

Meadows Way West 13.463
NG2 14.127
Gregory Street 15.067
Queens Medical Centre 15.612
University of Nottingham 16.380
University Boulevard 17.495

Compton Acres 15.913
Ruddington Lane 16.408
Wilford Lane 15.146

Southchurch Drive North 17.526
Rivergreen 18.057
Clifton Centre 18.438
Holy Trinity 19.251
Summerwood Lane 19.712
Clifton South 20.109
20.129

13A : to Trowell Jn

NETWORK RAIL

13A : to Trent Jns

Middle Street 18.193
Beeston Centre 18.741
Chilwell Road 19.354
High Road - Central College 19.615
Cator Lane 20.261
Bramcote Lane 20.603
Eskdale Drive 21.088
Inham Road 21.655
22.414
Toton Lane 22.398

B

C

WILKINSON STREET
TRAM DEPOT AND
CONTROL ROOM (NET)

Wheel Lathe
Sanding
CW
LC
Car Park
Wilkinson Street
49B
49B
49B

13D : to Kirkby-in-Ashfield

0.000 Hucknall (Park & Ride) 0.027
Brickyard Lane (ABCL) 0.890
Hucknall No.3 (UWC) 1.100
Butler's Hill 1.179

NETWORK RAIL

Moor Bridge (Park & Ride) 2.790
Bulwell Forest 3.771
Bulwell Forest (CCTV) 3.585
Bulwell 4.600

Highbury Vale 5.780
Basford Chemicals (UWC)
David Lane 6.526
Lincoln St (CCTV) 6.563
Basford 6.973
Highbury Vale Jn 5.882
0.000
0.147
Phoenix Park (Park & Ride) 1.244
Cinderhill 0.814
1.262
49B

December 2018

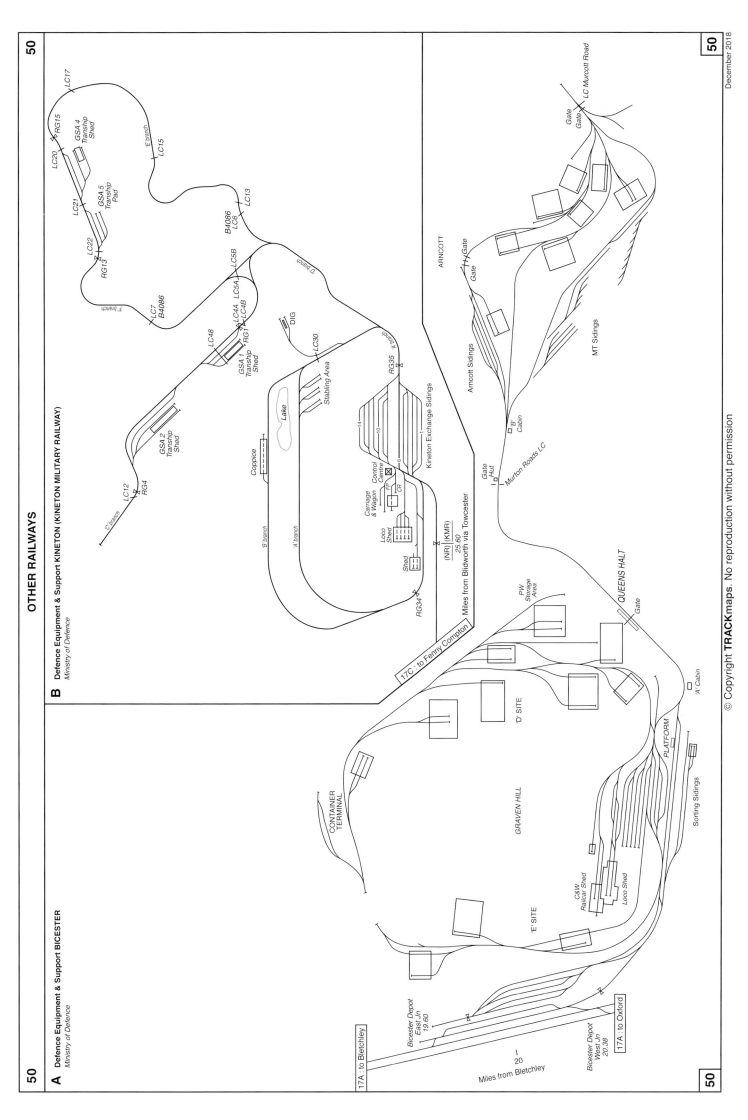

OTHER RAILWAYS

A Defence Equipment & Support BICESTER
Ministry of Defence

B Defence Equipment & Support KINETON (KINETON MILITARY RAILWAY)
Ministry of Defence

50   50

50   50

December 2018

Index

This index covers practically all the named locations relating to the National Network which appear on the maps to assist the reader in their search. Stations are listed in capitals, signal boxes with their codes and level crossings with their type. FP and Barrow crossings in the maps are not carried to the index. Locations of now-defunct assets are given in brackets. Other public service lines, light rail, Heritage lines, narrow gauge and other private lines are indexed by their line name and key stations only.

A

A1081 Bridge (Luton Airport Parkway)	9B
A14 Bridge (Kettering)	10A
A34 Bridge (Alderley Edge)	42B
A34 Bridge (Oxford)	17B
A34 Bridges (Cheadle)	43S
A38 Bridge (Breadsall)	12A
A38 Bridge (Lichfield)	25A
A38 Bridge (Willington)	26C
A38(M) Bridges (Aston)	20
A40 Bridge (Oxford)	17B
A41 Bridges (Chester)	28A
A41(T) Bridge (Watford)	2B
A414 Bridge (St. Albans)	9A
A42 Bridge (Lounge Jn)	14C
A421 Bridge (Bedford)	9C
A427 Bridge (Corby)	10C
A43 Bridge (Kettering)	10A
A442 Bridge (Lickey Incline)	23C
A45 Bridge (Birmingham International)	18C
A45 Bridge (Canley)	18B
A45 Bridge (Irchester)	9D
A452 Bridge (Berkswell)	18C
A454 Bridge (Darlaston)	21A
A46 Bridge (Bingham)	13B
A46 Bridge (Coventry)	18B
A46 Bridge (Sileby)	11A
A46 Bridge (Warwick Parkway)	19A
A46 Bridge (Widmerpool)	11C
A464 Bridge (Shifnal)	22A
A47 Bridges (Washwood Heath)	20
A483 Bridges (Wrexham)	27C
A494 Bridge (Shotton)	27B
A494 Bridge (Hawarden)	27C
A5 Bridge (Shenstone)	25A
A5(T) Bridge (Fenny Stratford)	3C
A5(T) Bridge (Milton Keynes)	3B
A50 Bridge (Blythe Bridge)	26B
A50 Bridge (Castle Donnington)	13C
A50 Bridge (Stenson)	26C
A50 Bridge (Stoke-on-Trent)	6B
A5020 Bridge (Crewe)	7A
A5047 Bridge (Edge Lane Jn)	38A
A5049 Bridge (Edge Lane Jn)	40A
A506 Bridge (Fazakerley)	40A
A51 Bridge (Weston)	6B
A511 LC (TMO)	14B
A5126 Bridges (Halton Jn)	29B
A5194 Bridge, Derby	11B
A537 Bridge (Macclesfield)	42B
A548 Bridge (Dee Marsh)	39B
A55 Bridges (Buckley)	27C
A55 Bridges (Saltney Jn)	27C
A55(T) Bridges (Chester)	28A
A553 Bridge (Bidston)	39A
A555 Bridge (Bramhall)	42B
A555 Bridge (Handforth)	42B
A555 Bridge (Hazel Grove)	43S
A555 Bridges (Heald Green)	43S
A556 Bridge (Hartford)	29A
A556 Bridge (Lostock Gralam)	42B
A557 Bridge (Widnes)	38B
A557(T) Bridge (Runcorn)	37A
A560 Bridge (Skelton Jn)	43S
A561 Bridge (Garston)	38A
A561 Bridge (Halewood)	37A
A570 Bridge (Rainford)	40A
A58 Bridge (St. Helens)	41B
A580 Bridge (St. Helens)	41B
A580 Bridge (Spellow)	40A
A580 Bridges (Golbourne)	29C
A590 Bridge (Milnthorpe)	31C
A6 Bridge (Chinley)	44B
A6086 Bridge (Corby)	10C
A66 Bridge (Appleby)	36C
A66 Bridge (Penrith)	32B
A689 Bridge (Kingmoor)	33C
A74(M) Bridge (Gretna Jn)	33A
A74(M) Bridge (Quintinshill)	33A
A75 Bridge (Gretna Green)	33A
Abbey Foregate Jn SB (AF)	27

Abbey Foregate LMD	27A
Abbey Jn, Nuneaton	5B
Abbey LC (TMO)	26B
Abbotswood Jn	23C
Abbotswood North Jn	23C
Abernethy's LC (UWC)	17B
ACCRINGTON	45B
Accrington EGF	45B
Accrington Viaduct	45B
ACOCKS GREEN	19A
Acrow Quarry	36B
Acrow Quarry GF	36B
Action Wells Jn SB (AW)	1
ACTON BRIDGE	29A
Acton Bridge Jn	29A
Acton Canal Wharf Jn	1
Acton Canal Wharf SB (ACW)	1
ACTON CENTRAL	1
Acton Grange Jns	29B
Acton Grange Vdcts, Manchester Ship Canal	29B
Acton Wells Jn	1
Adam Dales Viaduct	25A
Adam Viaduct	30A
ADDERLEY PARK	18C
ADLINGTON (Cheshire)	42B
ADLINGTON (Lancashire)	46C
Admiralty Sdg GF	33A
Admiralty Sidings Jn	33A
Adswood Road	43S
Agecroft North Jn	46C
Agecroft South Jn	46C
AIGBURTH	38A
AINSDALE	40B
Ainsdale LC (CCTV)	40B
Ainsdale Wheelchex	40B
AINTREE	40A
Aintree Station Jn	40A
Ais Gill Summit	36C
Ais Gill Viaduct	36C
Albert Edward Viaduct, Ironbridge	22C
ALBRIGHTON	22A
ALDERLEY EDGE	42B
Alderley Edge North Jn	42B
Alderley Edge South Jn	42B
Aldridge Jn	25A
Aldwinkle LC (UWC)	10B
Alexandra Dock Sdgs	40A
Alexandra Dock Tunnel	40A
Alexandra Docks	40A
ALFRETON	12A
Alfreton Tunnel	12A
Allerton East Jn	38A
Allerton Jn	38A
Allerton Jn SB (AN)	38A
Allerton TMD (AN)	38A
Allerton West Jn	38A
Allington East Jn	13B
Allington LC (MCB)	13B
Allington North Jn	13B
Allington SB (AL)	13B
Allington West Jn	13B
Allscott GF	27A
Alrewas LC (MCB) & SB (AS)	25A
ALSAGER	42A
Alsager LC (CCTV)	42A
Althorp Park HABD	4B
ALTRINCHAM	43S
ALVECHURCH	23B
Alvechurch Station Jn	23B
AMBERGATE	12A
Ambergate Jn	12A
AMERSHAM (LUL)	15B
Ampthill Tunnels	9C
Ancoats Viaduct	43N
Andrews LC (UWC)	23C
Angerton Hall LC (UWG)	34B
Angerton Hall No.2 LC (UWG)	34B
Angerton Hall No.3 LC (UWG)	34B
Anglesea Sidings	25A
ANSDELL & FAIRHAVEN	47B
Apesford LC (MG)	26B

Apethorne Jn	44A
APPLEBY	36C
APPLEBY EAST (disused)	36C
Appleby LC (TMOG)	36C
Appleby North SB (A)	36C
Appleby West Jn	36C
APPLEY BRIDGE	41A
APSLEY	2B
Apsley Manor Farm No.2 LC (UWC)	16B
Archers No. 1 LC (UWC)	26C
Ardley Summit	16C
Ardley Tunnel	16C
ARDWICK	43N
Ardwick East Jn	43N
Ardwick Jn	43N
Ardwick TMD (AK)	43N
Arena Tunnel, Birmingham	20
ARLEY (SVR)	24A
Arley HABD	25A
Arley Tunnel	25A
ARMATHWAITE	36D
Armathwaite Tunnel	36D
Armathwaite Viaduct	36D
Armington Jn	5B
Armitage HABD	6A
(Armitage Jn)	6A
Arnolds Flood Bridge	13B
ARNSIDE	34A
Arnside SB (AE)	34A
Arpley Extension Sidings	29B
Arpley Grid Iron Jn North	29B
Arpley Grid Iron Jn South	29B
Arpley Jn & Sidings	29B
Arpley Jn SB (AJ)	29B
Arriva Traincare Depot (CP), Depot	7A
Arten Gill Viaduct	36B
Asfordby Jn & GF	11C
Asfordby (Kirby Bellars) LC (AHBC)	10B
Asfordby Test Centre	11C
Asfordby Tunnel	11C
Ash Bridge Jn	43S
ASHBURYS	43N
Ashburys Aggregates Terminal	43N
Ashburys East Jn	43N
Ashburys West Jn	43N
Ashby Canal (Nuneaton)	5B
Ashby Jn, Nuneaton	5B
(Ashendon Jn)	16C
Ashfordby North Jn	11C
Ashfordby South Jn	11C
ASHLEY	43F
Ashton Canal (Guide Bridge)	44A
Ashton Canal (Reddish South)	43S
Ashton Moss North Jn	44A
(Ashton Moss South Jn)	44A
Ashton Viaducts	44A
Ashton-in-Makerfield	29C
ASHTON-UNDER-LYNE	44A
(Ashwell Branch Jn)	10B
Ashwell Gate House LC (MCBR)	10B
Ashwell LC (MCB)	10B
ASLOCKTON	13B
Aslockton LC (MCB-OD)	13B
ASKAM	34B
Askam LC (MCB) & SB	34B
ASPATRIA	35C
Aspatria Tunnel	35C
ASPLEY GUISE	3C
Aspley Guise LC (CCTV)	3C
Astley Bridge Jn	46B
Astley SB (AY)	43C
ASTON	20
Aston North Jn	20
Aston SCC (AN)	20
Aston South Jn	20
Aston Viaduct	20
Aston-by-Stone LC (CCTV)	6B
ATHERSTONE	5B
ATHERTON	46C
(Atlantic Dock Jn)	40A

ATTENBOROUGH	13A
Attenborough Jn	13A
Attenborough LC (CCTV	13A
Attenborough North Jn	5B
Attleborough Road Viaduct	5B
Attleborough South Jn	5B
AUGHTON PARK	40A
Aughton Road LC (CCTV)	40B
Avenue Sidings, Guide Bridge	44A
Averham Weir Viaduct	13B
Avon Viaduct, Rugby	5A
Ayhno Flyover	17C
Ayhno Jn	17C
AYLESBURY	15C
Aylesbury Carriage Sidings	15C
Aylesbury Jn	15C
Aylesbury Maintenance Depot	15C
Aylesbury Vale Jn	15C
AYLESBURY VALE PARKWAY	15C
Aylestone Viaduct, R. Soar	14B
(Aynho Park Jn)	17C

B

B' Group GF and Sidings, Kingmoor	33C
B4115 Bridge	18A
BACHE	28A
BAGILLT (disused)	27B
Bagillt LC (UWG)	27B
Baguley Fold Jn SB (BF)	43N
Bagworth	14B
Baileys LC (UWC)	26B
Bakers LC (UWC)	26B
Balderton LC (AHBC)	27C
Balderton Tunnel	27C
Balshaw Lane Jn	30B
BAMBER BRIDGE	46A
(Bamber Bridge Jn)	46A
Bamber Bridge LC (MCB)	46A
Bamber Bridge Stn GF	46A
BAMFORD	44C
Bamfurlong Jn	30A
Bamfurlong Sdgs Jn	30A
BANBURY	17C
Banbury Aggregate Terminal	17C
Banbury Depot Jn	17C
Banbury LMD	17C
Banbury North Jn	17C
Banbury Road Sidings	17A
Banbury South Jn	17C
BANK HALL	40A
Bank Head LC (UWG)	46A
Bardon Hill GF	14B
Bardon Hill LC (MCB) & SB (BH)	14B
Bardon Hill Quarries	14B
BARE LANE	31B
Bare Lane Jn	31B
Bare Lane LC (CCTV)	31B
BARLASTON	6D
Barlaston HABD	6D
Barlaston LC (CCTV)	6D
Barmoor Clough Tunnel	43E
Barnstone Tunnel (GCRN)	23A
BARNT GREEN	23B
Barnt Green Jn	23B
Barnt Green Single Line Jn	23B
Barnwell Farm LC (UWC)	17A
Baron Wood Tunnels	36D
Barrow Depot	34B
BARROW-IN-FURNESS	34B
Barrow-in-Furness SB (BF)	34B
BARROW-UPON-SOAR	11A
Barrow-Upon-Soar HABD	11A
Barthomley	7A
Barthomley (MWLG)	7A
Barton & Broughton Loop	31A
Barton Lane LC (AHBC-X)	13A
Barton North Jn	25A
Barton South Jn	25A
Barton Viaduct	31A
Basford Chemicals LC (UWC)	13D
Basford Hall Down Sidings	7A
Basford Hall Jn SB (BH)	7A

Basford Hall TMD (BA)	7A
Basford Hall Up Sidings	7A
Basford Hall Yard	7A
Basford Wood GF	7A
Baswich Viaduct	6B
Bath Row Tunnel	23B
Bathing Pool LC (UWG)	34A
BATTLEFIELD STEAM RAILWAY (BSR)	5C
(Bay Horse EGFs)	31A
BCN (Dudley Port)	21A
BCN (Monument Lane Jn)	20
BCN (Soho North Jn)	20
BCN (Soho South Jn)	20
BCN (Wolverhampton North)	22A
BCN (Wolverhampton)	21A
BEACONSFIELD	16B
BEARLEY	19A
Bearley Jn	19A
Beaumont Hill LC (UWC)	19A
BEBINGTON	37C
BECCONSALL (WLLR)	47D
BECKFOOT (RER)	33B
BEDFORD	9C
Bedford North Jn	9C
BEDFORD ST. JOHNS	9C
Bedford South Jn	9C
Bedford Station Jn	9C
BEDWORTH	5B
Beeches Farm LC (UWG)	27B
Beechwood Tunnel	18B
Beela Viaduct	31C
BEESTON	13A
BEESTON CASTLE & TARPORLEY (disused)	28A
Beeston Castle & Tarporley SB (BC)	28A
Beeston Down Sdgs	13A
Beeston South Jn	13A
Bell Busk Vdct (R. Aire)	36A
Bell House LC (UWG)	35A
Bell Lane, Leicester	10B
Belle Isle Jn	8A
BELLE VUE	43N
BELPER	12A
Belper GF	12A
Belper Yard	12A
Belsize Fast & Slow Tunnels	8A
Belvedere Viaduct	27A
Bennerley Viaduct	14A
Bennetts LC (UWC)	26B
BENTHAM	31B
Bentley Heath LC (CCTV)	19A
BERKHAMSTED	3A
BERKSWELL	18C
BERMUDA PARK	5B
Berry Lane LC (UWW)	3C
BESCAR LANE	41A
Bescar Lane LC (AHBC)	41A
Bescot Curve Jn	21A
Bescot Depot (BS)	21A
Bescot Jn	21A
Bescot Middle Jn	21A
BESCOT STADIUM	21A
Bescot Yards	21A
Bestwood Park Jn	13D
BEWDLEY (SVR)	24A
Bibbington Summit	43E
Bicester Depot East Jn	17A
Bicester Depot West Jn	17A
Bicester London Road LC (CCTV)	17A
BICESTER MILITARY RAILWAY (MOD)	50A
BICESTER NORTH	16C
Bicester South Jn	16C
BICESTER VILLAGE	17A
BIDSTON	39A
Bidston Dee Jn	39A
Bidston East Jn	39A
Bidston Moss Viaduct	39A
Bidston West Jn	39A
BILBROOK	22A
BINGHAM	13B
Bingham LC (MCB-OD)	13B
Bingham Road LC (UWC)	13B
Birch Coppice	25A
BIRCHWOOD	43D
Birdswood Tunnel (flyover)	29A
Birkbeck Viaduct	32A
BIRKDALE	40B
Birkdale LC (CCTV)	40B
Birkdale Sdgs, Southport	41A
BIRKENHEAD CENTRAL	39A
Birkenhead Central Carriage Sidings (disused)	39A
BIRKENHEAD NORTH	39A
Birkenhead North T&RSMD (BD)	39A
BIRKENHEAD PARK	39A
Birkenhead Sdgs, Dee Marsh	39C
Birkett Tunnel	36C
Birmingham & Fazeley Canal	25A
BIRMINGHAM AIRPORT AIR-RAIL LINK	18C
BIRMINGHAM AIRPORT TERMINAL 1	18C
Birmingham Curve Jn	26C
Birmingham Freightliner Terminal	20
BIRMINGHAM INTERNATIONAL	18C
Birmingham International North Jn	18C
Birmingham International South Jn	18C
BIRMINGHAM MOOR STREET	19B
BIRMINGHAM NEW STREET	20
Birmingham New Street PSB (NS)	20
BIRMINGHAM SNOW HILL	20
(Blaby Jn)	10B
BLACK COUNTRY LIVING MUSEUM	21B
Black Dyke LC (AHBC)	34A
BLACKBURN	46A
Blackburn Bolton Branch Jn	46A
Blackburn Bolton Jn	46A
Blackburn East Jn	46A
Blackburn Station Holding Sidings	46A
Blackburn Tunnel	46A
Blackburn West Jn	46A
Blackpool Carriage Sidings (BP)	47A
BLACKPOOL ELECTRIC TRAMWAY	47E
BLACKPOOL NORTH	47A
BLACKPOOL PLEASURE BEACH	47B
BLACKPOOL SOUTH	47B
BLACKROD	46C
Blackrod Jn	46C
Blackwell North Jn	23B
Blackwell South Jn	23B
Blackwell South Jn	12A
Blackwell Summit	23B
(Blainscough GF)	30A
BLAKE STREET	25A
BLAKEDOWN	24A
Blakedown (Churchill) Viaduct	24A
Blakedown LC (CCTV)	24A
Blea Moor SB (BM)	36B
Blea Moor Tunnel	36B
BLEASBY	13B
Bleasby LC (AHBC-X)	13B
Bletchington LC (UWC)	17B
BLETCHLEY	3B
Bletchley East Jn	3B
Bletchley Flyover Jn	3B
Bletchley Flyover North Jn	3B
Bletchley North Jn	3B
Bletchley South Jn	3B
Bletchley TMD (BY)	3B
Bletchley Up Yard	3B
Bletchley Yard	3B
Blisworth	4A
BLOXWICH	22B
BLOXWICH NORTH	22B
BLUNDELLSANDS AND CROSBY	40A
BLYTHE BRIDGE	26B
Blythe Bridge LC (CCTV)	26B
Blythe Viaduct, Hampton-in-Arden	18C
Boat Crossing LC (UWC)	23C
Boathouse Bridge Road	12A
Bodlondeb LC (UGW)	27B
Bog Jn	32C
BOLTON	46C
Bolton East Jn	46C
Bolton Road, Blackburn	46A
Bolton West Jn	46C
Bolton-le-Sands HABD	31B
Bolton-le-Sands LC (CCTV)	31B
BOOTLE	34C
Bootle Beck Viaduct	34C
Bootle Branch Jn	38A
Bootle Jn	40A
Bootle LC (MCG) & SB	34C
BOOTLE NEW STRAND	40A
BOOTLE ORIEL ROAD	40A
BORDESLEY	19B
Bordesley Down Yard	19B
Bordesley Jn	23B
Bordesley South Jn	19B
Bordesley Viaduct	19B
Borrow Beck Viaduct	31C
BOTTESFORD	13B
Bottesford LC (UWC)	13B
(Bottesford West Jn)	13B
Boulders Farm No.2 LC (UWC)	17B
Boultons LC (UWC)	26C
Bourne End Jn	3A
BOURNVILLE	23B
BOW BRICKHILL	3C
Bow Brickhill LC (CCTV)	3C
Bowness LC (UWG)	31B
Boxmoor Sidings, Hemel Hempstead	3A
Bradnocks Marsh HABD	18C
Bradnop Tunnel	26B
Bradshaw Brook Viaduct	46B
Bradshawgate Tunnel	46B
Bradwell Jn	42A
BRAMHALL	42B
Bramhall Jn	42B
Bramshall LC (AHBC-X)	26B
Brandon HABD	18B
Brandon Viaduct (R. Avon)	18B
Brandons LC (UWC)	26C
Branston GF (oou)	26C
Branston Jn, Burton	26C
Branston Up HABD	26C
Bransty Jn, Whitehaven	35A
Bransty SB (BY), Whitehaven	35A
Brassey LC (UWC)	10B
BRAYSTONES	35A
Braystones LC (UWC)	35A
BRAYTON (disused)	35C
Breadsall Jn	12A
Break Hills Hermitage Mill Viaduct	12A
BREDBURY	44A
Bredbury GF	44A
Bredbury High Level Tunnel	44A
Bredbury Sidings	44A
Brent Curve Jn	8B
Brent New Jn	2A
Brent Viaduct (Hjanger Lane)	16A
Brent Viaducts	2A
Brentingby LC (UWW)	10B
Brettles LC (UWC)	13B
Bretts LC (UWC)	10B
Brewery Fork Viaduct	43N
Brewery Jn	43N
BRICKET WOOD	2B
Brickyard & Lane LC (private)(ABCL)	13D
Bridge Street GF (oou), Northampton	4A
(Bridge Street Jn)	4A
Bridge Street Viaduct	26C
Bridgewater Canal (Patricroft)	43C
Bridgewater Canal (Runcorn East)	29B
Bridgewater Canal Vdct, Runcorn	37A
(Bridgewater Jn)	43N
BRIDGNORTH (SVR)	24A
BRIDGNORTH CLIFF RAILWAY	24A
BRIERFIELD	45C
Brierfield LC (MCB-OD)	45C
Brierfield Tunnel	45C
Brierley Hill Terminal	24A
Brierlow Sidings (oou) GF	44E
Briggs GF	44E
Brill Tunnel	16C
Brindle Heath Sidings	46C
Brinklow Jn	5A
BRINNINGTON	44A
British Salt GF, Middlewich	42B
BROAD GREEN	41B
Broad Oak LC (AHBC)	27C
BROADBOTTOM	44A
Broadholme	12A
Broadholme Viaducts (R. Derwent)	12A
BROMBOROUGH	37C
BROMBOROUGH RAKE	37C
Bromford Bridge	20
Bromford Bridge Jn	20
Bromham Viaducts	9C
BROMLEY CROSS	46B
Bromley Cross Jn	46B
Bromley Cross LC (FP) & Gate Box	46B
Bromley Street Jn	43N
Bromleys LC (UWC)	26C
BROMSGROVE	23C
Bromsgrove North Jn	23C
Bromsgrove South Jn	23C
BRONDESBURY	1
BRONDESBURY PARK	1
Brook Carriage Sdgs, Crewe	7A
Brook Hall Road LC (CCTV)	40A
Brooke Road LC (CCTV)	10B
Brookhay LC (AHBC)	25A
Brook's River Viaduct	10B
Brooksby LC (AHBC)	10B
Brookside Sidings, Guide Bridge	44A
Broome Lane LC (AHBC)	10B
BROWNHILLS WEST (CR)	22D
BRUNSWICK	38A
Brunthill Branch Jn	33C
Brush Traction, Loughborough	11A
BRYN	41B
(Buccleuch Jn)	34B
BUCKINGHAMSHIRE RAILWAY CENTRE	15D
BUCKLEY	27C
Bucknells Farm LC (BW)	16C
BUCKSHAW PARKWAY	30B
Buckshaw Parkway Jn	30B
Budbrooke Jn	19A
Bulcote LC (AHBC-X)	13B
Bullfields or Moor Lane Tunnels	46C
Bullocks No.1 (UWC)	43S
BULWELL	13D
Bulwell Forest LC (CCTV)	13D
Bulwell South Jn	13D
Burley Viaduct , R. Derwent	12A
BURN NAZE (disused)	47A
BURNAGE	43S
Burnden Jn	46C
BURNESIDE	31C
Burnham Bros LC (UWC)	19A
BURNLEY BARRACKS	45C
BURNLEY CENTRAL	45C
BURNLEY MANCHESTER ROAD	45C
Burnley Viaduct	45C
Burnside Higher LC (MCG)	31C
Burnside Lower LC (AOCL)	31C
Burnside Stn LC (UWG)	31C
BURRS COUNTRY PARK (ELR)	45A
BURSCOUGH BRIDGE	41A
Burscough Bridge Jn SB (BB)	41A
BURSCOUGH JUNCTION	47C
Burton Farm No.1 LC (UWC)	19A
Burton Farm No.2 LC (UWC)	19A
BURTON JOYCE	13B
Burton Joyce LC (AHBC-X)	13B
BURTON ON TRENT	26C
BURTON POINT (disused)	39C
Burtonwood GF (oou)	38B
BURY BOLTON STREET (ELR)	45A
Bushbury (Oxley) Jn	22A
Bushbury Jn	22A
Bushbury Viaduct	22A
BUSHEY	2B
Bushey Arches (R. Colne)	2B
Bush-on-Esk East Jn	33D
Bush-on-Esk No.1 LC	33D
Bush-on-Esk No.2 LC (AOCL)	33D
Bush-on-Esk No.4 LC (OC)	33D
Bush-on-Esk West Jn	33D
BUTLERS LANE	25A
BUTTERLEY (MR-B)	12A
BUXTON	43E
(Buxton Curve Jn)	43E
(Buxton Jn)	43E
Buxton No.1 Jn	43E
Buxton SB (BN)	43E
Buxton Up Relief Sidings	43E

C

C' Sidings, Wembley	2A
CAERGWRLE	27C
Caldew Jn, Carlisle	32C
Caldew Viaduct	32C
Caledonia Yard	19B
CALEDONIAN ROAD & BARNSBURY	8A
Calor Gas Sidings GF, Bedworth	5B
CALVELEY (disused)	28C
Calverleigh Farm LC (UWS)	26B
Calvert North GF	17A
Calvert South GF	17A
Calvert Waste Terminal	17A
Cambridge Street LC (UWC)	26C
Camden Carriage Sidings	1
Camden Jn South	1
Camden Jns	1
CAMDEN ROAD	8A
Camden Road Central Jn	8A
Camden Road East Jn	8A
Camden Road Incline Jn	8A
Camden Road Tunnels	8A
Camden Road Viaduct	8A
Camden Road West Jn	8A
Camden Viaduct	8A
Canal Farm Jn, Nuneaton	5B
Canal Sdgs, Warrington	29B

Name	Code
Canal Tunnel, Birmingham New Street	20
Canal Tunnels Jn	8A
Canal Tunnels, St Pancras	8A
Canal Viaduct (Gravelly Hill)	20
CANLEY	18B
Canning Street Jn	39A
Canning Street North LC & SB	
(derelict)	39A
CANNOCK	22B
CAPENHURST	37C
Capernwray Viaduct (R. Keer)	31B
CARK & CARTMEL	34A
Carleton Crossing LC (CCTV)	47A
CARLISLE	32C
Carlisle Carriage Sidings	32C
Carlisle North Jn	32C
Carlisle PSB (CE)	32C
Carlisle South Jn	32C
CARLTON	13B
Carlton LC (CCTV)	13B
Carlton Lane LC (UWG)	39B
Carlton Road Jn	8A
CARNFORTH	31B
(Carnforth East Jn)	31B
(Carnforth Furness & Midland Jn)	31B
Carnforth North Jn	31B
Carnforth South Jn	31B
Carnforth Station Jn SB (CS)	31B
CARPENDERS PARK	2B
Carr Lane LC (UWG)	39B
Carr Mill Viaduct	41B
Carriage Sdgs Middle SF, Wembley	2A
Carrington Street overbridge	13A
Carrs LC (UWC)	35C
Cart Lane LC (UWB)	34A
Carterhouse Jn LC (UWG)	37A
CASTLE BAR PARK	16A
Castle Bromwich Jn	25A
Castle Donington	13C
Castle Donnington Distribution Depot	13C
Castle Farm No.1 LC (UWG)	34C
Castle Foregate Sidings, Shrewsbury	27A
Castle Hill Tunnel	45A
Castle Mill Stream Bridge	17B
Castle Yard, Northampton	4A
Castlefield Jn	43N
CASTLETHORPE (disused)	3B
Castlethorpe North HABD	4A
CASTLETON	45A
Castleton Depot (closed)	45A
Castleton East Jn	45A
Castleton East Jn SB (CE)	45A
Castleton North Jn	45A
Castleton South Jn	45A
Cathcart Street LC (closed)	39A
Cattle Pens Viaduct	27A
Cauldwell EMUD, Bedford	9C
Causeway Tunnel	43G
Cavendish Street Tunnel	39A
Caverswall LC (MCB) & SB (CL)	26B
CAVERSWALL ROAD (FLR)	26A
Cedar Jn	8A
CEFN-Y-BEDD	27C
Cefn-y-Bedd Viaduct	27C
Cement Depot No.1 LC (Open)	32C
Cemetery Sdg, Nuneaton	5B
Cemetery Viaduct, Birmingham	20
Central Rivers Depot (CZ),	
Bombardier	25B
Central Tunnel, Liverpool	38A
Chaddesden	11B
Chaffers LC (TMOB)	45C
CHALFONT AND LATIMER (LUL)	15B
Chalfonts No.1/Misbourne Viaduct	16B
Chalfonts No.2 Viaduct	16B
Chapel Lane LC (MCG), Parbold	41A
Chapel LNW Tunnel,	
Chapel-on-le-Frith	43E
Chapel Milton Viaduct, Chinley	44B
CHAPEL-EN-LE-FRITH	43E
Chapel-en-le-Frith LC (UWG)	43E
Charlmont Road LC (FP) (R/G)	20
CHASETOWN (CR)	22D
CHASEWATER HEATHS (CR)	22D
CHASEWATER RAILWAY (CR)	22D
CHASSEN ROAD	43D
(Chatterley Valley DP)	42A
(Cheadle Heath South Jn)	43S
CHEADLE HULME	42B
Cheadle Hulme Nth Jn	42B
Cheadle Hulme Sth Jn	42B
(Cheadle Jn)	43S
Cheadle Village Jn	43S
Cheadle Wood Farm LC (UWC)	43S
CHEDDINGTOM WILD	3A
CHEDDINGTON	3A
CHEDDLETON (CVR)	26B
CHELFORD	42B
Chelford Loops	42B
Chelford North Jn	42B
Chelford South Jn	42B
(Chellaston East & West Jns)	13C
CHERRY TREE	46A
Cherry Tree GF	46A
Cherwell Viaduct	17A
CHESTER	28A
Chester East Jn	28A
Chester Engineers Sidings	28A
Chester Line Jn, Crewe	7A
Chester North Jn	28A
Chester PSB (CR)	28A
CHESTER ROAD	20
Chester South Jn	28A
Chester Station Yard	28A
Chester Train Care Centre (CH)	28A
Chester West Jn	28A
Chesterfield South Jn	12A
Chiltern Green HABD	9B
CHINLEY	44B
Chinley East Jn	44B
Chinley North Jn	44B
Chinley SB (CY)	44B
Chinley South Jn	44B
CHINNOR & PRINCES RISBOROUGH	
RAILWAY (C&PRR)	16B
CHINNOR (C&PRR)	16B
Chivers Coton Jn	5B
Chivers Coton Viaduct	5B
CHORLEY	30B
Chorley Tunnel	30B
CHORLEYWOOD (LUL)	15B
Christleton Tunnel	28A
Chunes LC (UWC)	22C
CHURCH & OSWALDTWISTLE	45B
Church Lane LC (CCTV)	6B
Church Road Tunnel	23B
Church Road, Liverpool	38A
Church Street LC, Wolverton	3B
Church Viaduct	45B
Churchyard Sidings	8A
CHURNET VALLEY RAILWAY (CVR)	26B
CLAPHAM (North Yorks)	31B
Clapham Viaducts, Bedford	9C
Clapham/Wenning Viaduct	31B
CLAVERDON	19A
Clay Cross North Jn	12A
(Clay Cross South Jn)	12A
Clay Cross Tunnel	12A
Clay Mills Jn	26C
CLAYDON (disused)	17A
Claydon L & NE Jn SB (CN)	17A
Claydon LC (AOCL)	17A
Clayton Bridge LC (CCTV)	44A
Clayton Bridge Viaduct	44A
CLC Viaduct, Bredbury	44A
Cleatop LC (UWG)	31B
Clerkenwell Tunnels	8C
Cliff Vale Terminal	26B
Cliffe Hill No. 1 & No.2 GFs	14B
Cliffe Vale Jn, Stoke	26B
CLIFTON	46C
Clifton & Lowther GSPs	32A
(Clifton Jn)	46C
Clifton Road Bridge (Rugby)	5A
Clintsfield LC (UWG)	31B
Clintsfield Viaduct	31B
CLITHEROE	36A
Clover-le-Dale LC (UWG)	40B
Club Gardens LC (BW)	13B
Club Lane LC (UWG)	47C
Coal Drops Viaduct, Miles Platting	43N
Coal Sdgs, Crewe	7A
Coalbrookdale Viaduct	22C
(Coalville Jn)	14B
Coalville Station LC (CCTV)	14C
Cobden Street Sidings	46C
Cobwall Viaduct	46A
Cockden Viaduct	45A
Cockshute Sidings, Stoke	26B
Codnor Park Jn	12A
CODSALL	22A
Cofton Jn	23B
Cogley Lane LC (UWC)	13B
Coleshill East Jn	25A
COLESHILL PARKWAY	25A
Coleshill West Jn	25A
Collier Lane Siding, Carlisle	32C
Collier's LC (UWC)	26B
Collyhurst Depot	43N
Collyhurst Tunnel	43N
COLNE	45C
(Colne Jn)	2B
Colne Viaduct	45C
Colne Viaduct, Bushey	2B
Colwich Jn	6A
Colwick LC (CCTV)	13B
Colwick Oil Depot (oou)	13B
Conder Viaduct	31A
(Coney Green Jn)	12A
CONGLETON	42B
Congleton Viaduct	42B
CONSALL (CVR)	26B
CONWAY PARK	39A
Cooks Lane LC (UWW)	10B
Cooks No.1 & No.2 LCs (UWC)	23C
Cooksholme LC (UWC)	23C
Cooperas Hill Tunnel	38A
Coopers LC (UWG), Bamber Bridge	46A
Coopers LC (UWG), Kidsgrove	42A
Copenhagen Jn	8A
Copenhagen Tunnel	8A
(Coppenhall Jn)	29A
Coppull Hall HABDs	30A
CORBY	10A
Corby Automotive Terminal	10C
Corby Run Round Sidings	10A
Corby Station North Jn	10A
Corby Station South Jn	10A
Corby Steelworks	10C
Corby Tunnel	10A
CORKICKLE	35A
Corks Farm No. 2 LC	25A
Cornbrook Viaduct	43N
Corporation Road Tunnel	39A
Corporation Yard Viaduct	19B
COSELEY	21A
COSFORD	22A
Cotehill/ High Stand Gill Viaduct	36D
Coton Hill Yard, Shrewsbury	27A
COTTESMORE (RRM)	10D
Cottons LC (UWC)	13C
Coundon Road LC (CCTV)	18B
COUNTRY PARK HALT (SVR)	24A
Coupland Viaduct	36C
COVENTRY	18B
COVENTRY ARENA	18B
Coventry Canal (Atherstone)	5B
Coventry Canal (Lichfield)	6A
Coventry Canal (Nuneaton)	5B
Coventry Canal (Polesworth)	5B
Coventry Canal (Stockingford)	25A
Coventry Canal (Streethay)	25A
Coventry Canal (Wilnecote)	25A
Coventry North Jn	18B
Coventry North Yard	18B
Coventry South Jn	18B
Covered way, Junction Rd Jn	8A
Cowburn Tunnel	44B
Cowburn Viaduct	44B
Cowdale Bar Viaduct	43E
Cowley Hill, St. Helens	41B
Cox's Walk LC (UWC)	13B
Crabtree LC (R/G)	41A
CRADLEY HEATH	24A
Crane Street Jn, Wolverhampton	21A
Crane Street Viaduct, Wolverhampton	21A
Crankley Point LC (R/G)	13B
Credley Heath LC (CCTV)	24A
Crescent Road LC (AHBC)	40B
Crescent Road Yard, Luton	9B
CRESSINGTON	38A
Cresswell LC (AHBC)	26B
Creswell Viaduct (M6)	6B
CREWE	7A
(Crewe Bank SB)	27A
Crewe Coal Yard SB (CY)	7A
Crewe Diesel Depot (CD)	7A
Crewe Down Holding Sidings	7A
Crewe Electric EMD (CE)	7A
Crewe Heritage Centre GF	7A
Crewe Independent Line Tunnels	7A
Crewe Junction SB (CJ), Shrewsbury	27A
Crewe North Jn	7A
Crewe PAD	7A
Crewe SCC (CE)	7A
Crewe Sorting Sdgs North SB (NY)	7A
Crewe South Jn	7A
Crewe Steelworks SB (SW)	7A
Crewe Works (ZC), Bombardier	7A
CRICH TRAMWAY VILLAGE	24B
Crick Tunnel	4B
CRICKLEWOOD	8B
Cricklewood Aggregates Terminal	8B
Cricklewood Curve Jn	8B
Cricklewood Depot Jn	8B
Cricklewood Depot SB	8B
Cricklewood Sidings	8B
Cricklewood South Jn	8B
Criftin Farm LC (UWC)	13B
Crilleys LC (UWC)	13B
Critchlows LC (UWC)	26B
Croal Viaduct	46B
Croes Newydd North Fork LC	
(MCB) & SB (CN)	27C
Croft Quarry	10B
CROMFORD	12A
Cromford Canal (Ironville)	12A
Crook Wheel LC (UWG)	34A
Cropredy HABD	17C
Crosby Garrett Tunnel	36C
Crosby Garrett Viaduct	36C
Crosfield's Crossing LC (CCTV)	29B
CROSTON	47C
Crow Nest Jn	46C
Crowdundle Viaduct	36D
Crown St. No.5 Tunnel	38A
Crown Street Jn	38A
Crown Street Tunnel, Liverpool	38A
(Crowthorne Jn)	44A
CUDDINGTON	42B
Culcheth Farm LC (UWG)	43C
Culgaith LC (MCB) & SB	36D
Culgaith Tunnel	36D
Cummersdale Viaduct	35C
CUMWHINTON (disused)	36D
Curborough Jn	6A
Currock GF	32C
Currock Jn	32C
Currock Yard	32C
Curzon Street Jn	20
Cutnall Green	24A

D

Dairy House Farm LC (UWG)	28C
DAISY HILL	46C
Daisyfield Jn	46A
Daisyfield SB (DS)	46A
Dale Lane GSP	40A
Dallam Freight Depot	29B
Dallam Jn	29B
Dallam Royal Mail Terminal	29B
Dallam Wheelchex	29B
Dalrymple LC (UWC)	35C
DALSTON	35C
Dalston Oil Depot GF	35C
Dalston Stn No.1 GF	35C
Dalston Stn No.2 GF	35C
DALTON	34A
Dalton Jn	34B
Dalton Jn SB (DJ)	34B
Dalton Tunnel	34A
Dane or Holmes Chapel Viaduct	42B
DANZEY	19A
DARK LANE (SGLR)	12B
Darlaston Jn	21A
DARLEY DALE (PR)	14D
DARWEN	46B
Darwen North Jn	46B
Darwen South Jn	46B
DAVENPORT	43S
Daventry International Rail Freight	
Terminal (DIRFT)	4B
Daventry North Jn	4B
Daventry South Jn	4B
Daw End Aquaduct	21A
Daw Mill Colliery	25A
Daw Mill East Jn	25A
Daw Mill West Jn	25A
Deal Street Jns	43N
Dean Lane	45A
Dean Lane LC (AHBC-X)	41A
Dean Royd Tunnel	45A
Dean Viaduct	42B
Deans Brook Viaduct	9A
DEANSGATE	43N
Deansgate Jn SB (DJ)	43S
Dee Marsh Jn SB (DM)	39C
(Dee Marsh Jn West)	39C

Dee Marsh North Jn	39C
DEE MARSH Shotton Works	39C
Deepdale	30C
Deepdale Jn	30C
Deepdale Tunnels	30C
DELAMERE	42B
DELPH (WLLR)	47D
Denbigh Hall North Jn	3B
Denbigh Hall South Jn	3B
DENHAM	16B
DENHAM GOLF CLUB	16B
DENT	36B
Dent Head Viaduct	36B
DENTON	44A
Denton Jn SB (DJ)	44A
Denton Station Jn	44A
Depot Jn, Longsight	43N
DERBY	11B
Derby Jn	11B
(Derby North Jn)	11B
Derby Square Jn	38A
Derby Station North Jn	11B
Derwent Jn, Workington	35B
Derwent/Workington Viaduct	35B
Desborough Summit	10A
Desford LC (AHBC)	14B
Devonshire Road Jn	47A
Diggle Jn SB (DE)	44A
DILHORNE PARK (FLR)	26A
Dingle Tunnel	38A
DINTING	44A
Dinting East Jn	44A
Dinting Lane LC (UWB)	44A
Dinting SB (DG)	44A
Dinting South Jn	44A
Dinting Vale Viaduct	44A
Dinting West Jn	44A
DISLEY	43E
Disley Tunnel (LNW)	43E
Disley Tunnel (Midland)	44B
Ditchburns LC (UWC)	15C
DITTON (disused)	37A
Ditton East Jn	37A
Ditton Reception Sidings	37A
Ditton Sidings GSP	37A
Ditton Viaduct	37A
Ditton West Jn	37A
Dock Jn North	8A
Dock Jn South	8A
Dock Street Sidings, Preston	30C
Docker Garth's Viaduct	31C
Docks Branch GF, Workington	35B
Dodds LC (UWC)	16B
Dodd's LC (UWG)	34B
DOLLIS HILL (LUL)	15A
Donnington Jn	27A
DORRIDGE	19A
Dorridge North Jn	19A
Dorridge South Jn	19A
Double to Single Jn	9C
DOVE HOLES	43E
Dove Holes Quarry	43E
Dove Holes Tunnel	43E
Dovefields LC (R/G)	26C
Dowlow Quarry	44E
Dowlow Sidings	44E
Down Salop Sidings	6B
Down Siding GF (Great Rocks)	43E
Downhill Carriage Sdgs	38A
Doxey Jn	6B
Drakelow East Curve Jn	14C
Drakelow West Curve Jn	14C
DRAYTON GREEN	16A
Drayton Green Jn	16A
Drayton Green Tunnel	16A
Drayton Road Jn	3B
DRIGG	34C
Drigg LC (MCG) & SB (D)	34C
Drigg Viaduct	34C
Drinkwater LC (UWC)	17B
Drybeck Viaduct	36D
DSE Viaducts & Arches	43N
Duckworths LC (UWG)	36A
DUDDESTON	20
Duddeston Jn	20
Duddeston Viaduct	19B
Dudding Hill Jn SB (DH)	8B
Duddon/Foxfield Viaduct	34B
Dudley Canal	24A
(Dudley Jn)	21A
DUDLEY PORT	21A
Dudley Tunnel	21A

DUFFIELD	12A
DUFFIELD (EVR)	12A
Duffield Jn HABD	12A
Duke Street LC (CCTV), Southport	40B
Duke Street LC, Mersey Docks	39A
Dukes Drive Viaduct	44E
Dukes Sdgs	34B
Dukes Wood LC (UWG)	40A
Dukinfield East Viaduct	44A
(Dukinfield Jn)	44A
Dukinfield West Vdct (Peak Forest Canal)	44A
Dunhampstead LC (AHBC)	23C
Dunnerholme LC (UWG)	34B
Dunstalls LC (UWC)	26C
(Durran Hill SB)	32C
(Duston North Jn)	4A
Dutton Viaduct	29A

E

Eagle Crossing LC	21A
Eamont Viaduct	32B
Earl Cowpers Viaduct, R. Nene	4A
Earles Branch	44C
Earle's Sidings SB (ES)	44C
EARLESTOWN	29C
Earlestown East Jn	29C
Earlestown South Jn	29C
Earlestown West Jn	29C
EARLSWOOD	19A
East Curve Viaduct, Guide Bridge	44A
(East Denham Jn)	16B
EAST DIDSBURY	43S
EAST LANCASHIRE LIGHT RAILWAY (ELR)	45A
East Langton HABD	10A
East Lune Viaduct	31B
East Middle Trench Sdgs	31B
East Midlands Control Centre	11B
East Midlands Gateway Freight Terminal (u/c)	13C
EAST MIDLANDS PARKWAY	11A
Eastcroft Depot, Nottingham	13A
EASTHAM RAKE	37C
Eaves Tunnel	43E
ECCLES	43C
Eccles LC (CCTV) (ML)	40B
Eccles SB (ES)	43C
Eccles Station Jn	43C
ECCLESBOURNE VALLEY RAILWAY (EVR)	12A
ECCLESTON PARK	41B
Eckington North Jn	23C
Eckington South Jn	23C
Eckington WILD	23C
ECML Bridge Covered Portal (HS1)	8A
EDALE	44B
Edale SB (EE)	44B
Eden Valley Loop	32A
EDEN VALLEY RAILWAY (Eden)	36C
Eden Viaduct	32C
EDGE HILL	38A
Edge Hill East Jn	38A
Edge Hill Maintenance Depot	38A
Edge Hill Reception Sidings	38A
Edge Hill West Jn	38A
Edge Lane Jn	38A
Edgeley Jn No.1 SB (EY1)	43S
Edgeley Jn No.2 SB (EY2)	43S
Edstone Aqueduct	19A
Edstone Hall No. 1 LC (UWW)	19A
(Egerton Street Jn)	38A
Egginton Jn SB (EN)	26C
Egginton LC (AHBC-X)	26C
Egleton LC (UWB)	10B
Ehen Viaduct	35A
Elford GF	25A
Elford Loop	25A
ELLESMERE PORT	37C
Ellesmere Port Docks	37C
Ellesmere Port SB (EP)	28A
Ellesmere Port West End Sdgs	37C
Ellesmere Port: East Yard Sdgs	28A
Elliots LC (UWC)	13C
Elm Grove LC (UWG)	39B
Elstow	9C
ELSTREE & BOREHAMWOOD	9A
Elstree Tunnels	9A
ELTON & ORSTON	13B
Elton Sidings & GSP	28A
Elton Wheelock Viaduct	42B
Elworth Jn	42B

Emergency Access LC (UWC)	36A
Endon LC (AOCL)	26B
(Engine Shed Jn)	30C
English Bridge Jn, Shrewsbury	27A
English Damside Viaduct	32C
ENTWISTLE	46B
ERDINGTON	20
Erewash Canal (Ilkeston)	14A
Erewash Canal (Long Eaton)	11B
Erewash Canal (Sheet Stores)	13A
Esk Viaduct	33A
Eskmeals Viaduct	34C
Etches Park T&RSMD (DY), Derby	11B
Etterby Exchange Sidings	33C
EUXTON BALSHAW LANE	30B
Euxton Jn	30B
Evelench LC (UWC)	23C

F

F' Sidings, Wembley	2A
FAIRFIELD	44A
Farington Curve (East Lancs) Jn	30C
Farington Curve Jn	30C
Farington Jn	30C
Farmer Johnson's LC (UWG)	28A
FARNWORTH	46C
Farnworth Tunnel	46C
Farrer's Viaduct (R. Wenning)	31B
FARRINGDON	8C
FAZAKERLEY	40A
Fazakerley LC (UWG)	40A
Fenny Compton Middle Jn	17C
Fenny Compton North Jn	17C
Fenny Compton Sidings	17C
Fenny Compton South Jn	17C
FENNY STRATFORD	3C
Fenny Stratford Jn	3C
Fenny Stratford LC (CCTV)	3C
Fenton Manor Tunnel	26B
Ferrett Lane LC (UWG)	41A
FFLINT	27B
Fflint Jn	27B
Fiddlers Ferry LC (UWG)	37B
Fiddlers Ferry Power Station	37B
Fiddlers Ferry Power Station SB (FF)	37B
Field House Farm LC (UWG)	42B
Finchley Road	8A
FINCHLEY ROAD & FROGNAL	8A
FINCHLEY ROAD (LUL)	15A
Findern LC (AHBC)	26C
Fine Lane LC (MCG)	25A
Fingham Brook Viaduct	18B
Finney Lane LC (UWG)	47C
Fishergate Tunnel	30C
FISHERGROUND HALT (RER)	33B
Fishermans Path LC (UWC)	40B
Fishpool Farm LC (UWG)	27B
FISKERTON	13B
Fiskerton LC (MCB-OD)	13B
FIVE WAYS	23B
FLIMBY	35B
FLITWICK	9B
Flitwick Jn	9C
FLIXTON	43D
Floriston HABDs	33A
Floriston LC (AHBC)	33A
FLOWERY FIELD	44A
Flyover Jn (summit), Bletchley	3B
Flyover Single Line Jn	3B
Foley Crossing SB (FY)	26B
Folly Lane	37A
Forders Sidings	3C
Forest House Farm LC (UWG)	42B
(Forks Jn)	32C
FORMBY	40B
Fosseway LC (AHBC)	25A
Foundry Lane, Ditton	37A
Foundry Wood Jn	18A
Four Ashes	22A
Four Lane Ends LC (R/G)	41A
FOUR OAKS	25A
Foxcover LC (UWC)	13B
FOXFIELD	34B
Foxfield LC (UWG) & SB	34B
FOXFIELD LIGHT RAILWAY (FLR)	26A
Freeby LC (UWW)	10B
FRESHFIELD	40B
Freshfield LC (CCTV)	40B
Frisby LC (MCB)	10B
Frisby SB(FY)	10B
FRODSHAM	28B
Frodsham Jn SB (FJ)	29B

Frodsham Tunnel	28B
Frog Lane LC (UWG)	41A
Fulwood Tunnel	38A
Furness Abbey LC (UWG)	34B
Furness Abbey Tunnel	34B
FURNESS VALE	43E
Furness Vale LC (MCB) & SB (FV)	43E
Fylde Road Viaduct	31A

G

Gade Valley Viaduct (M25)	2B
Galton Jn	21A
Galton Tunnel	21A
Gannow Jn	45C
GARSDALE	36C
Garsdale or Dandy Mire Viaduct	36C
Garsdale SB (G)	36C
Garstang & Catterall EGFs	31A
GARSTON (Herts)	2B
Garston Car Terminal (Ford Motor Co)	37A
Garston Freightliner Depot	38A
Garston Freightliner GF	38A
Garston Jn	38A
GARSWOOD	41B
Gas Works Tunnel	8A
GATHURST	41A
Gathurst Viaduct	41A
GATLEY	43S
Gauxholme Viaducts	45A
Gavray Jn	17A
Geddington HABD	10A
Geddington/Harpers Brook Viaduct	10A
Gerards Bridge Jn & GF	41B
GERRARDS CROSS	16B
Gibbet Hill Jn	18B
Gifford Street Portals	8A
GIGGLESWICK	31B
Gisburn Tunnel	36A
Glaston Tunnel	10A
GLAZEBROOK	43D
Glazebrook East Jn SB (GE)	43D
(Glazebrook West Jn)	43D
Glebe Street Jn	26B
Glen Parva GSP	10B
Glen Parva Jn	10B
(Glendon North Jn)	10A
Glendon Viaduct	10A
GLOSSOP	44A
GODLEY	44A
Godley Arches	44A
GODLEY EAST (disused)	44A
Golborne Jn	29C
Goldmire Quarry LC (UWG)	34B
Gonalston LC (AHBC)	13B
Goodridges LC (UWC)	10B
GOOSTREY	42B
Goostrey Jn	42B
Gordon Road Viaduct	16B
Gorsey Lane LC (UWC)	13B
GORTON	44A
GOSPEL OAK	8A
Gospel Oak Jn	8A
Goyt Cliff Viaduct	44B
Grammers LC (UWC)	13C
Grand Jns	20
Grand Union Canal (Acton Wells)	1
Grand Union Canal (Acton Wharf)	1
Grand Union Canal (Blisworth)	4A
Grand Union Canal (Bordesley)	23B
Grand Union Canal (Cheddington)	3A
Grand Union Canal (Crick)	4B
Grand Union Canal (Fenny Stratford)	3C
Grand Union Canal (Hemel Hempstead)	3A
Grand Union Canal (Kilsby)	4B
Grand Union Canal (Leamington Spa)	18A
Grand Union Canal (Mitre Bridge Jn)	1
Grand Union Canal (Northampton)	4A
Grand Union Canal (Northolt)	16A
Grand Union Canal (Saltley)	20
Grand Union Canal (Tyseley)	19B
Grand Union Canal (Wolverton)	3B
Grand Union Canal Aquaduct (Warwick)	18A
Grand Union Canal Viaduct (Denham)	16B
Grange Farm LC (UWC) (Launton)	17A
Grange Farm LC (UWC) (Warwick)	19A
Grange Jn	42A
GRANGE-OVER-SANDS	34A
Grange-over-Sands SB (GS)	34A
Granville Sidings	42A
Granville Street Tunnel	23B
Grassendale Tunnel	38A

GRAVELLY HILL	20
Grayrigg Loops	31C
GREAT CENTRAL RAILWAY (GCR)	23A
GREAT CENTRAL RAILWAY (N) (GCRN)	23A
Great Central Way Jn	15A
Great Howard Street Viaduct & Incline	40A
GREAT MISSENDEN	15C
Great Rocks Jn SB (GR)	43E
Great Rocks Tunnel	43G
GREEN LANE	39A
(Green Lane Jn)	39A
Green Lane LC (AHBC) (Saltney Jn)	27C
Green Lane LC (AHB-X) (Stewartby)	3C
Green Lane Tunnel	39A
Green Meadow Jn	44A
GREEN ROAD	34B
Green Road (AOCL)	34B
Green Road Viaduct	34B
GREENBANK	42B
Greenbank SB (GK)	42B
GREENFIELD	44A
GREENFORD	16A
Greenford (LUL) Bay Jn	16A
Greenford East Jn	16A
Greenford East SB (GE)	16A
Greenford South Jn	16A
Greenford West Jn	16A
Greens LC (UWC)	10B
Greens Viaduct (R. Wenning)	31B
Gregson Lane LC (UWG)	46A
(Grendon Underwood Jn)	15C
Gresford Bank	27C
Gresley Tunnel	14C
Gresty Bridge Depot	7A
Gresty Green East Jn	7A
Gresty Green Sidings	7A
Gresty Green West Jn	7A
Gresty Lane Down Sdgs GSP	7A
Gresty Lane Down Sidings	7A
Gresty Lane Jn	7A
Gresty Lane SCC (GL)	7A
Gresty Lane Sdgs	7A
Gresty Road, Crewe	7A
GRETNA GREEN	33A
Gretna Jn	33A
Gretton Viaduct	10A
Grid Iron Feeding Jn	29B
GRIMSTON (disused)	11C
Grimston Covered Way	11C
Grimston Tunnel	11C
GRINDLEFORD	44C
Grindleford WILD	44C
Griseburn LC (UWG)	36C
Griseburn Viaduct	36C
Grisedale LC (UWG)	36C
Grives Lane LC (AHBC)	12A
GUIDE BRIDGE	44A
Guide Bridge East Jn	44A
(Guide Bridge North Jn)	44A
Guide Bridge Stn Jn	44A
Guide Bridge West Jn	44A
Gunthorpe LC (BW - OMSL)	10B
GWERSYLLT	27C

H

HADDENHAM AND THAME PARKWAY	16C
HADFIELD	44A
HAG FOLD	46C
HAGLEY	24A
HALE	43S
Hale LC (CCTV)	43S
HALEWOOD	38B
Halewood East Jn	37A
Halewood Exchange Sidings	37A
Halewood West Jn	37A
Halewood, Jaguar Land Rover	37A
Hall Carleton LC (UWG)	34C
Hall End Jn	25A
HALL GREEN	19A
HALL I'TH'WOOD	46B
HALL ROAD	40A
Hall Road LC (CCTV)	40A
Hall Royd Jn	45A
HALTON (disused)	29B
Halton Jn	37A
HAMILTON SQUARE	39A
Hamilton Square Jn	39A
Hammerhouse Farm LC (UWC)	6B
HAMMERSMITH (MR-B)	12A
HAMPSTEAD HEATH	8A
(Hampstead Road Jn)	1
Hampstead Tunnel	15A
HAMPTON LOADE (SVR)	24A
HAMPTON-IN-ARDEN	18C
Hams Hall	25A
Hams Hall Jn	25A
HAMSTEAD	20
Hamstead Heath Tunnel	8A
Hamstead Tunnel, Kentish Town	8A
Hamstead Tunnel, Perry Barr	20
HANDFORTH	42B
Handforth Viaduct	42B
(Handsworth Jn)	21A
Handsworth Jn	20
Handsworth Memorial Cricket Club LC (UWC)	20
HANGER LANE (LUL)	16A
Hanslope Jns	4A
HAPTON	45B
(Harborne Jn)	20
Harbury Tunnel	18A
Hardendale Crossover	32A
Hardendale Quarry, Shap	32A
Hardstaffs LC (UWC)	12A
Harecastle HABD	42A
Harecastle Tunnel	42A
Harker: Kingstown	33C
HARLESDEN	2A
Harlesden Jn	2A
HARLINGTON	9B
Harlington Jn	9B
HARPENDEN	9A
Harpenden Jn	9A
Harpers Brook/Geddington Viaduct	10A
HARRINGTON	35B
Harrington Viaduct	35B
Harringworth/Welland Valley Viaduct	10A
Harrisons Sdgs EGF	32A
Harrisons Sidings	32A
Harrisons Sidings HABD	32A
HARROW & WEALDSTONE	2B
Harrow North Jn (LUL)	15B
Harrow South Jn	15B
Harrowden Jn	10A
Harrowden Jn HABD	10A
HARROW-ON-THE-HILL (LUL)	15B
HARTFORD	29A
Hartford CLC Jn	42B
Hartford East Jn	42B
Hartford Jn	29A
(Hartford LNW Jn)	29A
Hartford North Jn	42B
Hartford West Jn	42B
HARTLEBURY	24A
Hartlebury LC (CCTV)	24A
HATCH END	2B
HATHERSAGE	44C
Hathersage Viaduct	44C
HATTERSLEY	44A
HATTON	19A
Hatton Bank (foot)	18A
Hatton Bank Summt	19A
Hatton North Jn	19A
Hatton Station Jn	19A
Hatton West Jn	19A
Haverigg LC (AHBC)	34C
HAVERTHWAITE (LHR)	34D
Haw Lane LC (UWG)	36A
HAWARDEN	27C
HAWARDEN BRIDGE	39C
Hawkesbury Lane LC (CCTV)	5B
Hawkesbury Lane Up Sdg GF	5B
Haydock Branch Jn	29C
Haymarket Tunnel	39A
Hayside LC (UWC)	26C
HAZEL GROVE	43S
Hazel Grove East Jn	43S
Hazel Grove High Level Jn	43S
Hazel Grove SB (HG)	43S
Hazel Grove West Jn	43S
HAZELWELL (disused)	23B
Hazle Hall LC (UWC)	31B
HEADSTONE LANE	2B
HEALD GREEN	43S
Heald Green North Jn	43S
Heald Green South Jn	43S
Heald Green West Jn	43S
Heamies Bridge	6B
Heartland Park	20
Heartlands Park Sdgs GF	20
Heartlands Power Station (closed)	25A
(Heath Town Jn)	21A
Heathfield LC (UWG)	35C
HEATON CHAPEL	43S
Heaton Chapel Wheelchex	43S
Heaton Norris Jn SB (HN)	43S
HEATON PARK TRAMWAY, Prestwich	45D
HEDNESFORD	22B
Hednesford Jn	22B
HELLIFIELD	36A
Hellifield SB (HD)	36A
Hellifield South Jn	36A
Helm Tunnel	36C
HELSBY	28A
Helsby Jn SB (HY)	28A
Helsby West Cheshire Jn	28A
HEMEL HEMPSTEAD	3A
Hen Lane Bridge	18B
HENDON	9A
HENLEY-IN-ARDEN	19A
Herefore Storage Sdg	27A
Hermitage Brook Flood Opening	11A
Hesketh LC (UWG)	40B
Heskins LC (UWG)	47B
Hest Bank HABD	31B
Hest Bank Jn	31B
Hest Bank LC (CCTV)	31B
Hestham Hall LC (UWG)	34C
HESWALL	39A
HEYFORD	17B
HEYSHAM PORT	31B
Heysham Power Station	31B
Heysham Power Stn GF	31B
HEYWOOD (ELR)	45A
Heywood GF	45A
(Hibel Road)	42B
Hickling	11C
Hicks Lodge GF	14C
High Lane LC (UWG)	47C
High Oaks Jn	5A
High Peak Bridge, Whatstandwell	12A
High Tor Tunnels	12A
High Wapping Sidings	32C
HIGH WYCOMBE	16B
Higher Delacre LC (UWG)	42B
Highfields LC (UWG)	6B
Highgate Road Viaduct	8A
HIGHLEY (SVR)	24A
HIGHTOWN	40B
Hillhouse GFs	47A
Hillmorton Jns	5A
HILLSIDE	40B
Hilly Laid LC (TMOG)	47A
Hilton LC (MCG)	26C
HINCKLEY	10B
Hinckley Canal	10B
Hinderton Field Tunnel	39A
HINDLEY	46C
Hindlow (oou) GFs	44E
Hindlow Sidings	44E
Hindlow Tunnel	44E
Hinds LC (UWB)	10B
Hirst Hall Farm LC (UWC)	43C
Hitchin Branch Jn, Bedford	9C
Hives Farm LC (UWC)	10B
Hockley LC (CCTV)	26C
Hockley Tunnels	20
(Hoddlesden Jn)	46B
Hoghton LC (AHBC-X)	46A
Hoghton Tower Viaduct	46A
Hollands LC (Streethay)	25A
Holliday Street Tunnel	20
Holme Tunnel	45C
HOLMES CHAPEL	42B
Holmes Chapel HABD	42B
Holt Lane Tunnel	12A
Holts LC (UWC)	10B
HOLYWELL JUNCTION (disused)	27B
Home Farm LC (UWG)	42A
Hoods Mill LC (UWB)	10B
HOOTON	37C
Hooton North Jn	37C
Hooton South Jn	37C
HOPE (Derbyshire)	44C
HOPE (Flintshire)	27C
HOPE EXCHANGE (disused)	27C
Hope Exchange LC (UWC)	27C
Hope Works	44D
Horninglow Bridge Jn	26C
Horninglow Sidings, Burton	26C
(Horns Bridge)	12A
Horrocks LC (UWG)	36D
Horrocksford	36A
Horrocksford Jn SB	36A
HORSEHAY & DAWLEY (TSR)	22E
Horsfall Tunnel	45A
HORTON IN RIBBLESDALE	36C
HORWICH PARKWAY	46C
HOSCAR	41A
Hoscar LC (AHBC-X)	41A
Hospital LC (CCTV)	46A
HOUGH GREEN	38B
(Hough Green Jn)	38B
HOW WOOD	2B
Howe & Co's Sdg SB (HS)	36D
HOYLAKE	39B
Hubbards LC (UWC)	10B
HUCKNALL	13D
Hucknall No.3 LC (UWC)	13D
Hughenden Road Viaduct	16B
Humberstone Road Jn	10B
Humberstone Road Sidings	10B
HUMPHREY PARK	43D
HUNCOAT	45B
Huncoat Stn LC (MCB)	45B
Hunsbury Hill Tunnel	4A
HUNTS CROSS	38A
Hunts Cross SB (HC)	38A
Hunts Cross West Jn	38A
Huskisson Memorial	29C
HUYTON	41B
Huyton Jn	41B
Huyton Viaduct (R. Douglas)	46C
HYDE CENTRAL	44A
Hyde Jn	44A
HYDE NORTH	44A
Hyde Viaduct	44A
Hyde/Chiltern Green Viaduct	9B

I

Icknield Street Viaduct	20
IDRIDGEHAY (EVR)	12A
ILKESTON	14A
Ilkeston Jn	14A
INCE	30A
INCE & ELTON	28A
Ince & Elton LC (R/G)	28A
Ince Moss Jn	30A
Inkpens No.1 LC (UWC)	17B
Intersection Tunnel, Willesden	2A
Ipstones	26B
(Irchester Jn)	9D
Irchester Viaducts (R. Nene)	9D
IRLAM	43D
Irlam Vdct, Manchester Ship Canal	43D
Ironbridge Power Station	22C
Ironville Jn	12A
IRTON ROAD (RER)	33B
Irwell Bridge Jn	43N
Irwell Street Jn	43N
IRWELL VALE (ELR)	45A
ISLIP	17A

J

Jacksons LC (UWC)	26B
Jaguar Terminal (West Bromwich)	25A
(James Bridge Jn)	21A
JAMES STREET	38A
Jarvis Lane LC (UWW)	17A
Jefferies LC (UWC)	17C
Jericho LC (UWC)	10B
JEWELLERY QUARTER	20
Johnson Matthey LC (TMO)	36A
Johnsons No.2 LC (UWG)	34B
Jowett Sidings	9C
Junction Road Jn	8A

K

Katherine Street Tunnel	44A
KEARSLEY	46C
Keele Tunnel	6C
Keerholme LC (UWG)	31B
KEMPSTON HARDWICK	3C
Kempston Hardwick LC (AHBC-X)	3C
KENDAL	31C
KENILWORTH	18B
Kenilworth By Pass	18B
Kenilworth North Jn	18B
Kenilworth South Jn	18B
KENSAL GREEN	1
Kensal Green Jn	1
Kensal Green Jn (HL Line Jn)	1
Kensal Green Tunnels	1
KENSAL RISE	1

Name	Code
Kent Viaduct	31C
Kent/Arnside Viaduct	34A
KENTISH TOWN	8A
Kentish Town Jn	8A
Kentish Town Rd Viaduct	8A
Kentish Town Viaduct	8A
KENTISH TOWN WEST	8A
KENTON	2B
KENTS BANK	34A
Kents Bank LC (UWB)	34A
Kenyon Cutting	43C
(Kenyon Jn)	43C
(Ketley Jn)	27A
KETTERING	10A
Kettering North Jn	10A
Kettering South Jn	10A
Kettering Station Jn	10A
Ketton Cement Works	10B
Ketton LC (MCB)	10B
Ketton SB (K)	10B
Kibworth summit	10B
KIDDERMINSTER	24A
Kidderminster Jn	24A
KIDDERMINSTER TOWN (SVR)	24A
Kidderminster/Hoo Brook Viaduct	24A
KIDSGROVE	42A
Kidsgrove Jn	42A
KILBURN (LUL)	15A
KILBURN HIGH ROAD	1
Kilburn Viaduct	1
Kilby Bridge Jn	10B
Kilsby North HABD	4B
Kilsby Tunnel	4B
Kineton Jn	17C
KINETON MILITARY RAILWAY (MOD)	50B
King LC (UWC)	34B
King Street Depot, Blackburn	46A
Kingmoor Jn	33C
Kingmoor TMD (KD)	33C
Kingmoor Virtual Quarry LC	33C
Kingmoor Yard	33C
Kings Cross Aggregates Terminal	8A
KINGS CROSS THAMESLINK (disused)	8C
Kings Cross Tunnel North	8A
Kings Cross Tunnel South	8A
Kings Heath Traincare Depot	4A
KINGS LANGLEY	2B
Kings Mill No 1 LC (BW)	12A
KINGS NORTON	23B
Kings Norton Jn	23B
Kings Norton Sidings	23B
Kings Norton Station Jn	23B
KINGS SUTTON	17C
Kingsbury	25A
Kingsbury Branch Jn	25A
Kingsbury Jn	25A
Kingsbury SF (KY)	25A
KINGSLEY & FROGHALL (CVR)	26B
Kingswinford Branch (oou)	24A
Kingswinford Jn	24A
Kingswinford Jn GF (oou)	24A
KIRKBY	40A
(Kirkby Jn)	12A
Kirkby Lane End Jn	12A
Kirkby Muxloe LC (R/G)	14B
Kirkby South Jn	12A
KIRKBY STEPHEN	36C
Kirkby Stephen SB (KS)	36C
Kirkby Summit	12A
Kirkby Thore SB (KT)	36D
Kirkby Tunnel	12A
Kirkby Viaduct	34B
KIRKBY-IN-ASHFIELD	12A
KIRKBY-IN-FURNESS	34B
KIRKDALE	40A
Kirkdale Merseyrail Depot (KK)	40A
Kirkdale No.1 Tunnel	40A
Kirkdale No.2 Tunnel	40A
Kirkdale North Jn	40A
Kirkdale South Jn	40A
KIRKHAM AND WESHAM	47A
Kirkham North Jn	47A
Kirkham South Jn	47A
Kirkham West Jn	47A
Kirksanton LC (MCG)	34C
Kirtle Water Viaduct	33A
Kitson Wood Tunnel	45C
Knapton's LC (UWC)	17B
Knathole Viaduct	44B
Knighton Jn	10B
Knighton Old Sdgs	10B
Knighton Tunnel	10B
Knighton Viaduct	10B
Knowlhill Jn	3B
Knowsley Freight Terminal	40A
KNUTSFORD	42B

L

Name	Code
L & NW Jn, Derby	26C
Lady Brook Viaduct	43S
LAKESIDE (LHR)	34D
LAKESIDE and HAVERTHWAITE RAILWAY (LHR)	34D
(Lambrigg GF)	31C
Lancashire Enterprise Sdgs	30C
LANCASTER	31A
Lancaster South Jn	31A
Lancaster Canal (Carnforth)	31B
Lancaster Canal (Lancaster)	31A
Lancaster Canal (Preston)	30C
Lancaster North Jn	31A
(Lancaster Old Jn)	31A
Landor Street Jn	20
LANDYWOOD	22B
Langham Jn (MCB)	10B
Langham Jn SB (LN)	10B
LANGHO	36A
LANGLEY GREEN	21A
Langley Green West LC (CCTV)	21A
LANGLEY MILL	12A
Langley Mill HABD	12A
Langridge No. 2 LC (UWC)	26C
LANGWATHBY	36D
LAPWORTH	19A
Latchford	29B
LAUNTON (disused)	17A
Launton LC (AOCL)	17A
Lawden Road Viaduct	19B
Lawley Street Viaducts	20
LAWLEY VILLAGE (TSR)	22E
Lawsing LC (UWG)	31B
LAYTON	47A
LAZONBY AND KIRKOSWALD	36D
Lazonby Tunnel	36D
LEA GREEN	41B
Lea Green LC (UWC)	41B
LEA HALL	18C
Lea Wood Bridge	12A
Lea Wood Tunnel	12A
LEAGRAVE	9B
Leagrave Jn	9B
Leaming LC (UWG)	34A
LEAMINGTON SPA	18A
Leamington Spa North Jn	18A
Leamington Spa South Jn	18A
Leamington Viaducts	18A
LEASOWE	39B
Leasowe LC (CCTV)	39B
Leathersley Farm No.2 LC (UWC)	26C
Ledburn Jn	3A
Leeds & Liverpool Canal (Bamfurlong Jn)	30A
Leeds & Liverpool Canal (Blackburn)	46B
Leeds & Liverpool Canal (Bootle)	40A
Leeds & Liverpool Canal (Burnley)	45C
Leeds & Liverpool Canal (Burscough)	41A
Leeds & Liverpool Canal (Chorley)	46C
Leeds & Liverpool Canal (Church)	45B
Leeds & Liverpool Canal (Gathurst)	41A
Leeds & Liverpool Canal (Ince Moss Jn)	41B
Leeds & Liverpool Canal (Maghull)	40A
Leeds & Liverpool Canal (Old Roan)	40A
Leeds & Liverpool Canal (Rishton)	45B
Leeds & Liverpool Canal (Rose Grove)	45C
Leeds & Liverpool Canal (Sandhills)	40A
Leeds & Liverpool Canal (Wigan)	30A
Leeds Street Jn	40A
LEEK BROOK (CVR)	26B
Leekbrook Jn	26B
Leftwich (or Northwich) Viaduct	42B
Leggetts LC (UWC)	13B
LEICESTER	10B
Leicester Branch Canal	4B
Leicester Jn, Burton	26C
Leicester Loco Sdgs (LR)	10B
LEICESTER NORTH (GCR)	23A
Leicester North Jn	10B
Leicester South Jn	10B
Leigh LC (AHBC-X)	26B
LEIGHTON BUZZARD	3A
LEIGHTON BUZZARD RAILWAY (LBR)	3D
Lenton North Jn	13A
Lenton South Jn	13A
Leven/Plumpton Viaduct	34A
LEVENSHULME	43S
LEYLAND	30C
Lichfield Chord Jn	6A
LICHFIELD CITY	25A
Lichfield City Jn	25A
Lichfield North Jn	6A
(Lichfield Road Jn)	21
LICHFIELD TRENT VALLEY (HIGH LEVEL)	25A
LICHFIELD TRENT VALLEY (LOW LEVEL)	6A
Lichfield TV HL Jn SB (TV)	25A
Lichfield TV Jn	25A
Lichfield Up Sidings	6A
Lickey Incline	23C
Lidgate LC (UWC)	34B
LIDLINGTON	3C
Lidlington LC (CCTV)	3C
Lifford East HABD	23B
Lifford East Jn	23B
Lifford West Jn	23B
(Lightmoor Jn)	22C
Limbury Road GFs	9B
Limbury Road, Luton	9B
Lime Street Cutting	38A
Lime Street Tunnels	38A
Limestone Hall LC (MCG)	34C
Linby Station LC (ABCL)	12A
Lincoln Street LC (CCTV)	13D
Lindal Tunnel	34A
Lindby Colliery LC (ABCL)	13D
Lindridge Farm LC (UWB)	14B
Linslade Tunnels	3A
Lismore Circus Tunnel, Kentish Town	8A
Litchurch Lane Works (ZD), Bombardier	11D
Little Bourton LC (UWS)	17C
Little Bowden LC (R/G) (FP)	10A
Little Bridgeford Jn	6B
(Little Eaton Jn)	12A
LITTLE KEMBLE	16B
LITTLE SALKELD (disused)	36D
Little Salkeld Viaduct	36D
LITTLE SUTTON	37C
Little Viaduct, Alrewas	25A
Little Viaduct, Settle	36B
LITTLEBOROUGH	45A
Littleborough GF	45A
Littleborough Viaduct	45A
Littleton Mill LC (MCG)	37B
Littlewood Viaduct	12A
Littleworth Farm LC (UWC)	17A
Litton's Mill LCF (MCG)	29B
Liverpool Bulk Terminal	40A
LIVERPOOL CENTRAL	38A
Liverpool Central North Jn	38A
Liverpool Central South Jn	38A
Liverpool Docks	40A
Liverpool Exchange Viaduct	40A
LIVERPOOL LIME STREET	38A
(Liverpool Road)	43B
LIVERPOOL SOUTH PARKWAY	38A
Lobb Mill Viaduct	45A
Lock Lane Crossing LC (CCTV)	13C
LONDON EUSTON	1
LONDON MARYLEBONE	15A
London North Western Yd, Stoke	26B
London Rd Sdgs, Carlisle	32C
London Road Jn (Carlisle)	32C
London Road Jn, Derby	11B
(London Road Jn, Leicester)	10B
(London Road Jn, Nottingham)	13A
LONDON ST. PANCRAS INTERNATIONAL	8A
London Tunnel (HS1)	8A
Long Ashes LC (UWG)	32B
LONG BUCKBY	4B
LONG EATON	11B
Long Eaton Jn	13A
Long Eaton Town LC (CCTV)	13A
Long Lawford Jn	18B
Long Marsh LC (UWG)	34C
LONG MARTON (disused)	36C
Long Marton Viaduct	36C
Long Meg (or Eden Lacy) Viaduct	36D
LONG PRESTON	36B
LONGBRIDGE	23B
Longbridge Jn	23B
LONGPORT	42A
Longport Down Sidings	42A
Longport Jn	42A
Longport Repair Works (LT)	42A
Longsight North Jn	43N
Longsight South Jn	43S
Longsight TMD (MA) (LO)	43N
LONGTON	26B
Longton Viaduct	26B
LONGTOWN (MOD)	33D
Longwaite LC (UWG)	34C
Loop Jn, Quintinshill	33A
Lorne Street LC	39A
LOSTOCK	46C
LOSTOCK GRALAM	42B
LOSTOCK HALL	30C
Lostock Hall Jn	30C
Lostock Jn	46C
Lostock Works, Northwich	42B
LOUGHBOROUGH	11A
LOUGHBOROUGH CENTRAL (GCR)	23A
Loughborough East Jn (GCRN)	23A
Loughborough HABD	11A
Loughborough North Jn	11A
Loughborough South Jn	11A
(Lounge Disposal Point)	14C
Lounge Jn	14C
(Low Gill GF)	31C
(Low Gill HABD)	31C
Low House Crossing LC (MCB) & SB	36D
Low Mill HABD	35C
Low Mill LC (R/G)	35C
Low Moor LC (CCTV)	36A
Lowca Beck	35A
LOWDHAM	13B
Lowdham LC (MCB-OD)	13B
Lower Bentham Vdct (R. Wenning)	31B
Lower Park Street Tunnels	1
Lower Portland Farm LC (UWC)	12A
Lower Radway Green LC (UWG)	7A
Lowther Viaduct	32B
LOWTON (disused)	29C
Lowton Jn	29C
Loxley Lane LC (AHBC-X)	26B
Luffenham LC (CCTV)	10B
Lunds Viaduct	36C
Lune Viaduct	31B
LUTON	9B
LUTON AIRPORT CENTRAL TERMINAL (Luton DART)	9E
LUTON AIRPORT PARKWAY	9B
Luton Direct Air Rail Transit (under construction)	9E
Luton North Jn	9B
Luton South Jn	9B
Luton Up Sdgs GF	9B
Lydgate Viaduct	45C
LYE	24A
LYTHAM	47B

M

Name	Code
M1 Bridge (Bricket Wood)	2B
M1 Bridge (Castle Donnington)	13C
M1 Bridge (Elstree)	9A
M1 Bridge (Hunsbury Hill)	4A
M1 Bridge (Kirkby Muxloe)	14B
M1 Bridge (Narborough)	10B
M1 Bridge (Pinxton)	12A
M1 Bridge (Ridgmont)	3C
M1 Bridge (Trowell)	14B
M25 Bridge (Chorleywood)	15B
M25 Bridge (How Wood)	2B
M25 Bridge (Radlett)	9A
M40 Bridge (Banbury North)	17C
M40 Bridge (Banbury South)	17C
M40 Bridge (Bicester North)	16C
M40 Bridge (Bicester)	17A
M40 Bridge (Hatton)	19A
M40 Bridge (Kineton)	17C
M40 Bridge (Kings Sutton)	17C
M42 Bridge (Alvechurch)	23B
M42 Bridge (Birmingham International)	18C
M42 Bridge (Blackwell)	23B
M42 Bridge (Polesworth)	5B
M42 Bridge (Widney Manor)	19A
M42 Bridge (Wilnecote)	25A
M42 Bridge (Wood End)	19A
M5 Bridge (Hamstead)	20
M5 Bridge (Rowley Regis)	24A
M53 Bridge (Eastham Rake)	37C
M53 Bridge (Ellesmere Port)	37C
M53 Bridge (Leasowe)	39B
M53 Bridge (Upton)	39A

Location	Code
M54 Bridge (Bushbury Jn)	22A
M54 Bridge (Telford)	27A
M55 Bridge (Kirkham and Wesham)	47A
M55 Bridge (Preston)	31A
M56 Bridge (Ashley)	43F
M56 Bridge (Bache)	28A
M56 Bridge (Cheadle)	43S
M56 Bridge (Northenden)	43S
M56 Bridge (Preston Brook)	29A
M56 Bridges (Frodsham)	29B
M56 Bridges (Weaver Jn)	29B
M57 Bridge (Kirkby)	40A
M57 Bridge (Old Roan)	40A
M57 Bridges (Huyton)	41B
M58 Bridge (Old Roan)	40A
M6 Bridge (Admiralty Jn)	33A
M6 Bridge (Bamber Bridge)	46A
M6 Bridge (Bedworth)	5B
M6 Bridge (Birchwood)	43D
M6 Bridge (Bryn)	41B
M6 Bridge (Carnforth)	31B
M6 Bridge (Grayrigg)	31C
M6 Bridge (Holmes Chapel)	42B
M6 Bridge (Knutsford)	42B
M6 Bridge (Leyland)	30C
M6 Bridge (Orrell)	40A
M6 Bridge (Radway Green)	7A
M6 Bridge (Rickerscote)	22A
M6 Bridge (Shap)	32B
M6 Bridge (Tebay)	32B
M6 Bridge (Upperby)	32C
M6 Bridges (Newton-le-Willows)	29C
M6 Bridges (Penrith)	32B
M6 Bridges (Pettril Bridge Jn)	32C
M6 Slip (Bay Horse)	31A
M6 Toll Bridge (Anglesea)	25A
M6 Toll Bridge (Cannock)	22B
M6 Toll Bridge (Shenstone)	25A
M6 Toll Bridges (Coleshill)	25A
M6 Viaduct (Bescot)	21A
M60 Bridge (Ashton Moss North Jn)	44A
M60 Bridge (Clifton)	46C
M60 Bridge (Denton)	44A
M60 Bridge (Fairfield)	44A
M60 Bridge (Moorside)	46C
M60 Bridge (Patricroft)	43C
M60 Bridge (Urmston)	43D
M60 Bridges (Cheadle)	43S
M601 Bridge (Carnforth)	31B
M61 Bridge (Bamber Bridge)	46A
M61 Bridges (Horwich Parkway)	46C
M61 Bridges (Westhoughton)	46C
M62 Bridge (Patricroft)	43C
M62 Bridge (Winwick Jn)	29C
M65 Bridge (Darwen)	46B
M65 Bridge (Rishton)	45B
M67 Bridge (Denton)	44A
M69 Bridge (Croft)	10B
M69 Bridge (Shilton)	5A
MACCLESFIELD	42B
Macclesfield Canal	42B
Macclesfield Canal Aquaduct	43S
Macclesfield SB (MD)	42B
Macclesfield Tunnel	42B
MADELEY (disused)	22C
Madeley Chord Jn	6C
Madeley HABD	6C
Madeley Jn	22A
Madeley Jn	6C
Madeley South Jn	22A
Maesteg LC (UWG)	27B
MAGHULL	40A
Maghull LC (CCTV)	40A
MAGHULL NORTH	40A
MANCHESTER AIRPORT	43S
Manchester East SCC (AS/GB/SE/RJ)	43S
Manchester Freightliner Terminal	43N
Manchester International Depot	43N
Manchester International Freight Terminal	43N
Manchester Line Jn, Crewe	7A
MANCHESTER METROLINK	48
MANCHESTER OXFORD ROAD	43N
MANCHESTER PICCADILLY	43N
Manchester Piccadilly East Jn	43N
Manchester Piccadilly GF	43N
Manchester Piccadilly SB (MP)	43N
Manchester Piccadilly West Jn	43N
Manchester ROC	43N
Manchester Ship Canal Vdct, Runcorn	37A
Manchester South SCC (MS)	43S
Manchester Traincare Centre (LG)	43N
MANCHESTER UNITED FOOTBALL GROUND	43N
MANCHESTER VICTORIA	43N
Manchester Victoria East Jn	43N
Manchester Victoria West Jn	43N
Manisty Wharf, Ellesmere Port	37C
Mann Island Jn	38A
Manor Farm LC (UWC)	17A
MANOR ROAD	39B
MANSFIELD	12A
Mansfield Jn, Nottingham	13A
Mansfield Viaduct	12A
MANSFIELD WOODHOUSE	12A
Mansfield Woodhouse Jn	12A
Mantle Lane SB (ML)	14C
Mantle Lane Sidings	14C
Mantles Wood	15B
Manton Jn	10B
Manton Jn GF	10B
Manton Jn SB (MJ)	10B
(Manton North Jn)	10B
Manton South Engineers Sidings	10B
Manton Tunnel	10B
MARCHINGTON (disused)	26C
Marchington Old Stn LC (UWC)	26C
MARKET BOSWORTH (BSR)	5C
MARKET HARBOROUGH	10A
(Market Harborough Jn)	10A
MARPLE	44A
Marple North Tunnel	44A
Marple South Tunnel	44A
Marple Viaduct (R. Goyt)	44A
Marple Wharf Jn	44A
Marriots LC (UWC)	13B
Marsden/Nelson Viaduct	45C
Marsh Gibbon LC (UWC)	17A
Marsh House LC (CCTV)	37B
Marsh Lane Crossover	40A
(Marsh Lane Jn)	40A
Marsh Lane LC (ABCL)	16B
Marshfield Viaduct	36B
MARSTON GREEN	18C
Marston LC (AHBC-X)	3C
Marston Vale SCC (MV)	3C
Marston-on-Dove LC (AHBC)	26C
Martins Lane LC (R/G-X)	41A
Marylebone IECC (ME/OB)	15A
MARYPORT	35B
(Maryport Jn)	35B
Maryport LC (CCTV)	35B
MATLOCK	12A
MATLOCK (PR)	14D
MATLOCK BATH	12A
Matlock GF	12A
MATLOCK RIVERSIDE (PR)	14D
MAULDETH ROAD	43S
McKenzies LC (UWC)	12A
Meadow Lane Jn	13A
Meadow Lane LC (CCTV)	13A
Meadow Sidings, Toton	14A
Meadows Exchange Sidings, Ketton	10B
Meaford Crossing LC (CCTV)	6B
Meaford Old Hall Farm Viaduct	6B
Medlock Viaduct	43N
Meir Tunnel	26B
Melbourne Jn	26C
Melling Tunnel	31B
Melrose Avenue LC (UWG)	39B
Melton Jn & GF	10B
MELTON MOWBRAY	10B
Melton Stn SB (MN)	10B
MEOLS	39B
MEOLS COP	41A
Mercer's LC (UWG)	43F
Merchants Quay LC (UWG)	35B
Merry Lees LCs No.1, No2, & No.3 (UWC)	14B
Mersey Docks & Harbour Co Lines	39A
Mersey Tunnel	39A
Mersey Tunnel (Park Branch)	39A
Merseyrail (IECC) ASC (ML)	40A
Mickle Trafford Jn SB (MT)	28A
Mid Cannock Jn	22B
Mid Cannock Sdgs	22B
(Middleton Jn)	45A
Middleton Place LC (UWG)	34C
MIDDLETON WHARF (SGLR)	12B
Middlewich	42B
Middlewich Canal	29A
MIDDLEWICH LOOP (disused)	42B
Middlewich Loop East Jn	42B
Middlewich Loop West Jn	42B
MIDDLEWOOD	43S
Middlewood Tunnel	43S
MIDGE HALL (disused)	47C
Midge Hall LC (MCB) & SB	47C
(Midland Jn)	43N
MIDLAND METRO	21A
Midland Metro Depot	21A
MIDLAND RAILWAY - BUTTERLEY (MR-B)	12A
Midland Road Jn	8A
Midland Yard Jn, Nuneaton	5B
Midland Yard Jn, Walsall	21A
MILBROOK (Bedfordshire)	3C
Milburn Grange LC (UWC)	18B
Miles Platting	43N
Miles Platting Jn	43N
Milford & Brocton HABD	6A
Milford Jn	6A
Milford Tunnel	12A
Mill Dam LC (UWG)	34C
Mill Deeping LC (UWW)	10B
Mill Dyke LC (UWC)	13B
Mill Farm (UWC), Middlewood	43S
MILL HILL	46A
MILL HILL BROADWAY	9A
Mill Lane Jn, Northampton	4A
Mill Road depot, Rugby	5A
Mill Street LC (TMOG)	30C
Millbrook LC (CCTV)	3C
(Millers Dale Jn)	43E
Millers LC (UWG), Silecroft	34C
MILLOM	34C
Millom SB	34C
MILLS HILL	45A
Millstream Viaduct	17A
Millwood Tunnel	45A
Milnthorpe GF	31C
Milton Ernest Viaducts	9C
(Milton Jn)	26B
MILTON KEYNES CENTRAL	3B
Milton Keynes North Jn	3B
Milton Keynes South Jn	3B
Milton Viaduct, Black Brook, Chinley	44B
Milverton Jn	18A
Milverton Viaduct	18A
Mintholme LC (CCTV)	46A
(Mirehouse Jn)	35A
Misbourne/Chalfonts No.1 Viaduct	16B
MITESIDE HALT (RER)	33B
Mitre Bridge Jn	1
Mitre Bridge LC (CCTV)	1
Moat Farm No.1 LC (UWC)	16B
MOBBERLEY	43F
Mobberley LC (MCB) & SB (MY)	43F
Moco Farm LC (UWC)	17A
Moco Farm No.2 LC (UWW)	17A
Moira West Jn SB (MW)	14C
Mollington Viaduct	28A
MONKS RISBOROUGH	16B
Monks Siding LC (MCB) & SB (MS)	37B
Monmore Green Jn	21A
Monument Lane Jn	20
Moor Farm LC, Radford Jn	13A
Moor Farm No.1 LC (UWG), Millom	34C
MOOR PARK (LUL)	15B
Moorcock Tunnel	36C
MOORFIELDS	38A
MOORSIDE	46C
MORECAMBE	31B
Morecambe Jn	31B
Morecambe South Jn	31B
MORETON (Merseyside)	39B
(Mortimer Street Jn)	8A
Mortimer Street Viaduct	8A
Morton Jn	12A
Morton Road LC (MCB-OD)	13B
Moseley Tunnel	23B
MOSES GATE	46C
Mosley Street GF and Sidings	26C
Moss & Plums LC (FP)	13D
MOSS SIDE	47B
Moss Side LC (ABCL)	47B
Moss Tip LC (UWG)	34C
Mossband Jn	33A
MOSSLEY (Greater Manchester)	44A
MOSSLEY HILL	38A
MOSTON	45A
MOTTRAM STAFF HALT (disused)	44A
Mottram Viaduct Viaduct	44A
MOULDSWORTH	28A
Mouldsworth GF	42B
Mount Pleasant Tunnel	38A
MOUNTSORREL (GCR)	23A
Mountsorrel Stone Quarry	11A
Mow Cop LC (CCTV)	42A
Mucky Lane LC (UWK)	10B
MUNCASTER MILL (RER)	33B
MURTHWAITE HALT (RER)	33B
MUSEUM OF SCIENCE & INDUSTRY, MANCHESTER	43B

N

Location	Code
(Nadins Disposal Point)	14C
Nadins Swadlincote GF	14C
Napsbury HABD	9A
NARBOROUGH	10B
Narborough HABD	10B
Narborough LC (CCTV)	10B
Nash's LC (UWC)	26C
Nature Reserve LC (BW)	13A
NAVIGATION ROAD	43S
Navigation Road LC (CCTV)	43S
Naylors LC (UWC)	10B
NEASDEN (LUL)	15A
Neasden Depot (LUL)	15A
Neasden Freight Terminal	15A
Neasden Jn SB (NJ)	1
Neasden South Jn	15A
Neasden South Sidings	15A
Neilson Street Viaduct	18A
Neilsons Sidings	9D
NELSON	45C
NESTON	39A
NETHERFIELD	13B
Netherfield HABD	13B
Netherfield Jn	13B
NETHERTOWN	35A
Nettle Hill Viaduct (M6)	5A
New & Old Bank Sdgs, Toton	14A
New Ballast Sidings, Bescot	21A
NEW BIGGIN (disused)	36D
New Biggin Sidings	36D
New Bilton	5A
NEW BRIGHTON	39A
New Cliffe Hill: Stud Farm Quarry	14C
NEW LANE	41A
New Lane LC (AHBC)	41A
New Middle Sdgs, Crewe	7A
NEW MILLS CENTRAL	44B
New Mills Central SB (NM)	44B
NEW MILLS NEWTOWN	43E
New Mills South Jn SB (NS)	44B
New Mills Tunnel	44B
New Mills Viaduct	44B
New Street Tunnels, Birmingham	20
New Wetmore Depot & Sidings, Burton	26C
NEWARK CASTLE	13B
Newark Castle LC (CCTV)	13B
Newark Crossing	13B
Newark Crossing East Jn	13B
Newark Crossing South Jn	13B
Newbold Jn	5A
NEWBY BRIDGE HALT (LHR)	34D
Newcastle Jn	26C
NEWSTEAD	12A
Newstead LC (AHBC)	12A
Newton (Farm) LC (UWW)	26B
NEWTON for Hyde	44A
Newton Heath TMD	45A
Newton Jn, Bescot	21A
Newton Viaduct	44A
Newton Viaduct, Newton-le-Willows	29C
NEWTON-LE-WILLOWS	29C
Newton-le-Willows Jn	29C
Newtown Tunnel	44B
Newtown Viaduct	44B
Noose Lane LC (CCTV)	21A
Norbury Hollow LC (MG)	43S
Norbury Viaduct	43S
Normanton LC (10) (AHBC-X)	13B
North Acton Jn (LUL)	16A
North Erewash LC (CCTV)	13A
NORTH HARROW (LUL)	15B
North Jn, Appleby	36C
North London Waste Terminal, Cricklewood	8B
North Lune Viaduct	32A
(North Mersey Jn)	40A
(North Rode Jn)	42B
North Rode Viaduct (R. Dane)	42B
North Side Up Sdgs, Rugby	5A
North Stafford Jn, Crewe	7A
North Stafford Jn, Stenson	26C

Name	Code
North Tunnel Jns, Birmingham	20
NORTH WEMBLEY	2B
North Wembley Jn	2B
North, Bottom End Sidings, Carnforth	31B
NORTHAMPTON	4A
NORTHAMPTON & LAMPORT RAILWAY (NLR)	4E
Northampton No.2 Jn	4A
Northampton North Jn	4A
Northampton South Jn	4A
Northampton Up Sidings	4A
NORTHAMPTONSHIRE IRONSTONE RAILWAY	4D
Northchurch HABD	3A
Northchurch Tunnels	3A
Northenden GF	43S
Northenden Jn SB (NJ)	43S
Northenden, Langley Lane	43S
NORTHFIELD	23B
Northgate Street Tunnels	28A
NORTHOLT (LUL)	16A
Northolt Jn	16A
NORTHOLT PARK	16A
Northolt Park Jn	16A
NORTHWICH	42B
Northwich East Jn	42B
Northwich Oakleigh Sdgs	42B
Northwich South Jn	42B
Northwich Station Jn	42B
Northwich West Jn	42B
NORTHWICK PARK (LUL)	15A
NORTHWOOD (LUL)	15B
NORTHWOOD HALT (SVR)	24A
NORTHWOOD HILLS (LUL)	15B
NORTON BRIDGE (disused)	6B
Norton Bridge Jn	6B
Norton Jn & SB (NJ)	23C
NORTON LAKESIDE (CR)	22D
Norton LC (R/G-X)	29B
Norton SB (NN)	29B
Nortonside LC (UWC)	23C
NOTTINGHAM	13A
Nottingham and Beeston Canal	13A
Nottingham East Jn	13A
NOTTINGHAM EXPRESS TRANSIT (NET)	49
Nottingham Road Viaduct, Derby	12A
Nottingham TMD (NM)	13A
Nottingham West Jn	13A
NUNCKLEY HILL (GCR)	23A
NUNEATON	5B
(Nuneaton Midland Jn)	5B
Nuneaton North Jn	5B
Nuneaton South Jn	5B

O

Name	Code
(OA &GB Jn)	44A
OAKENGATES	27A
Oakengates Tunnel	27A
OAKHAM	10B
Oakham Crossing SB (OM)	10B
Oakham LC (MCB) & SB (O)	10B
Oakley HABD	9C
(Oakley Jn)	9C
Oakley Viaducts	9C
Octel Sdg GF	42B
Oddingley LC (MCB-OD)	23C
Oil Sdgs GF, Burn Naze	47A
Old Cliffe Hill Sdg	14B
Old Dalby Test Centre	11C
(Old Harpenden Jn)	9B
OLD HILL	24A
Old Hill (Blackheath) Tunnel	24A
(Old Oak Jn)	1
Old Oak Sidings, Willesden	1
OLD ROAN	40A
Old Side Exchange Sidings, Warrington	29B
Old Trent Dyke Viaduct	13B
Olive Mount Cutting	41B
Olive Mount Jn	41B
Olive Mount Tunnel	41B
OLTON	19A
Orams No.1 LC (UWG)	46A
Orams No.3 LC (UWG)	46A
Ordsall Lane Jn	43N
Oriel Road Tunnel	40A
Ormside Viaduct	36C
ORMSKIRK	40A
ORRELL	40A
ORRELL PARK	40A
Orston Lane LC (MCB-OD)	13B

Name	Code
Oubeck	31A
Overbury Street Tunnel	38A
OVERPOOL	37C
Oxenholme North Jn	31C
Oxenholme South Jn	31C
OXENHOLME: The Lake District	31C
OXFORD	17B
Oxford Canal (Heyford)	17B
Oxford Canal (Kilsby)	4B
Oxford Canal (Oxford North)	17B
Oxford Canal (Tackley)	17B
Oxford Canal Jn	17B
Oxford Canal, Rugby	5A
Oxford Down Sidings	17B
Oxford Engineers Sidings	17B
Oxford North Jn	17B
OXFORD PARKWAY	17A
Oxford Road East Jn	43N
Oxford Road West Jn	43N
Oxford Station North Jn	17B
Oxford Station South Jn	17B
Oxford Up Sidings	17B
Oxheys Loop	31A
Oxley (Stafford Road) Jn	22A
Oxley Sth Yd Shunters cabin (CS)	22A
Oxley T&RSMD (OY)	22A
Oxley Up Sidings	22A
Oxley Viaduct	22A

P

Name	Code
PADGATE	43D
(Padgate Jn)	43D
Padge Hall Farm LC (UWC)	10B
Pages LC (UWG)	47C
PAGE'S PARK (LBR)	3D
Paradise Jn	38A
PARBOLD	41A
Parbold LC (MCB) & SB (PD)	41A
PARK (disused)	43N
Park Farm No.1 (UWC)	19A
Park Farm No.2 (UWC)	19A
Park Hall Viaduct	25A
Park House Farm LC (MWLO)	34B
Park Lane Jn	25A
Park North (UWG)	34B
Park Royal Jn	16A
Park Royal Sidings	16A
Park South Jn	34B
Park South LC (MCB) & SB (PS)	34B
PARK STREET	2B
(Park Street Jn)	43N
Park Street Tunnel, Walsall	21A
Parkhead Viaduct	21A
Parkhouse LC (UWC)	35C
Parkside Jn	29C
Parrott's No.1 LC (UWG)	22A
PARTON	35A
Parton North Jn	35A
Parton South Jn	35A
PATRICROFT	43C
Pattersons LC (UWC)	10B
PEAK FOREST (disused)	43E
Peak Forest Canal (Guide Bridge East Jn)	44A
Peak Forest Canal (Woodley)	44A
Peak Forest Holding Sidings (Peak Forest Jn)	43E
Peak Forest South SB (PF)	43E
Peak Forest Tunnel	43E
PEAK RAIL (PR)	14D
PEARTREE	26C
Peasley Cross	41B
PEMBERTON	30A
Pemberton Tunnel	30A
Pendlebury Tunnels	46C
PENDLETON (disused)	46C
Pendleton Tunnels	46C
Pendleton Viaduct	46C
Penketh Hall LC (UWG)	37B
PENKRIDGE	22A
Penkridge Down & Up HABDs	22A
Penkridge Viaduct (R. Penk)	22A
Penrith GF and Sdgs	32B
Penrith Middle Jn	32B
Penrith North Jn	32B
Penrith South Jn	32B
PENRITH: The North Lakes	32B
Pensnett	24A
Pentre LC (UWG)	27B
Pentre Sea Wall	27B
PENYFFORD	27C
Penyfford Cement Works	27C

Name	Code
Penyfford LC (UWC)	27C
Penyfford SB (PD)	27C
Peover Viaduct	42B
PERIVALE (LUL)	16A
PERRY BARR	20
Perry Barr North Jn	20
Perry Barr South Jn	20
Perry Barr West Jn	20
Pershore Road Tunnel	23B
Peto/Betts Viaduct	21A
Petteril Bridge Jn	32C
Philips Park South Jn	43N
Philips Park West Jn	43N
Pic Tor Tunnel	43E
Pic Tor Viaduct	43E
Picko Tunnels	38A
Pilkington Viaduct	41B
Pilton Sdg LC (UWC)	10B
Pinfold LC (MCB)	26C
PINNER (LUL)	15B
Pinxton LC (CCTV)	12A
Pirton LC (AHBC)	23C
PITSFORD & BRAMPTON (NLR)	4E
PLEASINGTON	46A
Pleasington Golf Club No.1 LC (UWG)	46A
Pleasington Viaduct (R. Darwen)	46A
Pleck Jn, Walsall	21A
Plemstall LC (UWG)	28A
Plot LC (UWC)	13B
PLUMLEY	42B
Plumley West SB (PY)	42B
(Plumpton Jn)	34A
Plumpton Loop	32B
PLUMSTREE (disused)	11C
PMOL Depot, Stourbridge	24A
Poachins LC (UWC)	10B
POLESWORTH	5B
Polesworth North Viaduct	5B
Polesworth South Viaduct (R. Anker)	5B
Pony Crossing LC (UWC), Woburn	3C
Pool Hey LC (AHBC)	41A
(Port Carlisle Branch Jn)	32C
Port of Barrow	34B
Port of Heysham LC (UWG)	31B
Port of Workington	35B
PORT SUNLIGHT	37C
Portland Street LC (CCTV)	40B
Portobello Jn	21A
Portsmouth LC (R/G)	45C
Potters Lock No. 1 LC	14A
POULTON-LE-FYLDE	47A
(Poulton-le-Fylde Jn)	47A
Pound Land LC	21A
Power Box Sidings (Preston)	30C
POYNTON	42B
PRESCOT	41B
PRESTBURY	42B
Prestbury Tunnel	42B
PRESTON	30C
Preston Brook HABD	29A
Preston Brook Tunnel	29A
Preston Docks	30C
Preston Fylde Jn	30C
Preston North Jn	30C
Preston PSB (PN)	30C
Preston Ribble Jn	30C
PRESTON ROAD (LUL)	15A
Preston South Jn	30C
PRIMROSE HILL (disused)	1
Primrose Hill Jn	1
Primrose Hill Tunnels	1
Primrose Hill Viaduct	1
Primrose Viaduct	36A
PRINCES RISBOROUGH	16B
Princes Risborough Jn	16B
Princess Royal Distribution Centre	2A
Prologis Park	18B
Proof House Jn Viaduct	20
Proof House Jns	20
Pulford LC (AHBC)	27C
Pump House LC (UWG)	35A
Punch Bowl Viaduct	31B
(Pye Bridge Jn)	12A

Q

Name	Code
QUAINTON ROAD	15C
(Quainton Road Jn)	15C
Queen Aethelfreda Viaduct	37A
Queens Head Scrapyard	20
Queens Head Viaduct, Birmingham	20
QUEEN'S PARK	1
Queens Park Jn	1

Name	Code
Queens Road Depot (Metrolink)	48N
Quintinshill	33A
Quintinshill GSP	33A
QUORN & WOODHOUSE (GCR)	23A

R

Name	Code
RADCLIFFE (Notts)	13B
Radcliffe Viaduct	13B
Radford Jn	13A
RADLETT	9A
Radlett Aggregates Terminal	9A
Radlett Jn	9A
RADWAY GREEN (disused)	7A
Radway Green LC (CCTV)	7A
Radwell Viaducts	9C
Raikes Viaduct	46B
Railway Age Heritage Centre, Crewe	7A
RAILWAY TECHNICAL CENTRE (ZA)	11B
RAINFORD	40A
Rainford Jn SB (RJ)	40A
RAINHILL	41B
RAMSBOTTOM (ELR)	45A
RAMSGREAVE & WILPSHIRE	36A
Ratcliffe Jn	11A
Ratcliffe North Jn	11A
Ratcliffe-on-Soar Power Station	11A
RAVENGLASS (RER)	33B
RAVENGLASS AND ESKDALE RAILWAY (RER)	33B
RAVENGLASS for ESKDALE	34C
(Ravenhead Jn)	41B
Ravenhead Works	41B
RAVENSTOR (EVR)	12A
RAWTENSTALL (ELR)	45A
Ray Street Gridiron	8C
Rearsby LC (AHBC)	10B
Reception Emergency Power GF	43N
RECREATION GROUND (SGLR)	12B
Rectory Jn	13B
(Reddish Jn)	44A
REDDISH NORTH	44A
REDDISH SOUTH	43S
Reddish Viaduct	44A
REDDITCH	23B
Redhill Tunnels, Trent	11A
Regent Road LC (AOCL)	40A
Regents Canal (Camden Bank)	1
Regents Canal (Marylebone)	15A
Regents Canal (St. Pancras)	8A
Regents Canal Jn	8A
Reservoir Jn	17C
Ribble or Sherif Brow Viaduct	36B
RIBBLE STEAM RAILWAY	30C
Ribble Viaduct, Preston	30C
Ribble Viaduct, Settle	36B
RIBBLEHEAD	36B
Ribblehead GF	36B
Ribblehead Viaduct	36B
RICE LANE	40A
Rickerscote Jn	22A
RICKMANSWORTH (LUL)	15B
Rickmansworth North Sidings (LUL)	15B
Rickmansworth South Sidings (LUL)	15B
Ridgemont LC (CCTV)	3C
RIDGMONT	3C
Rigby Road Depot (Blackpool Trams)	47E
Rigg LC (UWG)	33A
Rippings LC (UWC)	10B
Rippins Main LC (UWC)	10B
Risehill Tunnel	36B
RISHTON	45B
Rishton Tunnel	45B
River Alne	19A
River Alt Viaduct	40B
River Alun (Caergwrle)	27C
River Alun (Rossett Jn)	27C
River Amber (Ambergate)	12A
River Anker Viaduct	5B
River Avon Viaduct (Eckington)	23C
River Avon Viaducts (Leamington)	18A
River Avon Viaducts (Warwick)	18A
River Blythe Viaduct	25A
River Bollin (Ashley)	43F
River Bollin (Macclesfield)	42B
River Brent (Neasden)	15A
River Brent Viaduct (Castle Bar Park)	16A
River Calder	35A
River Chater	10B
River Cherwell (Heyford)	17B
River Cherwell (Reservoir Jn)	17C
River Cherwell (Tackley)	17B
River Clywedog Viaduct	27C

Name	Code
River Cole (Earleswood)	19A
River Cole (Tyseley)	19B
River Cole (Whitlocks End)	19A
River Cole Viaduct	18C
River Colne (Radlett)	9A
River Colne Viaduct (Denham)	16B
River Dane (Middlewich)	42B
River Dee Viaduct (Hawarden Bridge)	27C
River Derwent (Ambergate)	12A
River Derwent (Derby)	11B
River Derwent Viaducts (Ambergate)	12A
River Devon (Bottesford)	13B
River Devon Viaduct (Newark)	13B
River Douglas Viaduct (Rufford)	47C
River Dove Viaduct	26C
River Ellen Viaducts	35C
River Erewash (Attenborough)	13A
River Erewash (Ilkeston)	14A
River Erewash (Ironville)	12A
River Erewash (Toton)	14A
River Erewash (Trowell)	14A
River Eye (Melton Mowbray)	10B
River Eye (Whissendine)	10B
River Gade	15B
River Gowy (Mickle Trafford)	28A
River Gowy (Stanlow)	28A
River Goyt (Whaley Bridge)	43E
River Great Ouse Viaduct, Bedford	9C
River Irwell (Manchester Victoria)	43N
River Irwell (Ordsall Chord)	43N
River Keer (Carnforth)	31B
River Leen	13A
River Leen Viaduct	13D
River Lune (Tebay)	32A
River Mersey (East Didsbury)	43S
River Mersey (Warrington)	29B
River Nene Viaducts, Northampton	4A
River Pettrill (Penrith)	32B
River Ribble Viaduct	31B
River Rother (Horns Bridge)	12A
River Soar (Barrow-upon-Soar)	11A
River Soar (Loughborough)	11A
River Soar (Narborough)	10B
River Soar Viaduct, Croft	10B
River Sow	6B
River Sowe (Coventry Arena)	18B
River Stour (Cradley Heath)	24A
River Tame (Bescot)	21A
River Tame (Darleston Jn)	21A
River Tame (Hamstead)	20
River Tame (Lichfield)	6A
River Tame (Washwood Heath)	20
River Tame (Water Orton)	25A
River Tame Flood Arches (Coleshill)	25A
River Tame Viaduct (Aston)	20
River Tern	27C
River Thame Bridge (Aylesbury)	15C
River Thame Viaduct (Haddenham & Thame Parkway)	16C
River Trent (Stoke on Trent)	26B
River Trent Viaduct (Armitage)	6A
River Trent Viaduct (Rugeley)	6A
River Trent Viaduct (Sheet Stores Jn)	13C
River Trent Viaduct (Stone)	6B
River Trent Viaduct, Chellaston	13C
River Trent Viaduct, Drakelow	14C
River Waver Viaduct	35C
River Welland (Market Harborough)	10A
River Wenning (Wennington)	31B
River Winster	34A
River Wreak	11A
River Yarrow Viaduct	30B
Riverside Sdgs, Northampton	4A
Roade Cutting	4A
Roade HABD	4A
ROBY	41B
Roby Jn	41B
ROCHDALE	45A
Rochdale Canal (Deansgate)	43N
Rochdale Canal (Hall Royd Jn)	45A
Rochdale Canal (Mills Hill)	45A
Rochdale Canal (Philips Park West Jn)	43N
Rochdale East Jn	45A
Rochdale West Jn	45A
Rochdale West SB (TH)	45A
ROCK FERRY	39A
Rock Ferry North Jn	39A
Rock Ferry South Jn	39A
Rockcliffe Hall Tunnel	27B
Rodidge LC (MCG)	25A
ROLLESTON	13B
Rolleston LC (MGB-OD)	13B
Rolleston Mill LC (UWC)	13B
ROMILEY	44A
Romiley Jn	44A
Rood End Yard	21A
Roodee Jn	28A
Roodee Viaduct (R. Dee)	28A
ROOSE	34B
ROSE GROVE	45C
Rose Grove West Jn	45C
ROSE HILL MARPLE	44A
Rossett Jn	27C
Rossett LC (R/G)	27C
Rothery LC (UWC)	35C
ROTHLEY (GCR)	23A
Round Oak Steel Terminal	24A
Roundham LC (R/G-X)	17B
Rowes LC (UWC)	26C
ROWLEY REGIS	24A
ROWSLEY SOUTH (PR)	14D
Royal Seaforth Container Terminal	40A
Ruabon Road Tunnel	27C
Ruckley Viaduct	22A
RUDDINGTON FIELDS (GCRN)	23A
RUFFORD	47C
Rufford LC (MCB) & SB (RD)	47C
RUGBY	5A
Rugby North Jn	5A
Rugby Rail Operating Centre	5A
Rugby Signalling Control Centre	5A
Rugby South Jn	5A
Rugby Trent Valley Jn	5A
Rugeley 'B' Power Station	6A
Rugeley Down GFs	6A
Rugeley North Jn	6A
Rugeley Power Station Jn	22B
(Rugeley South Jn)	6A
RUGELEY TOWN	22B
RUGELEY TRENT VALLEY	6A
Ruislip Depot (LUL)	16A
RUISLIP GARDENS (LUL)	16A
Ruislip Gardens Jn	16A
RUNCORN	37A
Runcorn Bridge (R. Mersey)	37A
RUNCORN EAST	29B
Runcorn Jn	37A
Runcorn Viaduct North (R. Mersey)	37A
Runcorn Viaduct South	37A
RUSDEN (RHTS)	9F
RUSDEN HISTORIC TRANSPORT SOCIETY (RHTS)	9F
RUSHCLIFFE HALT (GCRN)	23A
Russell Street Tunnel	38A
RUTLAND RAILWAY MUSEUM (RRM)	10D
RYDER BROW	43N
Ryecroft Jn, Walsall	21A

S

Name	Code
Sadler's LC (UWC)	23C
ST. ALBANS ABBEY	2B
ST. ALBANS CITY	9A
St. Andrews Jn, Birmingham	20
ST. ANNES-ON-THE-SEA	47B
ST. BEES	35A
St. Bees LC (MCB) & SB	35A
(St. Helens Canal)	41B
St. Helens Canal Viaduct	37B
ST. HELENS CENTRAL	41B
ST. HELENS JUNCTION	41B
(St. Helens Stn Jn)	41B
ST. JAMES (closed)	38A
St. James Tunnels	38A
St. John's Wood Tunnel	15A
St. Luke's Jn, Southport	41A
St. Mary's North Jn	12A
St. Mary's South Jn	12A
ST. MICHAEL'S	38A
St. Michael's Tunnel	38A
St. Pancras Signalling Room (HS1)	8A
St. Pancras Station Box	8A
SALFORD CENTRAL	43N
SALFORD CRESCENT	43N
Salford Hope Street	43N
Salford West Jn	43N
Salford, Windsor Bridge Sdgs	46C
Salop Goods Jn SB (SG), Crewe	7A
Salop Goods Loop Jn	7A
Saltcoats LC (MCG)	34C
Salthouse Jn	34B
Salthouse Jn GF	34B
Salthouse No. 1 LC (UWG)	34C
Salthouse No.3 LC (UWG)	34C
Salthouse Viaduct	34B
(Saltley PSB)	20
Saltney Jn	28A
SALWICK	47A
SANDBACH	42B
Sandbach North Jn	42B
Sandbach South Jn	42B
Sandford Brake Farm LC (UWC)	17B
SANDHILLS	40A
Sandhills Jn	40A
Sandicare Ballast Sidings	14A
Sandringham Avenue LC (UWG)	39B
Sandscale/Br. Cellophane LC (AOCL)	34B
SANDWELL & DUDLEY	21A
Sandy Lane LC (AHBC-X)	17B
SANKEY for Penketh	38B
Sankey Jn (Earlestown)	41B
(Sankey Jn) (Warrington)	38B
Sankey Viaduct, Earlestown	41B
Sankey Viaduct, Warrington	38B
Sark Viaduct (Eng/Scot border)	33A
SAUNDERTON	16B
Saunderton Summit	16B
Saunderton Tunnel	16B
(Sawley Jn)	11B
Sawley LC (CCTV)	11B
Saxelby Tunnel	11C
Saxondale LC (UWC)	13B
Scarrington Lane LC (19) (AHBC-X)	13B
Scholes Tunnel	41B
(Scout Green SB)	32A
Scout Tunnel	44A
Scropton LC (MCG) & SB	26C
Scropton Mill Lane LC (UWC)	26C
(Seacombe Jn)	39A
SEAFORTH & LITHERLAND	40A
Searchlight Lane HABD	6B
Searchlight Lane Jn	6B
SEASCALE	34C
Seaton Tunnel	10A
Seaton Viaduct	10A
SEER GREEN AND JORDANS	16B
(Sefton Jn)	40A
SELLAFIELD	35A
Sellafield SB (S)	35A
Sellafield Works	35A
Sellafield/Calder Viaduct	35A
SELLY OAK	23B
Selly Oak Viaduct	23B
Serjeants LC (UWC)	26B
SETTLE	36B
Settle Jn	36B
Settle Jn SB (SJ)	36B
Settle or Church Viaduct	36B
Severn Bridge Jn SB (SBJ)	27A
SEVERN VALLEY RAILWAY (SVR)	24A
Severn Viaduct	27A
Sewstern Lane LC (MSL-X)	13B
SHACKERSTONE (BSR)	5C
Shallowford HABDs	6B
Shap Quarry	32A
Shap Summit GSP	32A
Shap Up GF	32A
Sharnbrook Jn	9D
Sharnbrook Summit	9D
Sharnbrook Tunnel	9D
Sharnbrook Viaducts	9C
Sharston Jn	43S
Shaw's LC (R/G)	41A
Sheepwash Viaduct	12A
Sheet Stores Jn	13A
(Shelton Works)	42A
SHENSTONE	25A
Shenstone Viaduct	25A
SHENTON (BSR)	5C
Sherbourne Viaduct	18B
SHIFNAL	22A
Shifnal Viaduct	22A
Shilton HABDs	5A
SHIREBROOK	12A
SHIRLEY	19A
Shotlock Hill Tunnel	36C
SHOTTLE (EVR)	12A
SHOTTON HIGH LEVEL	27C
SHOTTON LOW LEVEL	27B
Shotwick	39C
Shotwick	39B
Shotwick GF	39C
SHREWSBURY	27A
Shrewsbury Line Jn, Crewe	7A
Shropshire Union Canal (Calveley)	28C
Shropshire Union Canal (Chester)	28A
Shugborough Tunnel	6A
Shugborough Viaduct (R. Trent)	6A
(Siddick Jn)	35B
Sideway Jn	6D
SILEBY	11A
Sileby Jn	11A
SILECROFT	34C
Silecroft LC (MCB) & SB	34C
Silkstream Jn	9A
Silo Curve Jn	8A
SILVERDALE	34A
Silverdale LC (AHBC)	34A
Silverdale Tunnel	6C
SINFIN CENTRAL (disused)	26C
SINFIN NORTH (disused)	26C
Single & Double Jn	3C
Single Line Jn (Bletchley)	3B
Sir Philip Rose's Viaduct	16B
Skeffington Road LC (TMO)	30C
Skelly Crag LC (MCG)	34B
Skelton Jn	43S
Skew Bridge	30C
Skew Bridge Jn	30C
Slade Lane Jn	43S
Sleights LC (CCTV)	12A
Slutchers Lane LC (FP)	29B
SMALL HEATH	19B
Small Heath North Jn	19B
Small Heath South Jn	19B
Smardale Viaduct	36C
SMETHWICK GALTON BRIDGE	21A
Smethwick Jn	21A
SMETHWICK ROLFE STREET	20
SMETHWICK WEST (disused)	21A
Smithdown Lane Tunnel	38A
SMITHY BRIDGE	45A
Smithy Bridge LC (MCB)	45A
SNIBSTON COLLIERY RAILWAY (Closed)	14E
Snow Hill Tunnel, Birmingham	20
Snow Hill Viaduct	20
Sod Hall LC (UWG)	47C
Soho East GF	20
Soho East Jn	20
Soho North Jn	20
Soho South Jn	20
Soho T&RSMD	20
Soho Viaduct	20
SOLIHULL	19A
Somerton LC (UWC)	17B
Songar Grange Farm LC (UWC)	19A
Sough Tunnel	46B
Soulbury Road HABD	3A
Souldern No.1 Viaduct	16C
Souldern No.2 Viaduct	17C
SOUTH GREENFORD	16A
SOUTH HAMPSTEAD	1
South Hampstead Tunnels	1
South Harrow Tunnel	16A
South Jn, Southport	40B
SOUTH KENTON	2B
SOUTH RUISLIP	16A
South Tunnel Jn, Birmingham	20
South West Sidings, Willesden	1
SOUTH WIGSTON	10B
South Yard, Crewe	7A
SOUTHPORT	41A
Southport Goods Yard GF	41A
Southport Sidings, Wigan	30A
Southport Stn Jn	41A
Southwaite HABD	32B
Sowe Viaduct	18B
Sowters LC (UWC)	12A
Specklies LC (UWC)	10B
Speke East Jn	37A
Speke Sidings	38A
Speke Sidings GF No. 1	38A
Speke West Jn	38A
SPELLOW (closed)	40A
Spellow No.1 Tunnel	40A
Spellow No.2 Tunnel	40A
Spencers LC (UWG)	31B
Spetchley HABD	23C
Spetchley North Jn	23C
Spetchley South Jn	23C
SPITAL	37C
Spon End Viaduct (Coventry)	18B
SPONDON	11B
(Spondon Jn)	11B
Spondon LC (MCB-OD)	11B
Spring Gardens Viaduct	44E
SPRING ROAD	19A

Name	Ref
Spring Road Covered Way	19A
SPRING VILLAGE (TSR)	22E
Springs Branch Depot, Wigan	30A
Springs Branch Jn	30A
Springs Branch Jn (Slow lines)	30A
Springs Branch No.1 Jn	30A
Spurrier's No.2 LC (UWC)	26C
SQUIRES GATE	47B
STAFFORD	6B
Stafford & Worcester Canal (Four Ashes)	22A
Stafford & Worcester Canal (Oxley)	22A
(Stafford Jn), Wellington (Salop)	27A
Stafford North Jn	6B
Stafford Royal Mail Terminal	6B
Stafford South Jn	6B
Stafford Trent Valley Jn No. 1	6B
Stainforth Tunnel	36B
Stainton Crossing	33C
Stainton Jn	33C
(Staley & Milbrook Jn)	44A
Stallington LC (CCTV)	26B
STALYBRIDGE	44A
Stalybridge Jn	44A
Stalybridge Old Tunnel	44A
Stalybridge Tunnel Jn	44A
Stalybridge Viaduct	44A
STAMFORD	10B
Stamford Tunnel	10B
Standedge Tunnel	44A
Stanford Road Viaduct, R Soar (GCRN)	23A
Stangrah Farm LC (UWG)	34C
STANLOW & THORNTON	28A
Stansfield Hall Jn	45A
Stanton Gate Down Sdgs	14A
Stanton Grove	40A
Stanton Tunnel	11C
Starr Gate Tram Depot (Blackpool Trams)	47F
Stathams LC (OMSL)	26B
Station Road LC (CCTV), Hoylake	39B
STAVELEY	31C
Staveley LC (ABCL)	31C
Staythorpe Crossing LC (MCB-OD)	13B
Steamtown, Carnforth	31B
STECHFORD	18C
Stechford North Jn	18C
Stechford South Jn	18C
Stechford Viaduct	18C
STEEPLE GRANGE LIGHT RAILWAY (SGLR)	12B
STEEPLEHOUSE JUNCTION (SGLR)	12B
STEEPLEHOUSE QUARRY (SGLR)	12B
Stenson Jn	26C
Stenson Raynors LC (UWC)	26C
STEWARTBY	3C
Stewartby Brickworks LC (CCTV)	3C
Stockbeck Viaduct	36A
(Stockingford)	25A
STOCKPORT	43S
(Stockport Canal)	44A
Stockport Carriage Sidings	43S
Stockport No.1 SB (ST1)	43S
Stockport No.2 SB (ST2)	43S
Stockport Viaduct	43S
Stockton Brook Tunnel	26B
Stoke Jn	26B
Stoke Lane LC (AHBC-X)	13B
Stoke Line Jn, Crewe	7A
STOKE MANDEVILLE	15C
Stoke North Jn	26B
Stoke Works Jn	23C
Stoke/Seven Arches Viaduct	26B
STOKE-ON-TRENT	26B
Stoke-on-Trent SCC (SOT/CH)	26B
Stoke-on-Trent Works (ZJ)	7B
Stokyn Lodge LC (UWC)	27B
STONE	6B
Stone Cabin LC (UWG)	34B
Stone Jn	6B
Stonebridge Jn	2A
STONEBRIDGE PARK	2A
Stonebridge Park Depot	2A
Stonebridge Park Repair Shops	2A
STONEHENGE WORKS (LBR)	3D
Stoneleigh Road Viaduct	18B
Stoney Low Tunnel	6C
Stoneyfield Viaduct	9A
Stoneyford Siding (oou)	12A
Stores Siding GF	2A
Stourbridge Jn GF	24A
STOURBRIDGE JUNCTION	24A
Stourbridge LMD	24A
Stourbridge Middle Jn	24A
Stourbridge North Jn	24A
STOURBRIDGE TOWN	24A
Stourbridge Viaduct	24A
Stowe Hill Tunnel	4A
Strand Road LC, Liverpool Docks	40A
STRATFORD-UPON-AVON	19N
Stratford-upon-Avon Canal (Lapworth)	19A
Stratford-upon-Avon Canal (Stratford)	19A
Stratford-upon-Avon Canal (Whitlocks End)	19A
STRATFORD-UPON-AVON PARKWAY	19A
STRINES	44B
STYAL	42B
Styal Jn	42B
Substation (Willesden) LC (UWC)	1
SUDBURY & HARROW ROAD	16A
SUDBURY HILL, HARROW	16A
Sudbury Jn (former Brent Jns)	2A
Sudbury LC (MCB) & SB (SY)	26C
Sudbury Viaduct (R. Dove)	26C
SUMMERSEAT (ELR)	45A
Summit East Tunnel	45A
Summit Tunnel	45A
Summit West Tunnel	45A
Sundon Jn	9B
Sunny Hill	26C
SUTTON COLDFIELD	20
Sutton Coldfield Tunnel	20
Sutton Cutting, St. Helens	41B
Sutton Forest LC (AHBC)	12A
Sutton Jn LC (CCTV)	12A
Sutton Oak, St. Helens	41B
SUTTON PARK (disused)	25A
SUTTON PARKWAY	12A
Sutton Tunnel	29B
Sutton Weaver GSP	29B
Sutton Weaver HABD	29B
(Swains Park Sdgs)	14C
Swainsley Viaduct, R. Derwent	12A
Swan Side Viaduct	36A
SWANBOURNE (disused)	17A
Swanbourne Siding	3B
Swannington LC (AHBC)	14C
SWANWICK JN (MR-B)	12A
SWINTON	46C
Switches Farm LC (UWC)	36A
(Sydney Bridge Jn)	7A
Syke Foot LC (UWG)	36D
Sysonby Grange LC (UWC)	10B
SYSTON	10B
Syston East Jn	10B
Syston North Jn	10B
Syston South Jn	10B
T	
TACKLEY	17B
Tackley LC (UWC)	17B
TAME BRIDGE PARKWAY	21A
Tame Valley Canal (Aqueduct)	21A
Tame Viaducts	44A
TAMWORTH (HIGH LEVEL)	25A
TAMWORTH (LOW LEVEL)	5B
Tamworth HABD	25A
Tamworth Viaduct (HL, R. Anker)	25A
Tamworth Viaduct (LL, R. Anker)	5B
Tarn Gate LC (UWG)	47A
Tasker Street, Walsall	21A
Tatterthwaite LC (UWG)	31B
Taylor Street	46A
Taylor's Lane Power Station	1
Taylors LC (UWC)	13B
Tebay North & South Jns	32A
Teigh LC (FPG)	10B
TELFORD CENTRAL	27A
Telford International Railfreight Terminal (TIRFT)	27A
TELFORD STEAM RAILWAY (TSR)	22E
Tesco' Covered Way	16B
THATTO HEATH	41B
THE GREEN (RER)	33B
THE HAWTHORNS	21A
THE LAKES	19A
The Oaks LC (UWG)	46B
THORNTON CLEVELEYS (disused)	47A
Thornton LC (TMOB)	47A
Thorpes Bridge Jn	43N
Three Spires Jn	18B
THURGARTON	13B
Thurgarton LC (AHBC)	13B
Thurmaston WILD	10B
(Tibshelf & Blackwell Branch Jn)	12A
TILE HILL	18B
Tinwell LC (UWC)	10B
TIPTON	21A
Toadmoor Tunnel	12A
TODMORDEN	45A
Todmorden Viaduct	45A
Todmorden Viaduct Jn	45A
Tolans LC (UWG)	39B
Tolney Lane Viaduct	13B
Tonge Viaduct	46B
Topley Pike GF (oou)	43E
Totley Tunnel	44C
Totley Tunnel East SB (TE)	44C
Toton Centre Jn	14A
Toton Loco Stabling Sidings	14A
Toton No.4 LC	14A
Toton North Jn	14A
Toton North Yard	14A
Toton South Jn (HL Lines)	14A
Toton TMD (TO)	14A
Toton West Yard	14A
Tottenham North Curve Tunnels	8A
TOWN GREEN	40A
Towneley LC (MCB)	45C
Townley Tunnel	45C
Trafford Depot & Control Centre (Metrolink)	48S
TRAFFORD PARK	43D
Trafford Park East Jn	43N
Trafford Park Sidings	43N
Trafford Park West Jn	43N
Trent & Merset Canal (Rugeley Town)	22B
Trent & Mersey Canal (Armitage)	6A
Trent & Mersey Canal (Castle Donnington)	13C
Trent & Mersey Canal (Chellaston)	13C
Trent & Mersey Canal (Colwich)	6A
Trent & Mersey Canal (Kidsgrove)	42A
Trent & Mersey Canal (Lostock Gralam)	42B
Trent & Mersey Canal (Middlewich)	42B
Trent & Mersey Canal (Sandbach)	42B
Trent & Mersey Canal (Stoke on Trent)	26B
Trent & Mersey Canal (Stone)	6B
Trent East Jns	13A
Trent Fields Viaduct	13B
Trent Gardens LC (UWC)	13B
Trent South Jn	13A
Trent Viaduct, Ratcliffe	11A
(Trent West Jn)	13A
(Trentham North & South Jns)	6D
Trind Sidings	3A
TRING	3A
Tring North Jn	3A
Tring South Jn	3A
Trowell North Jn	14A
Trowell South Jn	14A
Tuebrook Sidings	38A
Tulketh Viaduct	47A
Tunnel Road Tunnels, Edge Hill	38A
Tunnicliffs No. 1 LC (UWC)	26C
Tunstead Sidings GF	43G
Tunstead Works, Buxton	43G
Turton LC (AOCL)	46B
TUTBURY & HATTON	26C
Tutbury Crossing (MCB) & SB (TY)	26C
TYSELEY	19B
Tyseley Carriage Stabling Sidings	19B
Tyseley Depot (TS)	19B
TYSELEY LOCOMOTIVE WORKS (Vintage Trains Trust)	19B
Tyseley No.1 SB (TY1)	19B
Tyseley North Jn	19B
Tyseley South Jn	19B
TYSELEY WARWICK ROAD	19B
U	
Uffington & Barnack LC (MCG)	10B
Uffington SB (UN)	10B
ULVERSTON	34A
Ulverston Canal Viaduct	34A
Ulverston SB (UN)	34A
Underhill LC (UWG)	34B
UNIVERSITY	23B
Up Carriage Line GF, Wembley	2A
UPHOLLAND	40A
Upholland Tunnel	40A
UPPER HOLLOWAY	8A
Upper Holloway SB (UH)	8A
Upper Leigh LC (AHBC-X)	26B
Upper Park Street Tunnels	1
Upper Portland Farm LC (UWC)	12A
Upper Portland LC (AHBC)	12A
Upperby Bridge Jn	32C
Upperby Depot (CL)	32C
Upperby Holding Sidings	32C
Upperby Jn	32C
Upperby Yard GF	32C
Uppermill Viaduct (Saddleworth)	44A
UPTON	39A
URMSTON	43D
UTTOXETER	26C
Uttoxeter SB (UR)	26C
V	
Vale Royal	42B
Vale Royal Viaduct	29A
Vauxhall Jn, Birmingham	20
VERNEY JUNCTION (disused)	17A
Verney Junction LC (UWW)	17A
Very Light Rail Innovation Centre (Dudley)	21A
Victoria Road Tunnel Portal	38A
Virtual Quarry GF, Kingmoor	33C
Vitriol Works SB (VW)	45A
W	
Wadborough LC (AHBC)	23C
WADDESDON (disused)	15C
Wagon Repair GF	32C
WALKDEN	46C
Wallasey Bridge Road LC	39A
WALLASEY GROVE ROAD	39A
WALLASEY VILLAGE	39A
Wallside Sdg, Hall Road	40A
WALSALL	21A
Walsall Canal Aquaduct	21A
Walsall North Jn	21A
Walsall South Jn	21A
WALSDEN	45A
Waltham Nurseries LC (UWG)	34B
WALTON & ANFIELD (closed)	40A
WALTON (Merseyside)	40A
Walton Jn	40A
Walton Old Jn & Sidings	29B
WARCOP (Eden Valley Rly)	36C
WARCOP (Eden)	36C
Wards LC (UWC), Stamford	10B
Wards LC (UWG), Wennington	31B
Wards Sdg GF	10B
Warren House LC (MWL)	12A
WARRINGTON BANK QUAY	29B
WARRINGTON CENTRAL	38B
Warrington Central SB (WC)	38B
Warrington North Jn	29B
Warrington SB (WN)	29B
Warrington South Jn	29B
Warrington Viaduct	38B
WARRINGTON WEST (u/c)	38B
WARWICK	18A
WARWICK PARKWAY	19A
Washstones LC (R/G) (UWCM)	10B
Washwood Heath East Jn	20
Washwood Heath Viaduct	20
Washwood Heath West Jn	20
Washwood Heath Yards	20
Waste Bank Tunnel	36D
Water Eaton Jn	17A
Water Eaton Road Jn	3B
WATER ORTON	25A
Water Orton East Jn	25A
Water Orton West Jn	25A
Water Street Jn	43N
Water Works LC	10C
WATERLOO (Merseyside)	40A
Waterloo Branch Jn	38A
Waterloo LC (CCTV)	40A
Waterslack Quarry LC (UWG)	34A
Waterworks LC (UWC)	25A
Watery Road GF	27C
Watford East Jn (LUL)	15B
WATFORD HIGH STREET	2B
(Watford High Street Jn)	2B
WATFORD JUNCTION	2B
Watford Lodge Tunnel	4B
WATFORD NORTH	2B
(Watford North Jn)	2B
Watford North Jn (LUL)	15B
Watford North LC (ABCL)	2B
Watford South Jn	2B
Watford South Jn (LUL)	15B

Location	Ref
Watford Tunnels	2B
Watford Yard	2B
(Watling Street Jn)	8B
Wavertree Jn	38A
WAVERTREE TECHNOLOGY PARK	41B
Wavertree Viaduct	38A
Way & Works Jn, Derby	11B
Weasels Lodge LC (UWC)	17A
Weaste Depot	43N
Weaver Emergency Crossover	29A
Weaver Jn	29A
Weaver or Frodsham Viaduct	28B
WEDGWOOD	6D
Wedgwood LC (CCTV)	6D
WEDNESBURY TOWN (disused)	21A
(Wednesbury Town Jn)	21A
Wednesfield Heath Tunnel	21A
Weedon Viaduct	4A
Weer Lane LC (UWC)	26C
Weightmans Viaduct	13B
Weights Lane Jn	23B
Welland Valley/Harringworth Viaduct	10A
WELLINGBOROUGH	9D
(Wellingborough Branch Jn)	9D
Wellingborough North Jn	9D
Wellingborough South Jn	9D
Wellingborough Viaduct (R. Ise)	9D
WELLINGTON (Shropshire)	27A
Welsh Harp Viaduct (R. Brent)	9A
Wembley Aggregates Terminal	15A
Wembley Carriage Reception Sidings	2A
WEMBLEY CENTRAL	2A
Wembley Central GF	2B
Wembley Central Jn	
(former Sudbury Jn)	2A
Wembley European Freight Operating	
Centre Yard	2A
Wembley LMD (Chiltern)	15A
Wembley Mainline SB (WM)	2A
WEMBLEY PARK (LUL)	15A
WEMBLEY STADIUM	15A
Wembley Traincare Depot	2A
Wembley Yard SB (WY)	2A
Wembley Yard South Jn	2A
WENDOVER	15C
WENNINGTON	31B
(Wennington Jn)	31B
WEST ALLERTON	38A
West Bradford Road LC (TMO)	36A
(West Denham Jn)	16B
(West Deviation Jn)	37A
WEST HAMPSTEAD	8A
WEST HAMPSTEAD (LUL)	15A
West Hampstead North Jn	8A
West Hampstead PSB (WH)	8A
West Hampstead South Jn	8A
WEST HAMPSTEAD THAMESLINK	8A
WEST LANCASHIRE LIGHT	
RAILWAY (WLLR)	47D
West London Jn (Willesden)	1
West London Waster Refuse	
Transfer Station	16A
West Lune Viaduct	31B
West Midlands Signalling Centre	20
WEST RUISLIP	16A
West Ruislip Up Sidings	16A
WESTHOUGHTON	46C
Westminster Tunnel	40A
Weston Viaduct	28B
Westons LC (UWC)	26B
Wetmore Jn	26C
WHALEY BRIDGE	43E
WHALLEY	36A
Whalley Viaduct	36A
WHATSTANDWELL	12A
Whatstandwell LC (UWC)	12A
Whatstandwell Tunnel	12A
Wheelwright Lane LC	18B
Whissendine LC (MCB)	10B
Whissendine SB (WE)	10B
WHISTON	41B
Whiston Incline	41B
Whitacre East Jn	25A
Whitacre West Jn	25A
Whitbeck LC (AOCL)	34C
WHITEHAVEN	35A
Whitehaven Tunnel	35A
Whitehouse Jn	6A
Whitehouse Tunnel	16B
Whites LC (UWC) (Banbury)	17C
Whites LC (UWC) (Sheet Stores Jn)	13C
Whitley Viaduct	45A
WHITLOCKS END	19A
Whittle International GF	46A
Wichnor Jn	25A
Wichnor Viaduct	25A
WIDMERPOOL (disused)	11C
WIDNES	38B
Widnes Intermodal Rail Depot	37A
(Widnes Jn)	38B
WIDNES SOUTH (disused)	37A
Widnes Train Care Depot	37A
WIDNEY MANOR	19A
Wigan North Jn	30A
WIGAN NORTH WESTERN	30A
Wigan South Jn	30A
Wigan Station Jn	30A
WIGAN WALLGATE	30A
Wigan Wallgate Jn	30A
Wigan Wallgate SB (WW)	30A
Wigston North Jn	10B
Wigston South Jn	10B
WIGTON	35C
Wigton GF	35C
Wigton SB (WN)	35C
Wilkinson Street overbridge	13D
Wilkinson Street Tram Depot &	
Control Rm (NET)	49C
Wilkinsons LC (UWC)	13B
Willaston LC (CCTV) (Gresty Lane)	7A
Willersley Tunnel	12A
Willesden (Acton Branch) Jn	2A
Willesden Brent Sdgs Jn	2A
Willesden Brent Sidings	2A
Willesden Carr. Shed Nth SB (CN)	2A
Willesden Carr. Shed Sth SB (CS)	2A
Willesden Euro Terminal	1
WILLESDEN GREEN (LUL)	15A
Willesden High Level Jn	1
WILLESDEN JN HIGH LEVEL	1
WILLESDEN JN LOW LEVEL	1
Willesden North Jn	1
Willesden Suburban Jn	1
Willesden Traincare Centre	1
Willesden West Jn	8A
WILLINGTON	26C
Willington Down HABD	26C
Willington LC (AHBC)	26C
Willow Lane LC (UWC)	13B
WILLOW TREE HALT (WLLR)	47D
WILMCOTE	19A
WILMSLOW	42B
Wilmslow HABD	42B
Wilmslow North Jn	42B
Wilmslow Old Viaduct	42B
Wilmslow South Jn	42B
Wilmslow Viaduct	42B
WILNECOTE	25A
Wilpshire Tunnel	36A
Wiltshires LC (UWC)	26C
WINDERMERE	31C
Windmill Lane Tunnel	28A
Windridge LC (UWC)	25A
Windsor Bridge North Jn	43N
Windsor Bridge South Jn	43N
Wing LC (UWC)	10B
Wing Tunnel	10B
Wing Viaduct	10B
Wingfield Tunnel	12A
Winnington Works	42B
WINSFORD	29A
Winsford HABD	29A
Winsford SB (WD)	29A
Winsford South Jn	29A
WINSLOW (disused)	17A
Winslow LC (UWC)	17A
Winterbutlee Tunnel	45A
Winwick Jn	29C
WIRKSWORTH (EVR)	12A
WIRRAL TRANSPORT MUSEUM	39D
WISTASTON ROAD (EMD platform)	7A
WITTON	20
WOBURN SANDS	3C
Woburn Sands LC (CCTV)	3C
Wolvercot North Jn	17B
Wolvercot South Jn	17B
Wolvercot Tunnel	17A
WOLVERHAMPTON	21A
Wolverhampton Logistics Centre	21A
Wolverhampton North Jn	22A
Wolverhampton Viaducts	21A
WOLVERTON	3B
Wolverton Works (ZN)	3B
Wolverton/Haversham Viaduct	3B
WOOD END	19A
Wood End Tunnel	19A
WOODLEY	44A
Woodley Jn	44A
Woodleys Farm LC (CCTV)	3C
Woods LC (UWK)	10B
Woods Tenement Farm LC (UWG)	42B
Woodside Farm LC (UWC)	43C
Woodside LC (UWC)	35C
WOODSMOOR	43S
Woodsmoor LC (CCTV)	43S
(Woodstock Curve Jn)	17B
Woodstock Road Jn	17A
Woolton Road Tunnel	38A
Wootton Broadmead LC (CCTV)	3C
WOOTTON WAWEN	19A
Worcester & Birmingham Canal	
(Alvechurch)	23B
Worcester & Birmingham Canal	
(Dunhampstead)	23C
Worcester & Birmingham Canal	
(Lifford)	23B
Worcester & Birmingham Canal	
(Selly Oak)	23B
WORCESTERSHIRE PARKWAY (u/c)	23C
WORKINGTON	35B
Workington Main No.2 SB (WN2)	35B
Workington Main No.3 SB (WN3)	35B
(Workington North - 2010)	35B
Workington Yard	35B
Worleston Viaduct	28C
Wormleighton LC (UWB)	17C
Wraysholme LC (AOCL-B)	34A
WREXHAM CENTRAL	27C
Wrexham Exchange Jn	27C
WREXHAM GENERAL	27C
Wrexham North Jn	27C
Wyfordby LC (MGH)	10B
Wyke Cop LC (AHBC)	41A
WYLDE GREEN	20
Wymington Tunnel	9D
Wymondham LC (MCG)	10B
Wyre Viaduct	31A
WYRLEY & CHESLYN HAY (disused)	22B
Wyrley and Essington Canal	21A
Wyrley and Essington Canal Aquaduct	21A
WYTHALL	19A

Y

Location	Ref
YARDLEY WOOD	19A
Yarnfield LC	6B
Yarnton Lane (AHBC-X)	17B
Yarrow Viaduct	30B
Yew Tree Farm LC (UWC)	19A
York Way North Jn	8A
York Way South Jn	8A

Z

Location	Ref
Zulus LC (UWC)	13B

Engineer's Line References

This listing is intended to show all the relevant operational ELRs that appear in this book, those that were live in the last edition but now closed, out of use or lifted and those that have carried over from the original network onto Heritage lines. More information can be found about these codes on the excellent website by Phil Deaves (see Bibliography). The location of the start and finish boundary of each ELR can be found in the book from the map reference in the Location Index applicable to any of the locations named in the description. Some ELRs extend over several pages.

ABE	Allington West Jn to Barkeston East Jn		CDM	Deansgate (Manchester) and Dee Marsh (near Chester) Line
ABW	Abbotswood Branch		CEC	Carnforth East Curve
ACD	Allington Chord		CEH	Castleton East Jn and Heywood Line
ACW	Acton Canal Wharf to Willesden		CGJ	Carlisle Grand Jn Line (WCML Crewe to Carlisle)
AEG	Allerton East Jn to Garston Jn Curve		CHW	Chester and Warrington Line
AFE	Abbey Foregate Jn to English Bridge Jn Curve (Shrewsbury Curve)		CIL	Chester Independent Lines
			CMD	Colwich Jn to Macclesfield Line
AFL	Aintree Fork Line		CMP	Crewe and Manchester Piccadilly Line
AHX	Allerton to Hunts Cross Curve		CNB	Chinley North Jn and Buxton Branch
AJM	Ambergate Jn to New Mills		CNH	Crewe North and Holyhead Line
ALC	Aston and Lichfield City Line		CNN	Coventry and Nuneaton Line
AMJ	Ashton Moss Curve (Ashton Moss South to North Jns)		COL	Manchester and Ordsall Lane Jn Branch
AML	Attenborough to Meadow Lane Jn Line		CPC	Codnor Park Jn to Hammersmith (Midland Railway Centre)
AMS	Moira West Jn to Shackerstone		CPI	Castleton and Bolton Line
ANL	Acton and Northolt Line		CRC	Camden Road Jn to Camden Jn Line
APB	Ambergate to Pye Bridge Line		CRR	Chester and Rock Ferry Line
ASB	Ashwell Branch		CSD	Castleton Depot
ASC	Shackerstone to Coalville Line		CSG	Crewe Salop Goods Loop
ASE	Nuneaton Ashby Jn to Shackerstone Line		CTA	Clifton Jn to Accrington Line
AWL	Acton Wells Branch		CVL	Churnet Valley Line
AYS	Ashburys Yard Sidings		CVS	Chester South Jn to Chester North Jn
			CWJ	Camden to Watford Jn Line (DC Electric Lines)
BAG	Birmingham and Gloucester Line		CWK	Hamilton Square and West Kirby Line
BBB	Blackburn and Bolton Branch		CYC	Chinley Chord
BBM	Bletchley to Bedford Midland Branch			
BBS	Blackburn Sidings		DAP	Dalton Jn to Park South Jn Curve (Barrow avoiding line)
BCJ	Birmingham Curve Jn to Branston Jn		DBP	Derby to Birmingham (Proof House Jn) Line
BCP	Bacup Branch		DCL	Didcot and Chester Line
BCR	Blackpool Carriage Sidings		DEX	Derbyshire Extension Branch
BCS	Bletchley Carriage Sidings		DHF	Denbigh Hall Flyover
BCV	Bordesley Jn to Tyseley Line		DJH	Daisyfield Jn and Hellifield Line
BDH	Brent Curve Jn to Dudding Hill Jn		DJO	Denton Jn to OA&GB Jn Spur
BDN	Bridge Street Jn to Duston North Jn		DJW	Duffield Jn to Wirksworth Quarry Branch
BDS	Bidston West Jn to Seacombe Jn		DNT	Darlington to Tebay Line
BEA	Barnt Green Evesham and Ashchurch Line		DPJ	Dudley Jn to Pleck Jn Line
BEJ	Buxton and Edgeley Jn Branch		DSD	Dinting South Jn to Dinting East Jn Curve
BEN	Birkenhead and New Brighton Branch		DSE	Deal Street and Edge Hill Line
BFG	Stonebridge Park Depot		DSS	Down Side Sidings, Euston (lifted)
BFO	Bletchley Flyover			
BHI	Basford Hall Independent Lines		ECM	East Coast Main Line
BIK	Bickershaw Colliery Branch		EDE	Eden Valley Branch
BJW	Bescot Jn to Wichnor Jn (Lichfield) Line		EEE	Liverpool Curve (Earlestown South to West Jns)
BLT	Bletchley Depot		EHW	Edge Hill Jn to Park Lane Goods (Wapping Branch)
BNN	Bedford to Northampton Jn (lifted)		EJN	Edgeley Jn and Northenden Branch
BOK	Broad Street and Old Kew Line via Hampstead (North London Line)		EPS	Earles Private Sidings
			ETC	Edinburgh to Carlisle Line
BPH	Blisworth to Peterborough Line		EWG	Edge Hill Jn to Waterloo Goods
BPP	Philips Park No 1 Jn to Brewery Siding Jn (Miles Platting Connecting Line)			
			FCO	Farington Curve Jn and Ormskirk Line
BSC	British Steel Corby Branch		FHR	Farington Curve Jn and Hall Royd (Burnley) Jn Line
BSD	Bescot Sidings		FJH	Frodsham Jn to Halton Jn Curve
BSG	Bicester South Jn to Gavray Jn			
BSJ	Bootle Jn Crossover		GBS	Guide Bridge Sidings
BSN	Brunthill Stainton Sidings		GDW	Glossop to Dinting West Jn Curve Branch
BTS	Brent Sidings		GEC	Greenford East Curve
BUX	Buxton and High Peak Jn Line No 1		GES	GEC Siding: Stafford No.4 SB (lifted)
BYK	Bewdley to Kidderminster Curve (Kidderminster Loop)		GJC	Gannow Jn and Colne Branch
			GJH	Gretna Branch
CAW	Cricklewood to Acton Wells Line		GMC	Greater Manchester Council Branch (Woodley)
CBC	Carnforth Barrow and Carlisle Line		GOJ	Gospel Oak to Jn Road Jn Line
CBI	Canal Tunnels		GSG	Gresty Road Salop Goods
CBR	Castle Bromwich to Ryecroft (Walsall) Line		GSJ	Galton Jn to Stourbridge Jn (Galton Branch and Stourbridge Extn Line)
CCB	Cotgrave Colliery Branch			
CCG	Croxley Green Branch		GSM	Kettering North Jn and Melton Mowbray Line
CCS	Rock Ferry and Cathcart Street Goods Branch (Birkenhead Goods Extension Line)			

GSW	Glasgow and South Western Line
GTP	Gorton Jn to Throstle Nest South Jn Line (now Metrolink)
HAJ	Hadfield and Ardwick Jn Line
HBL	Hest Bank Jn to Bare Lane Jn Curve
HCM	Newcastle-Under-Lyme Branch
HCN	Hartford Curve (CLC Jn to LNW Jn)
HEG	Hartford East Goods Curve
HFB	Higham Ferrers Branch
HGC	Hazel Grove Chord
HHJ	Hooton and Helsby Jn Line
HHW	Hatton North Jn to Hatton West Jn Curve
HLB	Holwell Branch
HNO	Hartford Northwich Oakleigh Sidings Branch
HNR	Hanslope Northampton and Rugby Line
HNS	Heaton Norris and Guide Bridge Line
HOB	Haydock Park Branch (St Helens Branch)
HOK	Horrocksford Branch
HSA	Hatton and Stratford-upon-Avon Branch
HSJ	Handsworth to Stourbridge Jn Line
HTW	Heath Town Jn to Walsall Lichfield Road Jn
HWG	Hartford West Goods Curve
HXS	Hunts Cross to Southport Line
IMG	Ince Moss Chord
ISL	International Services Link Line
JRT	Junction Road Jn to Carlton Road Jn
KBC	Kingsbury to Baddesley Colliery Branch
KBS	Kirkham and Blackpool South Branch
KCS	Kidsgrove to Crewe South Line
KGC	Kensal Green City Lines
KGW	Kensal Green Jn to Willesden Low Level
KJW	Kingsbury Jn to Whitacre Jn Chord
KMG	Kingmoor Goods Line and Sidings (Carlisle)
KSL	Knighton Jn Swannington and Leicester Jn Line
KWD	Kingswinford Line
LCN	Lostock Jn to Crow Nest Jn (Hindley) Branch
LCS	Liverpool Edge Hill to Crown Street Goods Branch
LEC	London Euston to Crewe Line
LED	Little Eaton Jn to Denby (lifted)
LEL	Lifford West Jn to Lifford East Jn
LHL	Lostock Hall Lines (also known as Farington Old Curve)
LKD	Lakeside Branch
LLG	Low Level Goods
LLI	Liverpool Independent Lines
LMD	Longsight Depot Sidings
LSC	Leamington Spa and Coventry Line
LSN	Lenton South to North Jns Curve
LSS	Landor Street Jn to St Andrews Jn
LTV	Lichfield Trent Valley Curve
MAJ	Manchester and Allerton Jn Line
MAS	Manchester and Sheffield Line
MCG	Maryport and Carlisle Goods Lines
MCH	Macclesfield and Cheadle Hulme Line
MCJ	Marylebone to Annesley
MCL	Midland City Line
MHH	Morecambe and Heysham Branch
MIA	Manchester International Airport Rail Link Line
MIR	Mersey Loop Line
MJI	Madeley Jn to Ironbridge Line
MJS	Melbourne Jn and Sinfin Branch
MJT	Mansfield Jn to Trowell Jn Line
MLN	Main Line (Paddington to Penzance via Bath)
MPR	Miles Platting and Rochdale Line (part NR, part Metrolink)
MRH	Macclesfield and Rose Hill Marple Branch
MSD	Manchester South District Railway (now Metrolink)
MSL	Birmingham Moor Street Line
MSM	Morecambe South Jn and Morecambe Branch
MVB	Manchester Victoria to Bury (now Metrolink)

MVE	Manchester Victoria and Euxton Jn Line
MVL	Manchester Victoria and Huddersfield Line
MVM	Manchester Victoria and Miles Platting Line
MVN	Manchester Victoria and Normanton Line
MYC	Midland Yard Jn to Canal Farm Jn (Nuneaton North Chord)
NAJ	Neasden South to Ayhno Jn
NBS	Norton Bridge and Stone Line
NEC	Newcastle and Carlisle Line
NGD	Newcastle Goods Lines
NGJ	Newton-Le-Willows to Golborne Jn Curve (Parkside West Curve)
NJN	Neasden Jn Curve
NLI	North London Incline
NMA	Nuneaton Avoiding Line (Midland Jn to Abbey Jn)
NMB	North Mersey Branch
NMC	New Mills and Cheadle Branch
NMH	Northampton and Market Harborough Line
NMM	North Mersey Branch to Marsh Lane Jn Curve
NOB	Nottingham and Barnetby Line
NOG	Nottingham to Grantham Line
NSE	Newark Crossing Curve
NSN	Northwich South Jn to Northwich West Jn Line
NSS	North Stafford Jn and Stoke-On-Trent Line
NTM	Northampton Sidings
NWO	Nuneaton and Water Orton Line
OCD	Ordsall Chord
OLD	Oldbury Branch (lifted)
OLL	Ordsall Lane to Liverpool Road station
OLW	Ordsall Lane Jn and Windsor Bridge Jn Curve
OME	Olive Mount to Edge Hill Line
OOS	Old Oak Sidings, Willesden
ORG	Miles Platting Jn to Oldham Road Goods Line (Oldham Road Goods)
OWW	Oxford Worcester and Wolverhampton Line
OXC	Oxley Chord
OXD	Oxford Branch
OXW	Oxenholme and Windermere Branch
PBJ	Proof House Jn and Bushbury Jn Line
PBL	Perry Barr Loop (Perry Barr North to West Jns Curve)
PBN	Preston and Blackpool North Branch
PBS	Pye Bridge to Shirebrook Line
PDB	Preston Deepdale Branch
PJL	Parkside Jn to Lowton Jn Curve (Parkside West Curve)
PJW	Portobello Jn to Wolverhampton Loop (Portobello Loop)
PMJ	Peterborough to Manton Jn Line
PPA	Philips Park (Miles Platting) and Ashburys Branch
PPP	Philips Park Jn and Baguley Fold Jn Curve
PRA	Aylesbury Branch (Princes Risborough to Aylesbury)
PRC	Watlington Branch (Princes Risborough and Chinnor Branch)
PRG	Padiham to Rose Grove Branch (part lifted)
PSE	Pye to Shireoaks East Jn Line
PSR	Preston Strand Road Branch
PVS	Park Viaduct South (Nuneaton Station)
QLT	Queens Park London Underground Lines
RAC	Radford Jn to Linby Colliery Branch
RBS	Rugby Birmingham and Stafford Line
RDB	Runcorn Dukes Dock Branch
RDK	Ramsden Dock Branch (Barrow in Furness)
RDO	Regents Canal to Domestic Platforms Line
RGY	Rugby Goods Yards
RRN	Rugeley to Ryecroft Line
RSD	Rugby to Stamford Line
RTS	Rugby and Leamington Line
RUD	Ruddington Chord (Loughborough)
RYH	Romiley and Hyde Branch
SAC	Settle and Carlisle Line

SAG	St Andrews Jn to Grand Jn Curve		TSN	Trent South to Nottingham Line
SAJ	Stalybridge Jn and Guide Bridge West Jn Spur		TTA	Chinley to Ashburys Line
SAS	Stechford and Aston Line			
SBH	Springs Branch (Wigan) and Huyton Line		UCJ	Upperby Bridge Jn to Carlisle Caldew Jn
SCG	South Carlisle Goods Lines		UHL	Up High Level Arrival Line
SCL	Soho Curve		ULR	Carlisle Upperby Jn to London Road Jn
SCN	Weaste Branch		USS	Up Side Sidings, Euston
SCQ	Stoke-On-Trent to Caldon Low Branch (Waterhouses Branch)			
			WAR	Appleby North Jn to West Jn
SCR	Speke Jn and Cressington Branch		WAW	Willesden to Acton Wells Line
SCT	Seaforth Container Terminal Branch (from Bootle Branch Jn)		WBS	Windsor Bridge North Jn (Salford Crescent) and Southport Line
SDJ	Skelton Jn to Ditton Jn Line		WCG	Watford to Croxley Green Chord
SEN	Syston East Jn to Syston North Jn Curve		WCL	Willesden Carriage Lines
SFO	Stansfield Hall Fork [Todmorden Curve]		WCM	West Coast Main Line (north of Carlisle)
SHL	Shrewsbury and Hereford Line		WDB	Wrexham Central and Bidston Line
SHS	St Helens Line (formerly to Widnes)		WDJ	Walsall to Darlaston Jn Curve
SIL	Stock Interchange Line		WEE	Winwick to Earlestown East Curve
SJC	Wennington to Carnforth Furness and Midland Jn		WEF	Wembley European Freight Operating Centre
SJD	Skelton Jn and Deansgate Jn Curve		WEL	West Ealing Loop
SJO	Sandhills Jn and Ormskirk Line		WFL	Willesden Freightliner Depot
SJS	Stourbridge Jn to Stourbridge Town Branch		WGL	Wednesbury Goods Loop (Bescot Jn to Bescot Curve Jn) (lifted)
SJT	Stratford-on-Avon and Midland Jn Line		WGP	Wigston to Glen Parva Curve
SKN	St Andrews Jn to Kings Norton Line		WGS	Wembley InterCity Depot
SKW	Skipton and Wennington Line		WHM	West Hallam Branch
SLT	Stonebridge Park LUL Depot		WHT	Washwood Heath Sidings
SMA	South Manchester Airport Chord		WJK	Walton Jn and Kirkby Branch
SNJ	Sandbach and Northwich West Jn Branch		WJL	Weaver Jn and Liverpool Line
SPC	St Pancras to Chesterfield Line		WJP	Woodley Jn to Partington Branch
SRD	St Helens and Rainford Line		WKL	Wigan and Kirkby Line
SRS	Stonebridge Park Shop Sidings		WKS	Wolverton Works
SSJ	Sheet Stores Jn to Stenson Branch (Castle Donnington)		WLL	West London Line (includes West London Extension Line)
SSP	Soho South to Perry Barr South Jn Branch		WMB	Willesden Jn to Mitre Bridge Jn Curve
STO	Stoke Works Branch		WMO	Wavertree Jn to Downhill Carriage Sidings
STY	Styal Line (Wilmslow Jn to Slade Lane Jn)		WND	Wellington to Stafford via Donnington Branch
SVB	Severn Valley Branch		WNS	Wigston to Nuneaton South Line
SWH	Swanwick Branch		WOA	Walton Old Jn to Arpley Jn Curve (Warrington)
SYC	Shrewsbury and Crewe Line		WOP	Water Orton to Park Lane Jn Curve
SZS	Willesden South West Sidings		WOW	Wolverton Works
			WPS	Wyre Dock (Fleetwood) and Poulton-Le-Fylde Branch
TAH	Tottenham and Hampstead Line		WRM	Willesden Royal Mail Terminal
TCC	Toton to Clay Cross Line		WSA	Watford to St Albans Abbey Branch
TES	Trent East Jn to Sheet Stores Jn Curve		WSJ	Wolverhampton to Saltney Jn (Chester) Line
THA	Thame Branch		WTS	Willesden Through Sidings
THL	Toton High Level Goods Line		WYM	Wymington Slow Line
TPS	Trafford Park Sidings		WZS	Willesden Traction Maintenance Depot Sidings
TRL	St Pancras to Cheriton (Channel Tunnel Rail Link)			
TSB	Tyseley South Jn to Bearley Jn Branch			

Line of Route Codes

Lines on the Network are nowadays given a Line of Route code (LOR) which may run over a number of ELRs. LORs have their origin in the codes used in the early 1990's in BR's Western Region. These were extended nationally by Railtrack in the late 1990's as Possession Resource Information Database (PRIDE) codes and renamed LOR sometime after. More information can be found about these codes on the excellent website by Phil Deaves (see Bibliography). The LOR description is the one generally used within the industry. To find an LOR in this book, take the location name from the list below and search for it in the Location Index.

London North West (North) codes appearing in this book

NW1001	Armitage Jn (Incl.) to Preston Flyde Jn
NW1002	Penkridge Station (Incl.) to Trent Valley Jn No.1 (Stafford)
NW1003	Silverdale to Madeley
NW1004	Rugeley Town (Excl.) to Rugeley North Jn
NW1005	Kidsgrove Jn to Crewe South Jn
NW1007	Nantwich (Excl.) to Crewe South Jn
NW1009	Basford Hall Jn to Sandbach South Jn (Ind. Lines)
NW1011	Gresty Lane to Salop Goods Jn
NW1013	Crewe Sorting Sidings North to Gresty Lane
NW1015	Salop Goods Jn to Crewe North Jn (Chester Ind. Lines)
NW1017	Salop Goods Jn to Crewe Coal Yd (Liverpool Ind. Lines)
NW1019	Acton Grange Jn to Warrington South Jn (Helsby Lines)
NW1021	Winwick Jn to Golborne Jn (via Earlestown)
NW1023	Haydock Branch Jn to Kelbit P.S.
NW1025	Bamfurlong Sdgs Jn to Ince Moss Jn (Ince Moss Chord)
NW1027	Preston South Jn to Strand Road
NW2001	Weaver Jn to Liverpool Lime Street
NW2003	Runcorn to ICI Salt Works (Runcorn Dock Branch)
NW2005	Speke Jn to Garston Jn
NW2007	Allerton East Jn to Garston Jn
NW2009	Arpley Jn to Ditton East Jn
NW2011	Walton Old Jn to Arpley Jn
NW2015	Ordsall Lane Jn to Edge Hill
NW2017	Eccles to Weaste
NW2019	Parkside Jn to Lowton Jn (East Curve Lines)
NW2021	Earlestown South Jn to Earlestown West Jn
NW2023	Springs Branch Jn to Huyton Jn (St. Helens Lines)
NW2025	St Helens Station Jn to Ravenhead Jn
NW2027	Edge Hill Bootle Branch Jn to Regent Road LC
NW2029	Olive Mount Jn to Edge Lane Jn
NW3001	Crewe North Jn to Holyhead
NW3003	Chester East Jn to Acton Grange Jn
NW3005	Gobowen (Excl.) to Saltney Jn
NW3007	Wrexham Central to Bidston West Jn
NW3009	Chester North Jn to Chester South Jn
NW3011	Chester West Jn to Hooton South Jn
NW3013	Hooton South to Helsby Jn
NW3015	Llandudno Jn to Blaenau Ffestiniog
NW3017	Llandudno Jn to Llandudno
NW3019	Gaerwen to Amlwch
NW3021	Frodsham Jn to Halton Jn
NW3023	Edgeley Jn No. 2 to Mickle Trafford
NW3025	Skelton Jn to Partington
NW3027	Timperley to Altrincham (Metrolink Lines)
NW3029	Sandbach North Jn to Northwich West Jn
NW3031	Northwich South Jn to Northwich Station Jn
NW3033	Hartford East Jn to Hartford North Jn (East Gds Line)
NW3035	Hartford West Jn to Hartford North Jn (West Gds Line)
NW3037	Hartford CLC Jn to Hartford Jn
NW4001	Preston Ribble Jn to Cove LC
NW4003	Preston Fylde Jn to Deepdale Jn
NW4005	Preston Fylde Jn to Blackpool North
NW4007	Kirkham North Jn to Blackpool South
NW4009	Poulton to Burn Naze
NW4011	Morecambe South Jn to Morecambe
NW4013	Hest Bank to Bare Lane
NW4017	Morecambe Jn to Heysham Port
NW4019	Oxenholme to Windermere
NW4021	Upperby Jn to Rome Street Jn
NW4023	Upperby Jn to London Road Jn
NW4025	Currock Jn to Bog Jn
NW4027	Carlisle Yard Recess Sidings to Brunthill
NW4029	Mossband Jn to Busk-on-Esk
NW4031	Gretna Jn to Gretna Green (Excl.)
NW4033	Carnforth North Jn to Carlisle South Jn (Via Barrow)
NW4041	Dalton Jn to Park South Jn
NW5001	Crewe North Jn to Manchester Piccadilly
NW5003	Wilmslow to Slade Lane Jn (Styal Lines)
NW5005	Heald Green South Jn to Heald Green West Jn
NW5007	Manchester Airport to Heald Green North Jn
NW5008	Norton Bridge to Stone Jn
NW5009	Colwich Jn to Cheadle Hulme
NW5010	Glebe Street Jn to Caldon Quarry
NW5011	Heaton Norris Jn to Guide Bridge Station Jn
NW5012	Foley Crossing (Excl.) to Stoke Jn
NW5013	Denton Jn to Ashton Moss North Jn
NW5015	Hadfield to Ardwick Jn
NW5017	Dinting South Jn to Dinting East Jn
NW5019	Glossop to Dinting West Jn
NW5021	Stalybridge to Guide Bridge West Jn
NW6001	Manchester Piccadilly East Jn to Euxton Jn
NW6003	Castlefield Jn to Allerton Jn
NW6004	Water Street Jn to Deal Street Jn (Ordsall Chord Lines)
NW6005	Manchester Victoria East Jn to Windsor Bridge South Jn
NW6007	Deal Street Jn to Ordsall Lane Jn
NW6009	Windsor Bridge North Jn to Southport
NW6011	Bolton East Jn to Blackburn Bolton Jn
NW6013	Lostock Jn to Crow Nest Jn
NW6015	Wigan Wallgate to Kirkby
NW7001	Manchester Victoria West Jn to Hebden Bridge
NW7005	Castleton East Jn to Hopwood GF
NW7006	Todmorden Viaduct Jn to Stansfield Hall Jn
NW7007	Farington Curve Jn to Ormskirk
NW7009	Farington Curve Jn to Hall Royd Jn (East Lancs Lines)
NW7011	Farington Jn to Lostock Hall Jn (Lostock Hall Lines)
NW7013	Daisyfield Jn to Hellifield
NW7015	Padiham Power Station Sidings to Rose Grove West Jn
NW7017	Gannow Jn to Colne
NW7019	Thorpes Bridge Jn to GMC Siding (Incl.)
NW7021	Miles Platting Jn to Marsden
NW7023	Philips Park West Jn to Brewery Jn
NW7025	Philips Park West Jn to Ashburys West Jn
NW7027	Baguley Fold Jn to Philips Park South Jn
NW8001	Hunts Cross West Jn to Southport
NW8003	Paradise Jn to James Street (Stock Interchange)
NW8005	Sandhills Jn to Ormskirk
NW8007	Bootle Jn to Aintree Emergency GF
NW8009	Walton Jn to Kirkby
NW8011	Mann Island Jn to West Kirkby (via Loop)
NW8013	Canning Street Jn to Hooton South Jn
NW8015	Bidston East Jn to New Brighton (New Brighton Lines)
NW8017	Canning Street North to Rock Ferry South Jn
NW9001	Dore West Jn to Edgeley Jn No.1 (Hope Valley Lines)
NW9003	Chinley East Jn to Chinley South Jn (Chord Line)
NW9005	Chinley North Jn to Buxton
NW9007	New Mills South Jn to Ashburys East Jn
NW9009	Marple Wharf Jn to Rose Hill
NW9011	Romiley Jn to Hyde Jn
NW9013	Woodley Jn to Bredbury Sidings
NW9017	Hazel Grove High Level Jn to Northenden Jn
NW9019	Buxton to Brigg's Sidings
NW9021	Buxton to Hazel Grove East Jn
NW9901	Gargrave to Carlisle South Jn
NW9903	Settle Jn to Carnforth Station Jn
NW9907	Warcop to Appleby
NW9909	Corby Gates to Petteril Bridge Jn
NW9911	London Road Jn to Bog Jn (Newcastle Goods Lines)

London North West (South) codes appearing in this book

MD101	Euston to Armitage Jn (Excl.)
MD105	Hanslope Juntion to Rugby (via Northampton)
MD120	Camden Jn to Watford Jn (DC Lines)
MD130	Watford Jn to St. Albans Abbey
MD136	Harlesden Jn to Wembley Central (Willesden Carriage Shed lines)
MD137	Harlesden Jn to Wembley Central (Wembley Yard lines)
MD140	Bletchley to Bedford St. Johns (Incl.)
MD145	Camden Road West Jn to Camden Jn
MD150	Kensal Green Jn to Willesden Suburban Jn
MD155	Kensal Green Jn to Harlesden Jn (City Lines)
MD160	Willesden High Level Jn to Mitre Bridge Jn
MD166	North Pole Jn to Wembley
MD167	Mitre Bridge Jn to Acton Wells Jn (South West lines)
MD170	Acton Canal Wharf to Willesden Jn
MD175	Brackmills to Northampton South Jn
MD180	Rugby, Trent Valley Jn to New Bilton
MD232	Abbey Jn to Hinckley (Excl.)
MD233	Midland Yard Jn to Canal Farm Jn
MD301	Rugby to Penkridge (Excl.) via Birmingham
MD306	Birmingham New Street to Ashchurch (Excl.) via Dunhampstead
MD310	Barnt Green Jn to Redditch
MD315	Stechford South Jn to Aston South Jn
MD320	Proof House Jn to Bushbury Jn (via Bescot)
MD325	Soho South Jn to Perry Barr North Jn (Soho Lines)
MD330	Soho East Jn to Soho North Jn
MD335	Perry Barr West Jn to Perry Barr South Jn
MD340	Aston North Jn to Alrewas (Excl.)
MD345	Bescot Jn to Rugeley North Jn (Excl.)
MD350	Anglesea Sidings to Lichfield City
MD355	Lichfield TV Jn to Lichfield Trent Valley (Chord Line)
MD360	Walsall, Pleck Jn to Darlaston Jn
MD365	Portobello Jn to Wolverhampton Crane Street Jn
MD370	Bescot Curve Jn to Walsall Pleck Jn
MD401	Heyford to Bordesley Jn
MD405	Leamington Spa Jn to Coventry South Jn
MD410	Coventry North Jn to Nuneaton South Jn
MD415	Hatton Station to Stratford-upon-Avon
MD420	Hatton North Jn to Hatton West Jn
MD425	Tyseley South Jn to Bearley Jn
MD430	Droitwich Spa to Stourbridge North Jn
MD435	Small Heath South Jn to Stourbridge North Jn
MD440	Galton Jn to Smethwick Jn
MD445	Stourbridge Jn to Stourbridge Town
MD450	Stourbridge North Jn to Round Oak
MD455	Kingswinford Jn South to Pensett
MD460	Fenny Compton to Burton Dassett
MD501	Tamworth (Incl.) to Birmingham, Proof House Jn
MD545	Kingsbury Jn to Whitacre Jn
MD555	Nuneaton North Jn to Water Orton East Jn
MD560	Water Orton West Jn to Park Lane Jn
MD565	Castle Bromwich Jn to Ryecroft Jn
MD570	Landor Street Jn to King's Norton Jn (Camp Hill Lines)
MD575	St Andrew's Jn to Grand Jn
MD580	Lifford East Jn to Lifford West Jn
MD701	Marylebone to Ayhno Jn
MD705	Greenford West Jn to South Ruislip
MD710	Neasden South Jn to Harrow on the Hill
MD712	Amersham to Aylesbury
MD715	Neasden South Jn to Neasden Jn
MD720	Princes Risborough to Aylesbury
MD725	Aylesbury to Claydon L&NE Jn
MD736	Oxford North Jn (Excl.) to Denbigh Hall South Jn
MD740	Bletchley, Summit of Flyover to Fenny Stratford (Flyover Lines)
MD745	Bicester South Jn to Gavray Jn
MD801	Wolverhampton North Jn to Abbey Foregate (Excl.)
MD805	Oxley, Stafford Road Jn to Bushbury Oxley Jn
MD810	Madeley Jn to Ironbridge National Power Station

London North East (East Midlands) codes appearing in this book

LN3140	Bedford St. Johns (Excl.) to Bedford Station
LN3201	St. Pancras to Tapton Jn (Via Derby)
LN3204	Trent South Jn to Nottingham East Jn
LN3207	Trent East Jn to Clay Cross North Jn
LN3210	Jn Road Jn to Carlton Road Jn (Tottenham Lines)
LN3213	Moorgate to Kentish Town Jn
LN3214	Canal Tunnel Jn to Belle Isle Jn
LN3216	Farringdon Jn to Blackfriars
LN3219	Cricklewood Curve Jn to Dudding Hill Jn
LN3222	Brent Curve Jn to Dudding Hill Jn
LN3228	Trent East Jn to Sheet Stores Jn
LN3231	Wigston South Jn to Glen Parva Jn
LN3232	Wigston North Jn to Hinckley
LN3234	Syston East Jn to Syston North Jn
LN3237	Loughborough South Jn to Hotchley Hill
LN3246	Ambergate Jn to Matlock
LN3249	Lenton South Jn to Lenton North Jn
LN3252	Mansfield Jn to Trowell South Jn
LN3255	Radford Jn to Kirkby Lane End Jn
LN3261	Trent South Jn to Toton South Jn (High Level Lines)
LN3264	Attenborough Jn to Meadow Lane Jn (Attenboro' Curve)
LN3273	Codnor Park Jn to Shirebrook Jn
LN3340	Alrewas (Incl.) to Wichnor Jn
LN3501	Derby London Road Jn to Tamworth (Excl.)
LN3505	North Stafford Jn to Stoke Jn (Excl.)
LN3515	Melbourne Jn to Sinfin
LN3520	Sheet Stores Jn to Stenson Jn
LN3225	Knighton Jn to Leicester Jn
LN3535	Birmingham Curve Jn to Branston Jn
LN3601	Kettering North Jn to Manton Jn
LN3605	Corby BSC Works to Corby North
LN3610	Corby Automotive Terminal to Corby North
LN3615	Helpston Jn to Syston South Jn
LN3620	Melton Jn GF to Asfordby
LN3625	Nottingham East Jn to Newark Flat Crossing (Excl.)
LN3635	Allington West Jn (Excl.) to Netherfield Jn

Other codes which appear all or in part in this book

EA1310	Camden Road West Jn to Richmond
EA1320	Camden Road West Jn to Stratford
EA1360	Dudding Hill Jn to Acton Wells Jn
EA1370	Gospel Oak Jn to Barking Tilbury Jn West
GW103	Paddington to Uffington
GW110	Old Oak Common West to South Ruislip
GW117	Greenford East Jn to Greenford South Jn
GW130	Acton Wells Jn to Acton East
GW174	West Ealing to Greenford West Jn
GW175	Greenford South Jn to Greenford Station
GW200	Didcot to Heyford
GW277	Oxford North Jn to Oxford Parkway (Excl.)
GW300	Abbotswood Jn to Stoke Wks Jn via Worcester Shrub Hill
GW310	Wolvercot Jn to Norton Jn
GW370	Droitwich Spa to Cutnall Green
GW401	Ashchurch (Incl.) to Westerleigh Jn
GW730	Severn Bridge Jn to Newport, Maindee West Jn
GW731	Abbey Foregate to Ruabon
GW732	Abbey Foregate to English Bridge Jn (Loop Lines)
GW735	Shrewsbury, Crewe Jn to Nantwich
LN101	King's Cross to Shaftholme Jn
LN682	King Edward Bridge South Jn to Carlisle North Jn
LN768	Mansfield Woodhouse to Shireoaks East Jn
LN808	Dore Station Jn to Totley Tunnel East
LN854	Hall Royd Jn to Skelton Jn
LN860	Diggle Jn to Copley Hill East Jn
LN922	Whitehall West Jn to Hellifield South Jn
SC001	Gretna Jn to Glasgow Central (via Beattock)
SC031	Gretna Jn to Glasgow Central (via Kilmarnock)
SO280	Farringdon to Herne Hill

Bibliography

The Publisher is grateful for the access given by Network Rail to a significant range of internal documents, most particularly the Sectional Appendix, Weekly and Periodic Operating Notices, Signalling Notices and Isolation Diagrams. In addition, a large number of other references have been used, the most reliable of which are:

Railway Passenger Stations in Great Britain – A Chronology (4th Edition)
By Michael Quick
Railway & Canal Historical Society, Oxford OX2 0NP

Signalling Atlas and Signal Box Directory (3rd Edition)
By Peter Kay and David Allen
Signalling Record Society, Wallasey, CH45 4PZ

The Railway Data Series (20 volumes covering the British Isles, mile by mile)
By Michael Oakley
Sword Press, Sutton Coldfield, B73 5UL

The Railways of Great Britain – A Historical Atlas (3rd Edition)
By Colonel Michael H. Cobb
Patrick S. Cobb, Newbury, RG20 9LB

Minor Railways in the British Isles series (4 volumes of track plans)
By Peter Scott
Published by P Scott, Reading RG30 2DQ

Branch Line News
Published fortnightly by the Branch Line Society, Bristol BS34 8NP

The 'Signalling Digest' compiled by Andrew Overton
Published in the bi-monthly Signalling Record by the Signalling Record Society,
http://www.s-r-s.org.uk

Midland Railway System Maps (6 volumes covering Midland Railway lines)
By John Gough & Peter Kay
Peter Kay, Teighnmouth TQ14 8DP

The 'Trackwatch' column from Modern Railways Magazine
2004-2011, by the late Gerald Jacobs
2011-2014, by Mike Bridge
2015 onwards, by Martyn Brailsford

British Rail National Route Codes; Catalogue of Route Sections at 1st January 1973
British Rail National Route Code Catalogue: List of Route Sections at 1st April 1986

Websites:
http://www.railwaycodes.org.uk/index.shtml, a site by Phil Deaves which details ELRs, past and present, LORs, Signal Box codes and a host of other useful information
http://www.railscot.co.uk/, Ewan Crawford's wide ranging site and a source of much visual information.
http://maps.nls.uk/, the National Library of Scotland which includes UK-wide old OS mapping at different scales
http://www.old-maps.co.uk/, another source of old OS mapping
http://www.disused-stations.org.uk/, a source of information about station histories
http://www.whatdotheyknow.com/, a site collecting the results of FOI requests
http://www.google.co.uk/maps and Google Earth, site and software providing aerial photography, often at a range of dates and over which detailed distance measurement can be made.

Chains to Yards to Km Conversion Table

80 chains = 1 mile = 1.609 Km

Chains	Yards	Km equivalent	Chains	Yards	Km equivalent	Chains	Yards	Km equivalent
1	22	0.020	28	616	0.563	55	1,210	1.106
2	44	0.040	29	638	0.583	56	1,232	1.127
3	66	0.060	30	660	0.604	57	1,254	1.147
4	88	0.080	31	682	0.624	58	1,276	1.167
5	110	0.101	32	704	0.644	59	1,298	1.187
6	132	0.121	33	726	0.664	60	1,320	1.207
7	154	0.141	34	748	0.684	61	1,342	1.227
8	176	0.161	35	770	0.704	62	1,364	1.247
9	198	0.181	36	792	0.724	63	1,386	1.267
10	220	0.201	37	814	0.744	64	1,408	1.287
11	242	0.221	38	836	0.764	65	1,430	1.308
12	264	0.241	39	858	0.785	66	1,452	1.328
13	286	0.262	40	880	0.805	67	1,474	1.348
14	308	0.282	41	902	0.825	68	1,496	1.368
15	330	0.302	42	924	0.845	69	1,518	1.388
16	352	0.322	43	946	0.865	70	1,540	1.408
17	374	0.342	44	968	0.885	71	1,562	1.428
18	396	0.362	45	990	0.905	72	1,584	1.448
19	418	0.382	46	1,012	0.925	73	1,606	1.469
20	440	0.402	47	1,034	0.945	74	1,628	1.489
21	462	0.422	48	1,056	0.966	75	1,650	1.509
22	484	0.443	49	1,078	0.986	76	1,672	1.529
23	506	0.463	50	1,100	1.006	77	1,694	1.549
24	528	0.483	51	1,122	1.026	78	1,716	1.569
25	550	0.503	52	1,144	1.046	79	1,738	1.589
26	572	0.523	53	1,166	1.066	80	1,760	1.609
27	594	0.543	54	1,188	1.086			